Narrative Social Structure

Narrative
Social Structure

Anatomy of the Hadith Transmission Network,

610–1505

RECEP SENTURK

STANFORD UNIVERSITY PRESS

Stanford, California 2005

Stanford University Press
Stanford, California
© 2005 by the Board of Trustees of the
Leland Stanford Junior University

Library of Congress Cataloging-in-Publication Data

Senturk, Recep
   Narrative social structure : anatomy of the Hadith transmission
network, 610–1505 / Recep Senturk.
      p. cm.
   Includes bibliographical references and index.
   ISBN 0-8047-5207-9 (cloth : alk. paper)
   1. Hadith—Criticism, interpretation, etc.   2. Hadith—Authorities.
3. Discourse analysis.   I. Title.
BP136.3.S46 2005
297.1'2406—dc22

                                                    2005021506

Printed in the United States of America on acid-free, archival-
quality paper

Original Printing 2005
Last figure below indicates year of this printing:
14   13   12   11   10   09   08   07   06   05

Typeset at Stanford University Press in 10/14.5 Minion

To HARRISON WHITE, *my mentor in sociology;*

RICHARD BULLIET, *my mentor in history;*

NURAY, *my wife and eternal companion;*

and, ultimately, the PROPHET MUHAMMAD, *who inspired the scholars whose network I analyzed*

Contents

Figures, Tables, and Maps

Figures

Tables

Maps

Preface

My purpose in *Narrative Social Structure* is to convince my colleagues that it is high time for us to bridge the gaps among different strands of structural query, in particular literary and social, synchronic and diachronic, with the purpose of achieving a more sophisticated and authentic image of human action. The book thus aims to reconfigure the relations among linguistics, the humanities, and the social sciences in light of evolving knowledge in these fields, which repeatedly demonstrates that boundaries between disciplines are no more fixed than writing upon water.

But how? I try to demonstrate an approach through a study of the monumental network of traditional Muslim scholars whose capital was narrative. These scholars gained their identity from this narrative but also gave an identity to it. What they exchanged among themselves was small pieces of narrative about the sayings, actions, or silent approvals of the Prophet Muhammad (571–632). Muslims call this narrative *hadith* and consider it the second source of Islam after the Qur'an. Harrison White, who learned for the first time from me what *hadith* is, used to define it for his friends as "the table talk of Muhammad other than the Qur'an." Each hadith has two parts: the text, and the chain of its transmission. My greater focus here is on the latter. I combine the oldest and the most recent analytical tools from a variety of disciplines, such as sociology, linguistics, the humanities, and network analysis, to shed new light on the millennium-long hadith transmission network.

I nevertheless observe that we all have narratives as part of our capital and source of identity. The content and the style of narrative may vary, but the structures of the discourse networks reflect great similarities. From a broader perspective, each social actor is a narrator, and each social organization is a discourse network. It would be an illusion to think of a social group without a discourse about past, present, and future. Is this relationship accidental, or is there a deeper connection? Sociologists from earlier generations used to subscribe to the former view, but the new generation increasingly adopts the latter approach. Mine is also an argument for the deeper, fluid, and multiplex connections between words and deeds, which we need to explore further. I thus expand the work of Harrison White, Randall Collins, Jurgen Habermas, Andrew Abbott, Walter J. Ong, Michael Silverstein, and John Lucy while combining it with my initial inspiration from Ferdinand de Saussure.

My mentors, friends, students, and editors contributed, each in his or her own way, knowingly or unknowingly, to the evolution of this book in New York, Istanbul, Bochum, Atlanta, Troy, and Stanford over a decade. I should begin with my mentors: Harrison White and Serif Mardin in sociology, Richard Bulliet in history, Mustafa Azami in hadith, M. Emin Er in classical linguistics and Islamic disciplines, and Harold Berman in law. They guided me in direct and indirect ways. I also greatly benefited from the comments and support of Ron Burt, Eric Leifer, Hamid Dabashi, Priscilla Ferguson, Randall Collins, Douglas White, Charles Kadushin, Tom Snider, Mustafa Emirbayer, Stephan Reichmuth, Mahmut Kaya, Hayreddin Karaman, and Ismail Erunsal. While I was researching and writing this book, my discourse network included Jay Cross, Harun J. Frankel, David Gibson, Ali Nizamuddin, Mohamad Hammour, Asna Husin, Gabriel Haddad, Faik Bilgili, Kasim Kopuz, Tahir Ayar, Bekir Kuzudisli, Mehmet Ozsenel, Joseph Walsh, and John Yasin. My engineer friends Goksen Elkas, Tamir Wasfy, Fatih Porikli, Dawud Wong, Hasan Guclu, and Mehmet Demiroglu provided technical support and wrote programs for me. Necdet Yilmaz graciously volunteered to draw the maps. My friends from the Center for Islamic Studies (ISAM), Istanbul, in particular Tahsin Gorgun and Sukru Ozen, played a special role. I remember them all, and many others from different parts of the world, with profound appreciation and gratitude and apologize for not being able to mention their names individually.

The patient and gracious support of Mark Granovetter from the very beginning has been crucial for me along with the comments of my anonymous reviewer. Both helped and guided me on the way to completing the book. Kate

Wahl, my editor at Stanford University Press, was very enthusiastic about the book, providing me the energy I needed to apply the last touches. I am also grateful to John Feneron, in-house editor at Stanford University Press, for his meticulous work on this manuscript.

My parents, my father- and mother-in-law, and my sisters, in particular Zeynep, have always been there for me at every stage of research and writing, with love and sacrifice. There is one person to whom I owe more than to anyone else: Nuray, my wife, comrade, and support through every challenge I have faced with her endless love and care.

Smiling is a charity.

—*Hadith*

CHAPTER ONE

Introduction

A central problem in the social sciences and humanities today is that of accounting for the relationship between social and literary structures, on the one hand, and the interaction between synchronic and diachronic structures, on the other. In place of a single overarching "Structuralism," one instead sees structuralisms both in the social sciences and in the humanities, with striking gaps and unclaimed territories between them. In most structural research, observations are not made on the system as a whole but on some part of it. This has created a gap between social and literary structuralisms; a similar gap is also observable between synchronic and diachronic structuralisms. I suggest here instead that a social organization is also a discourse network comprising synchronic and diachronic relations. As an alternative to the current disjointed view of discourse and society, this book suggests a more integrative paradigm, which asserts that the social world is an outcome of the ceaseless synergy between words and actions on the diachronic and synchronic axes; therefore, we cannot give primacy in our research to the one at the expense of the other.

"A man's mirror is his actions, not his words," reads one line of a couplet by Ziya Pasha, a nineteenth-century Ottoman poet. This line simply reflects the worldwide popular view, distinguishing between actions and words while privileging the former over the latter. The justification for such a view comes in the second line of the couplet, "For the level of one's intelligence is reflected in his work" (Göçgün, 2001: 159–61). Sociological theory with its varying strands has also, since its inception, internalized this prevalent sentiment. It has grounded itself on a distinction between social action and discourse, giving priority to the former over the latter, if not exclusively focusing on the former. As a result, sociologists have left words to scholars in linguistics and the humanities.

Yet recently this conventional division of labor in the academy has come under attack and begun to erode. *Narrative Social Structure* also contributes to this process by arguing that words and deeds are ineluctably interrelated and that they jointly construct social structures. More specifically, the book, deriving from Ferdinand de Saussure's legacy, aims to bridge the gap between discursive and social structures, on the one hand, and the gap between synchronic and diachronic structures, on the other. Bridging these two gaps constitutes the two tasks that this book undertakes. Since I argue, along with Saussure, that conjoining words and deeds or discursive and social patterns must be on the diachronic axis, the two goals of this book are intrinsically related to each other.

As to the first goal of the book, Jurgen Habermas and Harrison White, among others, have already taken the initial steps. Although the founding fathers of sociology, such as Emile Durkheim and Max Weber, completely neglected the discursive dimension of social action, successive generations of sociologists increasingly realized the inseparability of discursive and social processes. The second generation of sociologists, led by Talcott Parsons, could no longer ignore discourse and incorporated it into their analyses, yet only as an epiphenomenon. Today the new generation of sociologists, including Andrew Abbott, Erving Goffman, Pierre Bourdieu, Robert Wuthnow, and William Labov, increasingly recognizes the inseparability of both structures.

As to the second goal of the book, much needs to be done because diachronic structures have long been ignored, and the promise of structuralism in this regard has yet to be fulfilled, although almost a century has passed since its first formalization in the work of Saussure. Saussure proposed two types of structures on the time axis: synchronic and diachronic. He also proposed two other types of structures on the analytical-level axis: micro and macro. The matrix produced by these four dimensions summarizes Saussure's strategy with respect to structural query. Structuralists from the humanities and the social sciences have neglected the diachronic structures, for the most part, and concentrated on the analytical-level axis. Presently, however, any attempt to couple discursive and social patterns needs to take into consideration the temporal constraints involved in discursive and social action. The *synchronic* approach to the analysis of social and discursive actions is based on a hypothetical and inauthentic concept of social process because social and discursive actions alike are embedded within temporal structures that can be ignored only at a cost.

With the goal of bridging this gap and coupling the structures of speech and action, I extend the query about structures in the discursive and social processes to the persistent patterns in their ceaseless interaction. I argue that without an uninterrupted synergy between discursive and social structures, daily social life would be impossible to imagine. With a focus on the patterns in the interface, I offer a new explanation, on both the macro and the micro levels, for the construction of authority in a discourse network through time. More specifically, the question this work revolves around is why some social actors gain more aggregate or individual authority than others in a discourse network.

I extend, in the course of doing that, the application of current methods of synchronic (cross-sectional) social network analysis to diachronic (cross-temporal) social networks. Presently, social network analysis concentrates primarily on synchronic structures and uses cross-sectional data. In turn, I relate my findings on diachronic social networks to the research on cross-sectional social networks or social organizations in general. In doing this, I have as my purpose to demonstrate how the study of cross-sectional networks and the study of cross-temporal networks can mutually give rise to each other.

Narrative Social Structure also maintains that structuralist query in the humanities can foster that in the social sciences, and vice versa. The search for patterns in discursive mechanisms has long been carried out in isolation from that in social mechanisms, and the relationship between the two has until recently been ignored. Currently, the gap between the two strands of structuralist query has become increasingly noticeable on both sides. I claim this territory for myself and argue that social behavior can be better explained and predicted if an approach is employed that explores the interaction between social and discursive patterns.

The empirical evidence from the analysis of the hadith transmission network substantiates my claims. It is the longest social network in history ever to be recorded in such great detail, from the seventh century to the present. Hadith includes all primary records concerning the Prophet Muhammad (571–632 CE) and is precisely defined as follows: "Hadith (narrative, talk) with the definite article (al-hadith) is used for Tradition, being an account of what the

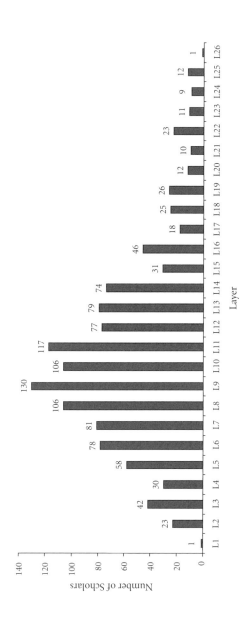

FIG. 1.1. The 26 Layers of Prominent Hadith Scholars, 610–1505

Prophet said, or did, or of his tacit approval of something said or done in his presence."[1] The Prophet Muhammad, born in Mecca, declared in 610 that he was the Messenger of God and invited people to Islam until his death in Medina. His flight from Mecca to Medina in 622, called the Hijrah, is considered the beginning of the Islamic calendar. Hadith literature, which consists of the anthologies of a great number of brief anecdotes and sayings of Muhammad, is the second source of Islam after the Qur'an, which, according to Muslims, comprises the direct revelations of God. Presently, more than a billion Muslims all over the world turn to hadith literature when they want to study and emulate the exemplary life and conduct of the Prophet Muhammad, commonly known as the *Sunnah*, meaning literally "tradition."

A hadith[2] (the plural is "ahadith") is a brief disjointed[3] narrative about the Prophet Muhammad transmitted orally and in writing through an extensively recorded network of narrators across generations. A generation is also called a *layer* (*tabaqa*) in the diachronic social network of hadith scholars, known as *muhaddithun*.[4] Only layers 1–26 of the hadith transmission network, extending from 610 to 1505 CE, are analyzed here, with a focus on the most prominent 1,226 narrators (see fig. 1.1) who had 13,712 connections among themselves. The beginning, 610, corresponds to the date Muhammad proclaimed his divine mission in Mecca, and the end, 1505, corresponds to the death in Egypt of the last prominent master of hadith, Suyuti. Geographically, the network served in the dissemination of Islamic knowledge from Spain, Africa, and the Balkans to central Asia and eastern Turkistan up to China and contributed to the integration of Islamic creed and practice.

The network of the most prominent hadith scholars, which is the focus of this book, comprised the most celebrated stratum among colleagues known as *huffaz*. This word is the plural of *hafiz*, which literally means "the guardian," "the one who memorizes and protects."[5] The term *hafiz* may also be used to refer to the people who committed Qur'anic scripture as a whole to memory, but that is not the meaning used here. The network of huffaz expanded with the spread of Islam until the tenth century CE, which corresponds to layer 11, around the fourth century after the Hijrah (AH), more precisely from 180 to 348 AH or 796–930 CE.[6] The number of huffaz reached its peak in layer 11, with 117 scholars. This number suddenly dropped to 77 scholars in layer 12, to 79 scholars in layer 13, and to 74 scholars in layer 14. From layer 15 on, the decrease in the number of huffaz became even more drastic: 31 scholars in layer 15, 10 scholars in layer 21, and only 1 scholar in layer 26. The curve is skewed to the left and has a tail to the right. This is significant because the left-hand side represents the era of authority formation, whereas the right-hand shows the era of authority claiming. Therefore, the flatness of the right-hand side and the eventual drop-off to zero are striking.

Being the longest of its kind in existence, the hadith transmission network can be used to explore longitudinal processes in social networks through time. The particular focus here is on exploring authority formation in a cross-temporal network. The analysis of the network of hadith scholars over centuries shows that interlayer brokerage (the ILB effect) and levels of reported speech (the LRS effect) work together uninterruptedly, on the macro and micro levels, to shape the social network and the behavior of the individual and aggregate social actors. These findings confirm the old structuralist tenet, developed earlier by Karl Marx, Weber, Durkheim, Parsons, Robert Merton, Ronald Burt, and White, that structural position is a better predictor of social action. Structural positions, however, are not merely a product of nontemporal social relations; rather, they are constructed temporally through discursive action.

Discursive action manifests itself in narrative or stories of countless types and lengths, implicitly assumed or actually told—entirely or in part. My approach to narrative in this study is *external*; I do not attempt to interpret the content of the narrative. Nor do I analyze how narrative has been interpreted and used in variable ways. Instead, I analyze the relation of narrative to the social network to which it gives life and form, and also through which it survives and disseminates. This approach concentrates more on the conditions that are vital for meaning to be possible. In line with this view, my interest is not solely in the conventional question of what narrative means or reflects but in *what narrative does socially.* The former question is based on the traditional referential approach to language use, which conceives of language only as a means of communication. However, this traditional referential paradigm has been recently expanded to other aspects of language use as well. Among them is the role of language use and discursive practices in establishing and maintaining social relations.

I maintain that there are persistent patterns conceivable to us in social and discursive processes, and in their interaction. These patterns are called *struc-*

tures. There has been a long tradition of query for such patterns in the human sciences, led by Saussure, M. M. Bakhtin, Roland Barthes, Michael Silverstein, and John Lucy. A similar research tradition in the social sciences has been led by Marx, Weber, Durkheim, George Simmel, Merton, White, and Burt. In the structuralist tradition, the explanation lies in the patterns of interrelations between the elements of an organization, discursive or social, micro or macro, synchronic or diachronic. I cross-fertilize these currently isolated structuralist traditions from linguistics, the humanities, and the social sciences and bring recent developments in all these fields to bear upon each other. From this perspective, I suggest in the following chapters that not only the relations *within* the discursive and social processes, uncoupled from each other, but also the interrelations *between* them should be a subject for structuralist query. An unexplored territory lies between the traditionally well established intellectual borders of the human and social sciences.

With the purpose of substantiating my claim, I empirically demonstrate how metalanguage implicitly configures our social networks whether we are aggregate or individual social actors. In my analysis of the hadith transmission network, I have found that a layer, a cohort of prominent scholars from one generation, is thinly connected to itself but thickly connected to past and future layers. Outward connections figure prominently in the network of preeminent scholars. Fewer than 3 percent of the total number of teacher ties are inward, that is, to teachers who are peers from the same layer. In contrast, more than 97 percent of ties are outward, that is, to earlier and later layers. These patterns, which I have analyzed below in greater detail on the macro and micro levels, persisted over nine centuries, from 610 to 1505. From a social network perspective, the role of prominent scholars in the hadith transmission network can be characterized as that of interlayer brokerage (again, the ILB effect), which brings them power. Yet the reason why prominent peers limit their connections to each other can be found in the discursive mechanisms involved in reported speech (again, the LRS effect).

Figure 1.2 illustrates how this phenomenon manifests itself in the hadith transmission network. In the interconnections of 26 layers observed here, only a very limited number of connections are to peers from the same layer. More concretely, only 880 (6.4 percent) of the total of 13,712 connections are inward, or synchronic, whereas 12,832 (93.6 percent) are outward, or diachronic. Yet the

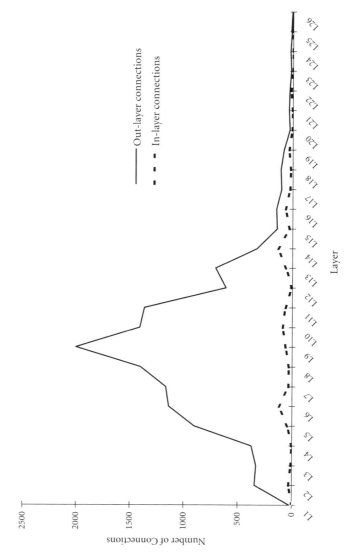

FIG. 1.2. Outward (Diachronic) and Inward (Synchronic) Ties over Time (Data from Layer 9)

ratio of synchronic connections to diachronic connections never exceeds 3 percent. This demonstrates that promising hadith students persistently avoided inward or in-layer connections with their peers by not accepting their narrative, because this would have increased the levels of reported speech unnecessarily. The forward-looking investment for a student was, as much as possible, in teacher connections to nonadjacent layers. Similarly, the foresighted investment for a prominent mentor was in students from the youngest possible layers.

The question of authority formation in the scholarly community has far-reaching implications for culture and society. The authority of the huffaz, who were part of the leading intellectual community of their time, known as the *ulama,* was not limited to the hadith transmission network. They were also highly influential both in the intellectual community and in Islamic society in general. Since there is no formal central authority in the Islamic community, the role of the *ulama* is crucial for the working of society. The authority of the *ulama* is increasingly drawing the attention of students of Islamic society.[7] By comparison with some other religious communities that are more familiar to sociologists, Islam lacks an authoritative central figure or institution like the church. Some may see the lack of a central authoritative institution as a weakness for Islamic society. Yet Richard Bulliet's recent exploration shows that in the absence of a single authority there have been multiple forms and sources of authority in Islamic society and culture: the Companions of the Prophet; the scholars, or *ulama;* and the saintly figures, or sufis (Bulliet 1994).

On a more general level, it is possible to observe in everyday life the metalinguistic pattern described above. Even if the content is the same and the report completely accurate, we still try to report a speech not from secondary sources but from the original source. In academic discourse networks, the same pattern is observable in scholarly citation. In writing a research report, for instance, we are expected to cite original but not secondary sources. There are firm social norms concerning reflexive speech. For example, it would be a grave mistake for a student to take a citation from the paper of a classmate rather than from the original source, even if the content and the wording are the same. If reporting from the original source is impossible because of social and temporal constraints, then we try to report a speech from the source closest to the origin. The same simple, common logic that characterizes our talk in everyday discourse lies behind what hadith transmitters did for centuries, yet in a more systematic way.

As we almost habitually try to manage the levels of reported speech, our social network gains its shape through an elusive process. We find ourselves embedded in a discourse network, a social system in which speech connects people to each other. I define discourse in this context as *interconnected speech*. This view of discourse is closely linked to the commonly used concept of narrative with a beginning, a middle, and an end, all interconnected. The interconnected structure of speech at once constructs and reflects the interconnections among speakers or social actors, whether or not they are aware of it.

Yet there are conceptual and methodological impediments to the implementation of this recently emerging approach in research. The problem that this recent orientation tackles is that of the long-ignored dynamics and mechanisms of the interplay between structures of action and structures of signification. Conceptually, there is a gap to be bridged between social and literary structuralism. Methodologically, analytical tools have yet to be developed for exploring the area between these two fields, although each field has developed tools to explore itself.

Scholars from the humanities and the social sciences are also calling for a more integrated approach to language use and social action. Among them are Habermas (1984), Hart (1992), John Shotter (1993), Silverstein (1993), Burns (1977), Abbott (1988b, 2001a, 2001b), White (1992, 1995), Bruner (1986, 1990), Desan, Ferguson, and Griswold (1988), Sewell (1992, 1994), Abrahamson and Fombrun (1994), Emirbayer and Goodwin (1994), Tilly, Goodwin, and Emirbayer (1995), and Tilly (1995). From this perspective, narrative ceases to be the significant other of science, for science itself has its own rather empirical narrative (White 1973; Somers 1992, 1995; Levine 1995). These scholars have acknowledged the mutual-influence process and have proposed causally reciprocal models as opposed to the earlier one-sided, reductionist, deterministic models. But how?

The interrelationship is not straightforward or self-evident. How do the two patterns work in interplay with each other in the construction, change, and perpetuation of social structures? This puzzle remains unsolved.

Structure of Inequality in Discourse Networks

Does discourse produce inequality and social stratification? If so, how? I demonstrate below that a discourse network is characterized by striking social inequality, which is perpetuated over centuries through elusive mechanisms. This finding is not peculiar to the hadith transmission network. Daily experience also shows that some narratives are socially more esteemed and authoritative than others. So are their producers and holders. A social actor can also be conceived as a narrator because everyday life is impossible without the telling and retelling of stories, our own and those of others. Likewise, a social network can also be conceived as a network of narrative because it is constructed and maintained through stories. The levels of reported speech in the stories we tell and retell bring about and sustain social inequality in a discourse network.

For instance, according to *Kitab Tadhkirah al-Huffaz*, the biographical dictionary of prominent hadith scholars by Abu Abdullah Shamsuddin Muhammad al-Dhahabi (d. 1348 CE), a major historian of Islam from the fourteenth century, only 1,176 scholars stood out among their colleagues as huffaz. They were noted, as Dhahabi's work demonstrates, among approximately 40,000 renowned figures in 21 layers of narrators. The proportion of huffaz is less than 3 percent within the population of Muslim scholars. According to Jalal al-Din Suyuti (d. 1505 CE), an eminent historian who came more than a century after Dhahabi, the number of scholars who gained broad public recognition as huffaz in the 24 layers from the time of the Prophet Muhammad until Suyuti's own time was only 1,188 (Suyuti 1984).

This illustrates how selective and competitive the process of intellectual stratification has been. Some of these scholars, perhaps, did not even envision in their lifetimes that their names would be included one day in the list of huffaz. They did the work and left the judgment about themselves to posterity, to the ever-evolving public view of future generations. One's place in the network of huffaz is thus retrospectively established and reestablished by later generations, after one's death.

What is even more striking, of all these highly noted scholars only six non-Arab men did work that gained almost unanimous recognition leading to their having been enshrined as the Six Canonical Books of Hadith. It was the public view of the broad scholarly community over generations, not a formal committee or central institution, that bestowed such authority on these works. We must also remember the underdeveloped condition of the means of communication at the time, by comparison with the technology that scholars employ today. Nor was the conferring of this worldwide social recognition instantaneous; stiff competition determined which books were to be considered the most authoritative. Furthermore, among these six books, the compilations of Muhammad bin Ismail al-Bukhari (d. 870 CE) and Muslim bin Hajjaj (d. 875 CE) gained the utmost authority. Yet the contest between these two continues and has yet to be resolved. Scholars still discuss which of these two compilations is the better one. Ibn Khaldun (d. 1406 CE) (1967, 447–63) reports that in his own time Western (North African) scholars considered the compilation of hadith by Muslim bin Hajjaj (*Sahih Muslim*) more authoritative than Bukhari's (*Sahih al-Bukhari*), whereas the opposite was true for the East. These compilations appear to be the two books most often cited in Islamic literature of the past and the present.

What guided the process of stratification in this discourse network? What bestowed unparalleled authority on a minute group of scholars and their narratives while depriving others of it? I demonstrate below that the huffaz were always the students of huffaz from previous layers. A student could not become a prominent scholar unless he was the student of one. This structure reminds us of the structure of Nobel Prize winners in modern academia. Zuckerman's work (1996) has documented the crucial role played by the social position of a prominent mentor in the prospective status of a student. Mullins (1973) undertook similar research on prominent social scientists, with similar results. Later, Collins (1998) conducted the most wide-ranging research on the issue by analyzing networks of philosophers in major civilizations from Japan to Europe and the Islamic world. These studies show parallels, which concern authority formation and stratification, in the social structure of intellectual discourse communities regardless of culture, time frame, and geographical location.

The observation about the stratification of discourse communities has far-reaching ramifications because it is not limited to intellectuals. Instead, each discourse network, whether or not it specializes in scholarly activity, is *stratified* rather than *flat*. In a narrative social structure, eyewitness narrative and narrators stand at the top of the pyramid, a social power explicitly reflected in the courtroom, in the news media, in historiography, in ethnography, and at the dinner table. "Being there" then, like "being here" now, empowers narrators with various identities: scientist, journalist, reporter, historian, witness, ethnographer, grandfather, and the like (Geertz 1983). For instance, narrators may appear in history as the apostles of Jesus, the Companions of Muhammad, the close circle of Marx, or a research team. Their authority goes almost unchallenged among adherents of the discourse network.

Eyewitness narrators thus constitute the core of the networks of narrative through which narratives are disseminated, originating in the circle of a prophet, in a laboratory, at a crime scene, in a "field," on a street corner, or at a dinner table. For the most part, the event and the witness gain this status *fortuitously*. One usually can do little to become a celebrated eyewitness, or to avoid becoming one; in general, it depends on a lucky or unfortunate accident. What makes the eyewitness so powerful is that there is no way to replicate a unique and transient event after it is witnessed. Events happen here and there and are mostly unplanned and unexpected.

Thus the status of witness cannot be replicated at will. Just as it is accidental that one witnesses a singular transient event, it is also accidental that a single event among an infinite number should gain social notability. If and when this happens, the eyewitness narrative is sought after by the public, the courts, newspaper readers, faithful followers, historians, or inquisitive students of a scientific field—a process that spontaneously instigates the formation of a narrative social structure.

Eyewitnesses enjoy the highest social status because, first, only they can speak independently, without reporting from anyone else; second, they alone can use object language in their speech, so that others who retell the story have to rely on eyewitnesses in their reported speech and thus cannot use object language; and, third, the speech of eyewitnesses is characterized by a *participatory* mode rather than a merely *reportorial* mode. Another reason why witnesses are so powerful in the discourse network is that reconstruction of an event at a later time depends on the narratives that eyewitnesses provide. Without eyewitness narratives, stories cannot gain the same authority. Furthermore, as our everyday experience also tends to demonstrate, those who retell stories are less esteemed than those who initially produce them, for the retellers are dependent on the producers.

Yet if eyewitnesses, who are at the core of the network, become unreachable, a constraint in network building, then discourse mediators emerge, each one adding a new level to the reported speech. Each additional level of reported speech means greater distance from the original teller and imparts less social authority to the narrative and to the narrator. The length of a narrative chain is inversely related to the faith it evokes in the public: the shorter the chain of narration, the more reliable the narrative.

Consequently, in daily life, we all habitually try to eliminate discourse mediators from our talk, for the purpose of keeping intervening levels of reported speech as few as possible. Compared with ordinary people, as the case of the huffaz illustrates, intellectuals are more self-conscious about this process. This is because the higher the number of discourse mediators in one's narrative, the lower one's status in the network of the narrative or discourse community. For this reason, we selectively establish connections with some social actors and report speech from them while avoiding others. In these processes, our social network gets shaped without our knowing how: out of our sight, metalanguage configures and reconfigures social networks.

Ironic Disappearance of the Huffaz

Huffaz ceased to exist as a class after the sixteenth century. After that time, as the work of al-Kattani (1982) demonstrates, the community of hadith scholars revered as huffaz only a very few exceptional scholars in each century.[8] Although Islam continued to spread even after the eleventh century to the Balkans, Africa, India, and the Far East, the size of the hadith transmission network began to shrink, and the curve tapered off until it completely diminished (see fig. 1.1). It is true that one cannot expect endless exponential growth in the size of a network of narrative, because of the quantitative constraints, yet the decline in the number of huffaz poses a question.

Is it not intriguing to see the demise of an intellectual class, after it has played the lead role for so many centuries? Figure 1.1 implies a long process of decline that has proved irreversible. Something happened during the eleventh century that made the network of huffaz begin to shrink ever more despite the continued spread of Islam and the increase in the Islamic population. Why did the network of huffaz contract despite the enlargement of Islamic geography? This paradox still begs for an explanation. It is easy to explain the formation and expansion of the network because it corresponds historically to the rise and spread of Islam. By contrast, the way the size of the network tapered off from the eleventh to the sixteenth century is a challenging puzzle.

The answer to this paradoxical question, I suggest, lies in the changing modes of narration, from predominantly oral (during the time of expansion, from layers 1 to 11) to predominantly written (from layers 21 to 26). This stage is known among the historians of hadith as the period of "compilation," *tadwin*. With the spread and institutionalization of education, the tension between memory and manuscript was resolved in favor of the latter. Writing had been in increasing use since the advent of Islam, but only as an aid to memory. Later, however, memory became an aid to writing, and scholarly communities willingly accepted becoming dependent on writing. This change in the mode of discourse had a clear impact on the social organization of scholars, which is best illustrated in the example of the huffaz.

Moreover, the beginning of the decrease in the number of huffaz correlates with the rise of the Six Canonical Books of Hadith. These books made the rigorously authenticated ahadith so accessible and convenient to students that they did not feel the need to repeat the primary research. Manuscripts gained so much trust and commanded so much authority that they conquered the space traditionally dominated by memory. The public gained easy access to "solid" (*sahih*) ahadith. Consequently, "weak" (*daif*) ahadith were marginalized to a great extent—another reason why interest decreased in extensive memorization of ahadith.

An additional major factor that contributed to the disappearance of the huffaz class can be found in the reconfiguration of relations between rival schools of thought in Islam. The efforts of the huffaz in their struggle against the Mutazilites and the Shiites contained the influence of these schools to a limited group. After this notable victory, the huffaz consolidated the relations among four major schools of law and brought them together under one banner, the People of Tradition and Community, or the *Ahl al-Sunna wa al-Jama'ah*, commonly known today as the Sunnite school. The term *Sunnite* today indicates a school of theology, and its followers are divided into four schools of law: Hanafi, Maliki, Shafii, and Hanbali.

The consolidation among opposing intellectual powers, which had served as the fuel of intellectual dynamism in the early phase of Islamic history, had a

negative impact on the level of networking activity among scholars and the volume of connections between generations. The decreasing intellectual tension
had also decreased the level of intellectual dynamism within the scholarly community. Collins (1998) observes a similar stagnation in the case of Japanese intellectuals. The consolidation of four schools of Islam under the banner of Sunnite identity was, however, one of the most remarkable achievements of Muslim
scholars in terms of the social integration of a worldwide community and
peaceful coexistence among otherwise conflicting denominations.

   Ironically, these great achievements by the huffaz in developing the technology of discourse (Ong 1982), standardizing the protocols of transmission, or
"interaction rituals" (Collins 1998), and consolidating the tensions within the
Islamic community were terminal for their network. The huffaz employed their
legendary retentive memories with remarkable success in decreasing the need
for memory on the part of the public. They painstakingly sifted reliable narratives from forged ones and offered them to the public in an easily accessible format, without knowing that their very success would eventually undermine their
necessity as a group. In a literate or writing-dependent society, a scholar who
relied on his memory became, as a social type, someone from a bygone era.
From then on, ahadith were to survive for the most part through manuscripts,
but not through memory. Scholars passed down bulky manuscripts of hadith
anthologies, such as the Six Canonical Books of Hadith, but not individual ahadith from memory (Sezgin 1956). The scholars' very success unintentionally
prepared their end.[9]

Authority Formation from Levels of Reported Speech

   In the absence of centralized formal regulations and institutions, the network of scholars, particularly in medieval times, was the image of a market in
which there was stiff competition. The conventional view might suppose at first
sight that students were attracted to particular teachers because they were more
knowledgeable. Yet the analysis in this book concludes otherwise, demonstrating how the network position of scholars determined who their students were
and thus determined the level of their social prominence.

   Narrative Social Structure aims to reveal the structure of authority formation
in a discourse community in which social actors are embedded both as tellers

and listeners. The scholarly and intellectual community, like other discourse communities, deals with symbolic structures. Scholars and intellectuals produce, exchange, and transmit symbols. Narrative is the main if not the only way in which they, like other social actors, think, organize, and market their ideas (Danto 1985). Not only the human and social sciences but also the hard sciences still depend on narrative (Nash 1994). Furthermore, not only oral cultures (Ong 1982) but also the literate and even computerized cultures depend on narrative (Schank 1990). New technologies seldom replace old ones completely; instead, they tend to open up new possibilities and to coexist with older ones.

Thus most of the symbolic structures circulating in the scholarly community are organized, stored, and marketed through narration. In the scholarly community, doing is saying. Furthermore, talk, and in particular reflexive speech, easily defined as talk about talk, connects scholars to each other and to previous and future generations. Scholars maintain the life of narratives by retalking about them, and narratives in turn maintain the network of the scholarly community. Unlike what most social theory would uphold, the words of the actors in a discourse network are their deeds. Consequently, social authority formation in the scholarly community cannot be treated separately from the narrative with which its members deal.

Each discourse network develops around a narrative, whether it is called "science," "history," "religion," or "literature" or goes under the name of a less formally organized set of everyday stories. Generally speaking, a discourse network is a social organization, or a social organization is a discourse network. Without speech and narrative, it is impossible to imagine the construction and operation of a social system, a firm, a university, a gang, a family, a state, a market, or the like. A narrative and a network arise simultaneously. Soon thereafter, a metanarrative develops from their interaction. These three structures give life to and influence one another, and thus a change in one brings about changes in the others. The three—narrative, social network, and metanarrative—intertwine to constitute a metastructure, a social organization.

One such metastructure is the hadith transmission network. Narratives of and about the Prophet Muhammad and the social network of his Companions and Successors developed gradually alongside an evolving metanarrative, called the Sciences of Hadith, a literal translation of *'ulum al-hadith*. Science, in this context, is not defined according to modern norms. The name "Sciences of Hadith" indicates the literature about the corpus of hadith narrative. Departing from the conventional approach that focuses on only one of these elements, the focus here is on the metastructure, the hadith narrative, the hadith transmission network, and the Science of Hadith, jointly emerged and reproduced. The process of narration maintains the metastructure and its building blocks in interaction with each other.

A single narrative might be of interest to several disciplines. In this case, since the content is common property, identity comes from genre. Scholars, just like other social actors, derive their identities from the *type* of narrative they deal with. Those who deal with the empirical narrative are called scientists. Humanists are those who deal primarily with the fictive narrative. Critics and theorists deal with metanarrative. Far from being stable, disciplinary borders are continuously redrawn by each generation, with consequences for the identities of the disciplines' practitioners. Historians, sociologists, theologians, and novelists keep a vigil to protect the borders of their disciplines—that is, the borders of their discourse networks—by reproducing not only the narrative but also the specific style of narration that distinguishes them from others who deal with the same narrative.

Knowledge, as an increasing number of scholars from a wide range of disciplines argue, is but a type of narrative, not only in preliteral societies, as Ong (1982) sees them, but also in highly literate, even computerized, modern and postmodern societies (Danto 1985; Schank 1990; Bruner 1986, 100–118). For instance, modern science, philosophy, and education, and the communities that increasingly fill up endless cyberspace, depend on narrative. The evolving technology of discourse does not threaten the place of narrative as the foundation of social actions, ties, and organizations, but it changes the mode of narrative production, dissemination, and marketing, with a clear impact on the configuration of social networks. Likewise, despite the evolving technology used in recording and reporting, the narrative construction of social networks still relies on reported speech, or metalanguage. The persistent mutual interdependence of discursive and social structures is best illustrated by the advent of cyberspace societies, whose life depends solely on discourse.

Social narratives and networks become possible through evolving reported speech; the transmitters and what they transmit are far from being fixed.[10] Their internal fabric relies heavily on reported speech because narrative is a report of what happened, without which we cannot do. Narrative disseminates through reported speech. All traditions—religious, scientific, philosophical, legal, political, artistic, or otherwise—are transmitted to succeeding generations through reported speech.

Furthermore, without reported speech, indirect connections in social networks would be impossible. Suppose that our language did not allow us to report the speech of others. Our relations would then remain limited to our direct interlocutors. Regardless of the technology employed, reported speech is used to activate relations with those who are absent from the current setting. As these relations are activated, the interlocutors strategically expand the discourse network beyond those who are present.

Possibilities for social narrative and social networks are mutually dependent. One is impossible without the other; they are jointly and mutually constructed and reconstructed: no social network without a social narrative, and no social narrative without a social network. If this is so, then why is there a gap between literary and social structuralism? This deep-rooted institutional and conceptual gap blinds researchers to the everyday joint processes created by discursive and social dynamics. Because of this gap, we ignore how everyday life employs both discursive and social structures simultaneously. In fact, our daily life is impossible without a strong link between these two structures and without their perfectly synchronic operation. This is true not only for individual social actors on the micro level but also for corporate or aggregate social actors on the macro level.

Narrative Capital from Weak Ties in a Discourse Network

Authority formation in a discourse network is based not only on the accuracy of reported speech but, more important, also on the network's proximity to the source, as reflected in the geodesic distance between source and speaker. Paradoxically, greater network proximity (lesser geodesic distance) between a speaker and the original source is produced by greater temporal distance between the nodes in a chain of narration.

Proximity to the original narrator is a desired property of a social network of narrators and can be measured through analysis of the network path between the two narrators. In the hadith transmission network, the path distance between a scholar and the Prophet is closely related to the length of the scholar's life, or his longevity, which could mislead us into thinking that age is what attracted students to particular mentors. Age was important only when it brought about shorter chains, which I measure below, using geodesic distance between the Prophet and the scholar with greatest longevity. Great longevity serves as an indication of a shorter chain only if the aged mentor commenced his studies not only in early youth but also under long-lived masters with shorter chains (Bulliet 1983).

In the hadith transmission network, therefore, social capital rather than age or knowledge played the most crucial role in attracting students. Scholars with desirable network connections were characterized both by the shortest narrative chains and by an extended number of parallel chains. They attracted students from remote parts of the Islamic world. The narrative capital of prominent scholars derived directly from the configuration of their social networks.

There was a clearly fortuitous aspect of the process of acquiring and using such a network. The accumulation of valuable narrative chains began at an early age, mostly under the supervision of old patrons and teachers who wanted to survive through their students. Families also played a very crucial role in supporting young pupils emotionally and financially in their hadith education, and especially in their travels abroad. Furthermore, some renowned scholarly families consistently produced scholars over several centuries, with grandfathers teaching grandsons but not with fathers teaching sons (Bulliet 1972; Shakir 1982).

This investment in knowledge at a very young age became social currency only after an age threshold was reached, a threshold marked by the moment when a scholar's layer began to meet its demise. Longevity, contingent upon the conditions mentioned above, made scholars with the shortest chains of narrative stand out. Only then could their social capital be put in use. Otherwise, if there had been many scholars who all had chains of the same length, they would not have been so appealing to students, regardless of their age and knowledge. Contrary to what is generally assumed, it was not the age or knowledge that counted but rather a particular configuration of the scholar's social network, one that would permit seekers of knowledge to reach the original source with a minimum number of discourse mediators.

The density of connections to the outside, in particular to nonadjacent social actors, is a striking network configuration, which results from attempts to reduce the levels of reported speech. One would expect, as I did at the outset of this study, the members of a prominent group to be closely linked to each other. On the contrary, the analysis below shows that the prominent scholars, as individuals and as a group, were closely linked to those who were far removed from them. In contrast to my initial expectation, they were distant from their own cohort. The network of the prominent, aggregate or individual, is therefore characterized by an extremely high frequency of weak ties to the outside of their own group.

Prominent scholars thus act as brokers of interlayer discourse and bridge the holes between layers. In this connection, weak ties, social capital, and structural holes play an important role in the process of authority formation in the intellectual community (Coleman 1988, 1990; Granevetter 1973; Burt 1992). Likewise, the same scholars playing the role of interdisciplinary discourse broker also bridge the gaps between various disciplines. By employing these perspectives, I not only extend social network analysis to discourse networks but also open a new area of application for the perspective that emphasizes the role of social network configuration in the process of competition. I also demonstrate that discourse networks are no different from other social networks with respect to competition and authority formation, on both the individual and the aggregate levels.

Basic Structure: Waves with Changing Lengths and Heights

The hadith transmission network encompasses both universal and provincial features. These can be distinguished from each other through a comparison with analogous intellectual networks from other civilizations. This will contribute to uncovering the basic structure of intellectual networks on the universal level, at the same time demonstrating the peculiar features of the network of huffaz. More clearly stated, to what extent are there characteristics of the hadith network that arise from historically specific forms of narrative discourse among Muslim scholars, and to what extent is there a universal mechanism of intellectual narrative discourse?

Sociologists, from Weber to Merton, Zuckerman, and Collins, have tried to prove that there is a universal structure to the networks of intellectuals. *Narra-*

tive Social Structure also follows the same conviction and aims to demonstrate the universal structure of the network of prominent intellectuals from the fresh angle outlined above. It does so without disregarding the provincial features emerging from peculiar historical conditions or the specific content of the discourse.

I argue that the universal structure and provincial features of the structure of intellectual networks reflect a wavelike pattern. Relations are consistently distributed in the time line, with the majority being diachronic; that is, relations are to prominent figures from preceding generations and to figures from subsequent generations who are yet to become prominent. In contrast, the number of synchronic connections to contemporaries remains strikingly low.

As an example, figure 1.3 demonstrates how the connections of layer 9 are distributed within that layer as well as to previous and subsequent generations. The former is indicated as UP (upstream), and the latter is indicated as DOWN (downstream), whereas the growing distance between layer 9 and the layer to which it is connected is marked by increasing numbers.

The topology typifies all the networks for prominent intellectuals, with variations in temporal distance and volume or frequency of connections reflecting changing conditions within or around the network. The height of the wave indicates the volume of the connections between the two generations under consideration: the higher the wave, the denser are the relations. The breadth of the wave demonstrates the duration of the connections between them. We will return to this discussion in greater detail.

The network of each scholar can also be summarized as a wave overlapping other waves on the time line. It arises with the connections to the earliest possible generation and ends with the connections to the latest possible generation. Scholars who were born around the same time are usually treated together as a cohort, a layer. Beginnings and ends of waves, representing their networking activity, may overlap, more or less. Yet their greatest interest would not be in each other but in the past and future generations outside each cohort.

The eminent intellectual invests his time and energy in the past and the future in order to control the present. Success in the present over rivals from his own generation depends on the degree of his reach toward adjacent generations upstream and downstream. Diachronic or vertical ties bring him what syn-

Volume of Connections

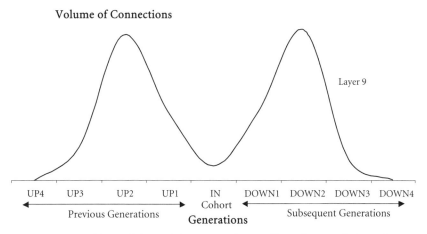

FIG. 1.3. Wave Shape of the Basic Structure of an Intellectual Network (Data from Layer 9)

chronic or horizontal ties cannot: not only vast knowledge and experience but also social status and prominence.

In the beginning of the hadith transmission network, the waves were high, and the distance between the two edges was large. This was an outcome of intense rivalry over the shortest chains. The maximal span of relations was kept as large as possible, to make chains as short as possible. This reached its peak at layers 11 and 12, around 900–1000 CE.

The downswing began around layer 14 and continued until layer 19, parallel to decreasing competition over the shortest chains. The emphasis shifted around this time, from the shortest chains to interpretation of the texts of narrative from divergent perspectives, which opened a new venue for competition.

The hadith transmission network began to show features of a rational discourse network as primary interest shifted from preserving the tradition to interpreting it creatively. Opposing juristic and theological interpretations of hadith had competed until the point where the overwhelming prevalence of the four schools of law in the Sunnite world succeeded in containing the Shiite school to particular areas, such as Iraq. The change from proliferation of rival schools to intellectual and religious consolidation can best be observed in the *madrasa,* or school system. Each madrasa initially belonged to only one of the four schools of law; later, education was offered in all four schools. Likewise, earlier law books were dedicated to a single school, whereas later ones adopted a comparative approach to all the existing schools. The same development took place in the Sunnite schools of theology, the Asharites and the Maturidites; both have been considered legitimate by the majority of the Sunnite world.

This indicates a great achievement by the huffaz in securing the lofty place that hadith deserved after a long struggle against philosophers and jurists who championed the primacy of reason: the Falasifa, the Mutazilite, and the People of Opinion (*ahl al-ra'y*). As consolidation was achieved, hadith literature was unanimously accepted as the second source of Islamic law and theology, after the Qur'an and before rational analogy (*qiyas*), which is considered the third source.

While the wave persistently preserved its shape, its length and the height, representing the network of prominent scholars, underwent adjustments parallel to these shifts and swings, until the final stabilization of the discipline of hadith. The immutable and mutable features demonstrate that universal structures and provincial features alike have been at work in the long history of the hadith transmission network. They can be disentangled for the purpose of exploring their respective contributions in particular historical settings and periods.

The maximal span that prevailed in the time of competition for the shortest chains, and the increased volume of connections corresponding with higher levels of networking activity in the hadith transmission network, can thus be seen as reflections of the peculiar historical conditions of the time, whereas the wave shape of the network of an individual hafiz is common to all prominent intellectuals, regardless of time, geography, and discipline. Below, I will comparatively analyze the data on the network of philosophers (Collins 1998), Nobel Prize winners (Zuckerman 1996), and prominent sociologists (Mullins 1973), to demonstrate this commonality in the shape of the network. Some of the earlier studies, such as the ones by Merton (1973, 1993), Zuckerman (1996), and Collins (1998), have already pointed out the importance of vertical ties in the particular networks they analyzed, and this work allows me to carry the argument on to the universal level. The networks of prominent intellectuals from the disciplines analyzed by the above-mentioned scholars have a stronger resemblance to the second phase of the hadith network, when hadith narration became routinized and standardized after having firmly secured a place for itself in the intellectual landscape in the tenth century CE. Yet, at times, they may also resemble the early phase of the hadith network. This may occur in the presence of strong emphasis on demanding that a scholar's claim to authority, or his authenticity as a scholar, be validated in some stipulated fashion. The Japanese philosophers, for instance, traveled to China in order to have shorter chains, although they could have linked themselves to the network through local teachers who had longer chains. However, the usual emphasis in philosophy is not on the maximally shortest chains. The shifting tension between inheritance and innovation or tradition and reason determines the maximal span of the wave, shaping the network of intellectuals.

Narrative, Meaning, and Society

What does narrative mean for its bearers and receivers? Briefly put, its meaning is contested by intellectuals who are anchored in different disciplines and schools. Also, meaning changes over time. Similarly, the same narrative may have different meanings for jurists, philosophers, theologians, preachers, historians, rulers, and the lay public. Yet all Muslims are expected to revere the tradition of the Prophet Muhammad, if from divergent perspectives, and to try to interpret it in the most exhaustive way possible and emulate its moral principles. The *Sunnah*, which literally means "custom and tradition," is what the Prophet Muhammad set before his followers as the best example of good conduct. Muslims are required to internalize the Prophet's example. Hence they have recorded his actions and sayings in great detail for transmission to future generations of Muslims. Therefore, the relations and actions of Muslims are colored if not completely shaped by the Sunnah of the Prophet Muhammad, the ideal for all pious Muslims. This approach has influenced the lives of large populations dispersed over a wide geographical area throughout history. Currently, all over the world, more than one billion Muslims, around one-fifth of the world's population, turn to these traditions for religious and moral guidance. Islamic theology and law still derive heavily from hadith literature, second only to the Qur'an.

The present approach to narrative, which is characterized by *externality*, looks at narrative and its social role from outside. More concretely, the main focus of this book is the interplay between social narratives and networks. The content of narrative, that is, knowledge or meaning, is not the primary interest of the present study. In other words, this is not a study about hadith literature as such; it is a study about how the discursive structure of tradition as a monumental social narrative is related to the magnificent social network through which it is disseminated across time and space. This is the aspect most neglected by current scholarship on the tradition and on other major narratives from other cultures.

The type of literary study that structuralism helps one envisage would not be primarily interpretive; it would not offer a method that, applied to literary works, produces new and hitherto unexpected meanings. Rather than a criticism that discovers or assigns meanings, it would be a poetics that strives to define the conditions of meaning. Granting new attention to the activity of reading, it would attempt to specify how we go about making sense of texts and to show the interpretive operations on which literature itself, as an institution, is based (Culler 1975, vii).

Newly emerging perspectives from the social sciences and the humanities can help shift or at least broaden the classical paradigm of hadith studies, still completely preoccupied with the undeniably important but conventional question of the extent to which the tradition deserves our faith. If the classical referential perspective on discourse, which characterizes the traditional paradigm, is replaced with a new, constitutive perspective on speech, new questions become possible. Likewise, the classical impressionistic and individualistic approach of historians to hadith transmission needs to be improved if not completely replaced with a structural perspective.

Only as we go beyond the traditional paradigm does it become possible for us to discover iterative patterns and structures in the texts and transmission networks of ahadith as well as in the interplay between the two. This book hopes to take a step in this new direction. It uses modern concepts and methods from the humanities as well as the social sciences not only to unearth iterative patterns in the literary and social structure of narrative but also to identify patterns in their interaction as they evolve as a metastructure.

By contrast with existing studies on the hadith tradition, studies confined by the traditional paradigm, my approach to hadith is *explanatory*. We have to keep in mind that even if the age-old debate over the reliability of ahadith is resolved, we will still need an explanation for the phenomenon of hadith transmission, regardless of opinions about the authenticity of particular narratives. Suppose we concluded that the monumental body of literature is completely reliable or completely unreliable or somewhere in between; this judgment would still not be able to offer an explanation for the rise of the social and literary structure of the tradition itself. We would still need to find out how and why the system worked the way it did, by analyzing the lives and networks of scholars.

Narrative Social Structure sets out to bridge two gaps on the conceptual and empirical levels: one is between literary and social structures, and the other is between synchronic and diachronic structures. On the conceptual level, chapter 3 is dedicated to the first issue, whereas chapter 5 is dedicated to the second. The rest of the book is an empirical implementation of this approach on different analytical levels. In this analysis, center stage is occupied by the contrast between diachronic and synchronic and between discursive and social structures. In accordance with the interpretive framework suggested here, the tension between these structures is maintained throughout the study; by contrast with conventional practice, however, the tension is not resolved in favor of one side, through reductionism.

Chapter 2, which follows this introduction, introduces the hadith tradition and the monumental hadith transmission network in relation to other overlapping narrative traditions and networks in Islamic history. Chapter 3 sheds more light on the theoretical questions this book aims to raise. Chapter 4 provides a closer look at the historical sources of social network data, their reliability, and the problems encountered in using them with modern methodology. Chapter 5 outlines the methodological problems in analyzing cross-temporal or time-stratified networks.

Chapter 6 looks at the broader picture by analyzing the connections among layers in the hadith transmission network on the macro level. Again on the macro level, chapter 7 explores the larger social and cultural structures in which the hadith transmission network was embedded by analyzing the brokerage role that huffaz played between different domains of Islamic discourse; chapter 7 further expands some of the questions already raised in this introductory chapter about the overlap between narratives and networks in Islamic history. Chapter 8 takes the analysis to the micro level by analyzing patterns in the networks of the three most prominent scholars from each layer. The findings on both levels confirm each other and demonstrate the effects of levels of reported speech (LRS) and interlayer brokerage (ILB) on authority formation in an intellectual community.

I close the loop, in chapter 9, by tying the argument back to cross-sectional networks and social organizations in general. In this connection, I discuss the role of vertical and outward ties to social power. I also link the macro and micro analyses by concluding that the authority of a social actor, whether the actor is corporate or individual, comes from extensive outward network connections.

CHAPTER TWO

Social and Literary Structure of *Isnad*

Whose Narrative?

The social network, more than a millennium long, of hadith scholars through which ahadith came down to us is traditionally known as the *isnad* system, involving countless numbers of scholars throughout the widespread geographical area of Islam. The intellectual preoccupation of these scholars is known as the science(s) of hadith. Here, the term *science (al-'ilm)* simply refers to a systematized body of knowledge. The science of hadith, as an academic study, is primarily a literary discipline dealing with narratives about the Prophet Muhammad, yet it has far-reaching ramifications for Islamic culture and society. If the Qur'an is divine knowledge, then the Sunnah of the Prophet Muhammad is its concrete and living embodiment. Aisha, the wife of the Prophet Muhammad, when she was asked about his conduct, replied that he was the walking Qur'an. Islam has two foundational scriptures or narratives, organically tied to each other, along with a multistream of interpretive traditions or metanarratives emerging around them.

A system of narration is constituted by narrators and listeners, texts of narrative, metanarrative(s), and the social network in which both the listeners and the tellers are embedded. The process of narration ties all these elements together. Within the context of hadith narration, these elements correspond to the master of hadith, the student of hadith, the text(s) of hadith, the metanarratives of hadith, and the *isnad* system, respectively. Below, I will discuss all these components and the way they are linked to each other within the context of the hadith transmission network, or *isnad* system. I will show how both narrative and its holders are embedded in a stratified structure, one that has helped determine whose narrative will gain more authority. The decision on the relative authority of a narrative is made by scholars, who critically examine texts and chains of transmission.

The question this chapter aims to answer is, What is the logic behind this system of stratification? I shall return to this issue shortly and in greater detail in the discussion of the methodology of hadith. Yet to begin with, Ibn Khaldun's account of hadith can help us as an outline of this logic. Ibn Khaldun designated a chapter in his *al-Muqaddima* to the sciences of his time, among which the science of hadith occupied a distinguished place (Ibn Khaldun, *The Muqaddimah*, 2:447–51):

> The sciences concerned with Prophetic traditions (*hadith*) are numerous and varied. One of them concerns abrogating and abrogated traditions. . . . Two traditions may be mutually exclusive, and it may be difficult to reconcile them with the help of interpretation. If, in such a case, it is known that one is earlier than the other, it is definite that the latter (tradition) abrogates (the earlier one). This is one of the most important and difficult sciences of tradition.
>
> Another of the sciences of tradition is the knowledge of the norms that leading *hadith* scholars have invented in order to know the chains of transmitters, the (individual) transmitters, their names, how the transmission took place, their conditions, their classes, and their different technical terminologies. This is because general consensus makes it obligatory to act in accordance with information established on the authority of the Messenger of God. This requires probability for the assumption that the information is true. Thus, the independent student must verify all the means by which it is possible to make such an assumption.

Having introduced the subject matter and its significance, Ibn Khaldun illustrates the process through which the relative reliability of a hadith is determined by the critics:

> He may do this by scrutinizing the chains of transmitters of traditions. For that purpose, one may use such knowledge of probity, accuracy, thoroughness, and lack of carelessness or negligence, as the most reliable Muslims describe a transmitter possessing.
>
> Then, there are the differences in rank that exist among transmitters.
>
> Further, there is the way the transmission took place. The transmitter may have heard the *shaykh* (dictate the tradition), or he may have read (it from a book) in his presence, or he may have heard (it) read in the presence of the *shaykh* and the *shaykh* may have written (it) down for him, or he may have obtained the approval of the

shaykh for written material (*munawala*), or he may have obtained his permission to teach certain traditions (*ijazah*).

The process of critical scrutiny of narratives eventually leads to a hierarchical system of narrative and narrators. A set of concepts is produced and employed for the purpose of indicating their place in the refined stratification:

<Then there is difference> with regard to the (degree) of soundness or acceptability of the transmitted material. The highest grade of transmitted material is called "sound" by (the hadith scholars). Next comes "good." The lowest grade is "weak." (The classification of traditions) includes also: "skipping the first transmitter on Muhammad's authority" (*mursal*), "omitting one link" (*munqati*), "omitting two links" (*mu'dal*), "affected by some infirmity" (*mu'allal*), "singular" (*shadhdh*), "unusual" (*gharib*), and "singular and suspect" (*munkar*). In some cases, there is a difference of opinion as to whether (traditions so described) should be rejected. In other cases, there is general agreement that (they should be rejected). The same is the case with (traditions with) sound chains. In some cases, there is general agreement as to their acceptability and soundness, whereas, in other cases, there are differences of opinion. *Hadith* scholars differ greatly in their explanation of these terms.

Then, there follows the discussion of terms applying to the texts of the traditions. A text may be "unusual" (*gharib*), "difficult" (ambiguous, *muskhil*), "(affected by some) misspelling (or misreading)," or "(containing) homonyms" (*muftariq*), or "(containing) homographs" (*mukhtalif*).

On all these points, hadith scholars have laid down a canon explaining the (various) grades and terms, and adequate to protect the transmission from possible defects.

Ibn Khaldun's account briefly demonstrates the rationally constructed and extremely self-reflexive system of traditional scholars of hadith.[1] Below, I will briefly survey both the evolving history and the rather dynamic and fluid system of the hadith transmission network.

A Structure from Reflexive Speech

"All those who listen to me shall pass on my words to others and those to others again; and may the last ones understand my words better than those who listen to me directly." With these words, the Prophet Muhammad concluded his farewell sermon, which he gave atop his camel in the middle of the Arabian Desert, near Mecca, during his farewell pilgrimage (631 CE). The Prophet's

Companions, following his oft-repeated instructions, as they had usually done since the beginning of Muhammad's Prophethood, carefully recorded in their memories the exact words they heard and the exact deeds they saw, in order to convey them to their families, friends, and tribes, and especially to the next generations. One wonders if they ever imagined the extent to which their speech, reported over and over by subsequent narrators from east to west, would contribute to the timeless social-literary monument that the hadith transmission network became.

Hadith, the reflexive speech[2] by which we know retrospectively what the Prophet said and what he did not say, constituted the impetus for a network of narrators. In an attempt to control fictive narrative, narrators of hadith from subsequent generations ensured that they learned the authorities through which the narrative had reached down to them. This stemma or chain of authorities came to be called the *isnad* (literally, "support" or "backing"). Within a few centuries of the Prophet's demise, chains of narrators had grown longer.

From this process emerged the structure of hadith, with its two elements: the chain of narrators (the *isnad*) and the narrative text (the *matn*), together constituting a new style of narrative. For interpretation, the chain needs to be contextualized in time and space as part of a larger network of narrators, and the text needs to be contextualized in the metanarrative as part of larger network of narratives. Thus a reader has to pay attention to time and space in the chain as well as in the text. The following example from Bukhari's hadith compilation is a better illustration of this point. Dates of death, according to the Hijrah calendar,[3] and names of the places where the narrators lived have been added, to help the reader visualize the dissemination of narrative across generations in time and space:

> [Bukhari (194–256, Bukhara) wrote], Al-Humaidi Abd Allah ibn az-Zubair [d. 143, Mecca] related to us saying: Sufyân [107–198, Mecca] related to us, saying: Yahya ibn Sa'id al-Ansâri [d. 143, Medina] related to us, saying: Muhammad ibn Ibrahim at-Tamimi [d. 120, Medina] told me that he heard 'Alqamah ibn Waqqâs al-Laithi [d. 80, Medina] say: I heard 'Umar ibn al-Khattab [d. 24, Medina] say on the pulpit: I heard the Apostle of God [d. 10, Medina], peace be upon him, say: "*Behold, the actions are but [judged] according to the intentions; and, behold, unto every man is due but what he intended. Thence, whoso migrateth for the sake of this world or to wed a woman, his migration is [accounted] for that unto which he migrated*" [Asad 1981, 3–4].[4]

Reflexive speech, as mentioned above connected generations of narrators to each other, thus playing the most crucial role in the construction and perpetuation of the network. Object language usually establishes ties between present actors, but reflexive language has the power of engaging actors in a widespread network, thereby demonstrating explicitly the relationship between literary and social structures. Without the reflexive power of language, it would have been impossible to interconnect multitudes of narrators in a social network.

The protocol of narration or reporting speech came under close scrutiny among hadith narrators because of its consequences for the authenticity of narration. There are multiple phrases used to indicate the transmission of narrative from one scholar to another. Each one of these phrases reflects a type or aspect of the connection between the teller and the listener (es-Salih 1988, 70–84). (See also the discussion of the fifth principle of hadith criticism, in "Methodology of Hadith Criticism: Usul al-Hadith," below.) For instance, the phrase "I heard from X" is not the same as "from X." The former specifies coexistence in time and space as well as direct hearing, whereas the latter keeps all these elements ambiguous. Similarly, "X told me" is not the same as "X said." The former clearly specifies direct and personal contact, whereas in the latter this is not clear.

Attempts to codify and rank protocols of reported speech did not gain unanimous support from the narrators. Yet the *isnad* and the hadith are classified according to the phrases used to indicate reported speech (Koçyiğit 1975, 117–31).[5] For instance, the famous Bukhari, author of the most respected hadith compilation, considered all phrases used in reporting speech to mean that the teller and the listener were in each other's presence and that the narration was direct because, he argued, this was the only acceptable way of secure transmission. For the majority, however, who used less strict criteria, his standards were hard to attain.

Authorities in the chain of narrative are linked to each other through reported speech until the chain reaches the Companion who narrates a brief story about the Prophet or a saying by him. Therefore, hadith employs both reported speech and narrative in the chain of authorities and in the actual text of narrative. In the chain and in the text of hadith, language use displays different patterns and thus should be treated differently in each context.

The structure of hadith makes explicit the ways in which literary and social structures bear upon each other by systematically recording what goes un-noticed in daily life. In hadith, the structure in which the narrators and the narrative are embedded, and which is only hinted at, to varying degrees, in other narrative social structures, is made explicit in writing. Both the text and the chain of previous narrators are narrated. The cultural subtext that comes with the narrative, without which it is impossible to interpret the narrative structure, is called *metanarrative* (White 1973; Waugh 1984; Somers 1995).

From the time of the demise of the Prophet Muhammad, in 632, a social structure and a critical approach developed around hadith narration, which transformed this artifact from a conventional narrative into a "science" with formal rules and terminology. The political, religious, and legal importance of hadith in social life, as the second scripture of Islam after the Qur'an, reinforced this process. The size of the network grew as Islam spread to other nations. Later, however, despite the continuous expansion of Islamic territories, the size of the network shrank.

Protocols of reporting speech and producers of narration are common to all social networks. We are all implicitly aware of them because we strategically employ them in our day-to-day life. Yet they remain relatively unexposed, and, as sociologists and linguists, we do not emphasize their power to shape our knowledge and relations.

Content, Form, and the Spread of a Narrative Network

How do the content and the form of narrative bear upon the spread of a narrative network? Current studies on hadith are silent on the relationship between the literary structure of ahadith and the configuration of the hadith transmission network because these studies are characterized by the traditional referential approach to narrative, which concentrates solely on how narrative reflects what is assumed to be reality itself. In this respect, however, White's work (1987) on the content of the literary form of narrative is illuminating, as is Ong's (1982) on oral and literary uses of language.

As Ong (1982) and Eco (1994, 127–28) argue, some narrative structures are more likely than others to spread and consequently become associated with larger networks of narrators. Ahadith with shorter sentences (that is, an additive style), mnemonic (formulaic) structures, and stories as their content were more likely to spread than were longer texts containing plain prose and those dealing with legal injunctions. Ong's study of orality and literacy argues that narrative is the most convenient way for an oral culture to store and organize knowledge (1982, 31–77). There are, however, constraints on length and structure because of the limitations of human narrative in an oral culture. In line with Ong, although from a different point of view, Eco argues that "disjointed" narrative is more appealing, and that all cult narratives share the disjointed structure (1994, 127–28).[6]

A hadith has the form of a brief narrative, a "sound bite," or a snapshot from the life of the Prophet, unencumbered by causal or chronological context. What did hadith narrators intend to do by creating this form? White (1987) argues that not only the text but also the form of a narrative has content. From this perspective, it is possible to ask what meaning the form of a hadith narrative carries. First of all, this form of narrative fostered the identity of hadith scholars, in distinction to those who practiced other forms of narrative. The disjointed, plotless, and unsequential form differentiated hadith narrators from other communities[7] that dealt with hadith: storytellers (*qussas*), historians, and biographers, who presented their material in a coherent chronological order, a logic that was achieved by extensive use of fiction, according to hadith narrators (Suyuti 1972). Narrative thus constructed, however, proved to be more appealing to the general public, which constituted a niche for the fictive mode of narrative about the Prophet, in contradistinction to the empirical mode of jurists and hadith narrators. The dislike of certain hadith scholars for storytellers and even for historians, and the apologetic reaction of others in defense of history, are well-known facets of Islamic intellectual history.

Chronological sequence was not a major concern for hadith narrators. Aristotle defined plot (mythos) as the "arrangement of incidents" to be imitated by the narrative through mimesis (Chatman 1978, 43). Ricoeur (1984) argues that mimesis is not straightforward: the mimetic process is a symbolic or allegoric representation in language of the universal human experience of temporality in actual or fictive events (White 1987, 169–84). Conversely, Barthes argues that "narrative's function is not to represent, it is to constitute a spectacle."[8] For Barthes, the coherence, unity, and naturalness of the text out of sequence are "myths" to be denied by the critic, whose task is to ceaselessly break and interrupt the narrative text and disregard its seemingly natural divisions (Barthes 1974, 13–16; Barthes 1988, 95–150).[9] Anyway, for early hadith narrators linear time was not an integral part of events, because the concept of linear time came into Arab culture late in the Caliphate of Umar, the architect of the Hijrah calendar.

More important, there seems also to be a crucial pragmatic concern illustrated in the form of hadith. Disjointed narrative proved to be a mnemonic structure—more memorable, easier to recall and disseminate, and more compatible with the functioning of the oral mind (Ong 1982). Thus, the more broken a text, *à la* Barthes, the easier its dissemination.[10] I conjecture, in this connection, that hadith owes its large spread primarily to its disjointed form. If hadith had taken the form of a single long, integrated text, then only a select few who had the dedication and means could have had access to it.[11] The most widespread hadith is usually referred to as *mutawatir*. One can also conjecture that narrators whose repertoires include mnemonic narratives are those who will become more prominent.

Rise of the *Isnad* System

The question of what gave rise to the hadith transmission network still remains to be fully addressed from a social and cultural perspective. It is not my primary purpose here, nor is it entirely possible, given the current level of knowledge, to formulate a completely persuasive answer to this question. Thousands of manuscripts that are scattered all over the world, and that could shed light on the issue, have yet to be published. However, I can cite some converging interests, which may be considered probable factors that contributed to the emergence of the hadith transmission network: (1) the Prophet's constant injunctions to his Companions on transmitting his words to others; (2) the efforts of converts to learn the teachings of the Prophet; (3) the efforts of states and jurists to preserve the integrity of one of the sources of law; (4) the social status that society bestowed on scholars who dealt with narratives concerning the Prophet; and (5) sectarian conflicts, with those involved striving to support their own views on the narratives of the Prophet and destroy the narratives of the other side.

The historical roots of the hadith transmission network can be traced back to the pre-Islamic culture of Arabia. The "bookless" culture of pre-Islamic Arabia required unlettered Arabs to make extensive use of memory in their cultural and daily affairs. Memorizing poems and genealogies of tribes, families, and famous figures was an integral part of this culture, especially for the cultivated few. With the advent of Islam, memorization found a new area of application: Arabs began memorizing the Qur'an and the words of the Prophet. Later, after the demise of the Prophet, when knowing the ties among hadith narrators became important, they began memorizing the connections between narrators, a body of knowledge formally very similar to that of tribal or familial genealogies.

According to various historical accounts, there is no clear beginning to the creation of the hadith transmission network and the sciences of hadith that evolved during the first two centuries of Islamic history. The hadith transmission network was rooted in the attempts of Muslims to preserve the integrity of the teachings of the Prophet Muhammad, which, they soon realized, depended on a reliable transmission network. Forgery, motivated by sectarian and political interests or simply by mythical and fictional impulse, was against the interests of the Companions of the Prophet, the new converts, and the state. The Companions of the Prophet were entrusted by the Prophet to protect his legacy from forgery. It was also in the interest of the new converts to learn the authentic teachings of the Prophet. Furthermore, it was in the interest of the state to protect one of the principal bases from which Islamic law was derived. These efforts eventually led to the transformation of narrative from an art into a "science" and resulted in the establishment of the "science(s) of hadith," with its numerous branches, alongside the emergence of the transmission network of hadith that has survived for fourteen centuries, until today.

Writing accompanied memorization from the beginning of hadith transmission, continually increasing in significance (Abbott 1957–1972; Gellens 1990; El-Moudden 1990). Memorization of the Qur'an and hadith is considered in Islam a type of worship (Smith 1993; Cragg 1973; Coward 1988; Graham 1987). In the first layer, only a few mastered writing and were allowed to write hadith. Others relied on memory. In this oral culture, memory was valued more highly than writing;[12] even the Prophet himself was unlettered. The number of ahadith memorized by a narrator was, by definition, correlated with the level of his knowledge.

One after another, great inventions by the collectivity of scholars emerged in scattered places. They contributed to the evolution of a narrative social structure. Muslims innovated a special unit of exchange, hadith; a special type of social relation, *riwaya,* meaning exchange of hadith; a special identity, *muhaddith,* meaning expert in hadith; a special network, *isnad,* meaning a tracing of knowledge to its source, or simply support; and special criteria for distinguishing various types of transmission chains. To ensure the proper operation of the network, they also innovated formal rules regulating the whole process, *usul al-hadith,* or the methodology of hadith. These rules determined inclusion in and exclusion from the hadith transmission network, and thus the scholarly activity of the narrators, the moral standards of their behavior, their relationships with each other (as teachers and students), and the authenticity of ahadith in circulation. There emerged multiple identities and descriptors, such as hafiz, "well known," "obscure," "trustworthy," and "liar," showing ranks and structural positions of the narrators and conflicts over attempts to control the process of narrative dissemination.

Despite all these efforts toward control, forgery continued, leaving devout followers of the Prophet with an obligation to painstakingly search for his authentic narratives. More than others in the Muslim community, *al-muhaddithun,* scholars of hadith, devoted their lives to this task and made it a vocation. According to Abbott (1957–72, 2:2), "On the whole, the traditionists, especially the pious ones who refused to serve the government as judges, paid greater attention to the *isnad*'s than did the rank and file of the legal profession and the rank and file of the historian."

An Expanding Network and Shifting Centers

The hadith transmission network must be perceived against a larger historical background. External forces on the hadith transmission network reveal themselves when we look at the shifting centers of hadith through time: (1) Mecca (610–620), site of the genesis of Islam; (2) Medina (620–661), site of the first Islamic state under the Prophet and his successors; (3) Syria (661–749), site of the Umayyad Empire; and (4) Iraq (749–1258), site of the Abbasid Empire. These cultural centers, with hadith as an integral part, were at the same time political centers of their eras, a fact that demonstrates the linkage between Islam's political and cultural history.

The number of hadith narrators who populated a city gives us a quantitative measure for determining the center of hadith narration. Ibn Hibban's work, *Mashahir Ulama' al-Amsar wa A'lam Fuqaha al-Aqtar* (Renowned Scholars of Cities and Outstanding Regional Jurists) demonstrates the polycentric structure of Islamic culture by documenting the fluctuations in the number of scholars over time in the important cities of each period. (Ibn Hibban; see fig. 2.1). In Mecca, the total number of Muslims did not exceed a few hundred. They gathered around the charisma of the Prophet and bore the pressures of rebelling against the dominant religion, culture, and structure (Dabashi 1989). In Medina, however, the total number of Muslims, who came from a variety of social, cultural, and religious backgrounds, reached into the thousands.[13]

Disciples of the Prophet came to be known as the Companions. The most commonly accepted criterion for being considered a Companion was to have had a direct tie to the Prophet in his lifetime. Those who lived at the same time as the Prophet but without a direct tie to him are called *al-Muhadramun*. In the time of the Companions, Medina remained the center of hadith, although new centers began to emerge with Medina's 152 narrators, 23 of them being among the most prominent. They occupied themselves primarily with teaching hadith to the younger generations, called Successors (layers 2–4). Among themselves, however, there was very little narrative exchange.

In the time of the Successors—those who had a direct tie to at least one Companion—Syria, and in particular Damascus, capital of the Umayyad Empire, emerged as the center of hadith, with 172 hadith narrators. The number of narrators who lived in Mecca was 70, a number that later on dropped even further, during the time of the Successors of Successors—those who had a direct tie to at least one Successor (layers 5–7). In the time of the Successors of Successors, Iraq emerged as the center: Basra, with 107 narrators, and Kufa, with 98.

The life spans of generations overlap and are indeterminate (see fig. 2.2). The death of the last narrator from a layer marks that layer's end. The era of the Companions (layer 1) ended in 110 AH/728 CE; that of the Successors (layers 2–4) in 180 AH/796 CE; that of the Successors of Successors (layers 5–7) in 220 AH/835 CE; that of the Successors of Successors of Successors (layers 8–10) in 260

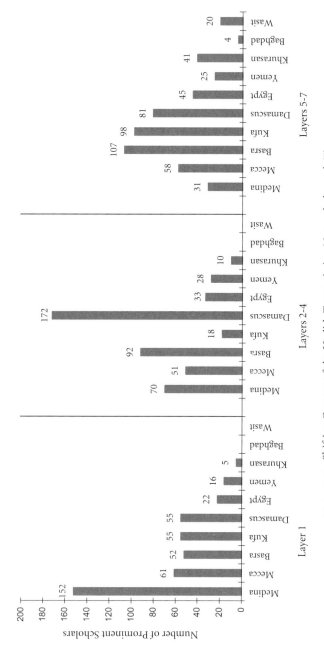

FIG. 2.1. Shifting Centers of the Hadith Transmission Network through Time

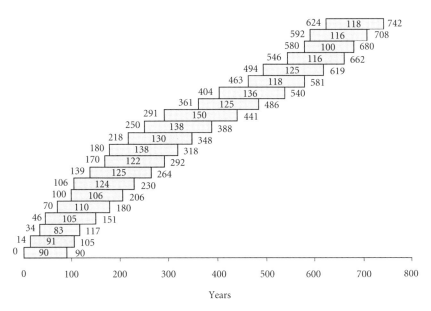

F I G . 2 . 2 . Longevity of Layers. For each layer, the first number (unshaded, left) indicates the beginning, the second number (shaded, center) indicates the duration, and the third number (unshaded, right) indicates the end. The dates are according to the Hijra calendar, whose first year corresponds to 622 CE.

AH/873 CE; and that of the Successors of Successors of Successor of Successors in 300 AH/912 CE. Companions lived between 10 BH and 110 AH (120 years); Successors lived between 12 and 180 AH (168 years); their Successors lived between 110 and 220 AH (110 years); their Successors lived between 180 and 260 AH (80 years); and their Successors lived between 220 and 300 AH (80 years) (Çakan 1993, 70–80).

Rise of Narrative Genres and Canons

The Prophet was concerned that his Companions might confuse the Qur'an with hadith. Hence he prohibited those who were incompetent in writing from writing down ahadith while he strongly encouraged everyone to write down the Qur'an. It was quite possible that Arabs who were new to writing might not be able to distinguish in their notes what was meant to be the Qur'an as opposed to hadith. Yet the literate and well-educated Companions got special permission and encouragement to record ahadith in writing. However, the general attitude toward recording ahadith had been ambivalent among the Companions because of their concerns that future generations might place equal importance on hadith and the Qur'an. But, after the Qur'an's authority was completely established, this risk waned during the time of the Rightly Guided Caliphs; consequently, attempts to collect ahadith and write them down increased.

Hadith compilation as a literary genre presents a great diversity: the *sahih* type (collections of authentic ahadith), the *sunan* type (topically organized ahadith), the *musnad* type (ahadith organized by the name of the Companion), the *juz* type (small collections of adhadith), and the like. Each type serves a different need.

The spreading institutionalization of hadith education (Okic 1959, 101–2, 105–14; Stanton 1990; Makdisi 1981, 1991)[14] also contributed to the canonization of certain collections as being the most reliable, ensuring a perception of reliability to the students of hadith.[15] These collections, usually referred to as "the Six [Most Reliable] Books," included books authored by Bukhari (d. 256 AH) (Fadel 1995), Muslim (d. 261 AH) (Robson 1949), Tirmizi (d. 273 AH), Nasai (d. 303 AH), Ibn Maja (d. 273 AH), and Abu Dawud (d. 275 AH) (Speight 1970). All these late authorities were non-Arabs, a fact that illustrates how hadith spread across lands and layers within a polycentric structure (Bulliet 1979, 8).[16]

Hadith compilation reached its peak with the emergence of the Six Reliable Books, which gained the highest authority among thousands of other collections. These compilations were later synthesized into single works, commented upon, and abridged for public use. They are still highly regarded by Muslims, with numerous scholarly works produced on them in each generation. After the Qur'an, they have served as the second scripture of Islam in Islamic law, theology, and mysticism. The divergent interpretive voices and communities around hadith narrative reflect the multistream, polyphonic, and polycentric structure of the network of traditional intellectuals.

Rise of Metanarrative Genres

Metanarratives of hadith can best be understood in contradistinction to each other: the methodology of hadith (*usul al-hadith*), the methodology of Islamic law (*usul al-fiqh*), commentaries on hadith compilations, and the biographical dictionary literature (*rijal, tabaqat,* and *tarikh*). Each metanarrative tradition developed a rather distinguished perspective (these perspectives are discussed below) on the same narrative material.

Hadith narration remained an excessively self-critical and self-reflective activity regarding ties, identities, and networks, but not only about narrative texts. The sciences of hadith, which emerged gradually parallel to the formation of the hadith transmission network, document the way hadith narrators examined their own network (Robson 1953). A survey of this literature will show that narrators developed differentiated views of hadith, its narrators, and the types of their ties. Furthermore, they analyzed patterns in the transmission networks of hadith to determine the degree of reliability. This critical activity created a system of thought through which narratives, narrators, and chains were brought together to create a larger structure.

How hadith narrators reflected on and examined their own networks and the networks of others manifests itself in metanarrative. Metanarrative—with valuation as an integral part—assigns identities to narrators, narratives, their ties, and their networks. This complicated order is difficult to penetrate without considerable study and contemplation. These parts developed relationally and remain interdependent with each other. Narratives mediate ties to other identities. The intermeshing of these identities creates a metastructure of actors, narratives, and metanarratives. Employing these constructs, metanarrative ironically both warns and assures the public about the reliability of narrative. Metanarrative genres of hadith give the impression of a bloody battlefield: identities are attacked and defended quite apart from conflicts over interpretation of the content of narrative. The outcome, however, as Silverstein argues for metalanguage (Silverstein 1993; see also Gombert 1992), is structural coherence variably achieved, perceived, and used by actors and onlookers.[17] The historical manifestation of structural coherence is the rise of the different schools of law, which made sense of hadith and its transmission network in contradictory terms.

Metanarrative is an emergent structural property of narrative social structure. It emerges—as both reflection and medium of construction—gradually parallel to the development of narrative social structure and takes various forms that are based on the criteria used in the self-reflection and examination of the narrators. These criteria are derived from culture and are based on broader epistemological questions.

Methodology of Hadith Criticism: Usul al-Hadith

Parallel to the emergence of hadith compilations in volumes, a new genre also emerged: critique of hadith. Scholars of hadith referred to it as the science(s) of hadith (*ulum al-hadith*), the science of the terminology of hadith (*'ilm mustalah al-hadith*), or the methodology of hadith criticism (*usul al-hadith*). This genre developed gradually over centuries.

Among early scholars of hadith, the rules and criteria governing their study were meticulous, but some terminology varied from scholar to scholar, and principles began to be systematically written down, scattered among various books. One of the outstanding and groundbreaking works is *Al-Risalah* of al-Shafi'i (d. 204), the introduction to the *Sahih* of Muslim (d. 261), and *the Jami'* of al-Tirmidhi (d. 279); many of the criteria of the early scholars (for instance, those of al-Bukhari) were deduced by later scholars through careful study of the integrity of reporters and *isnad*s that were accepted or rejected by the early scholars.

One of the earliest examples of a comprehensive work is the one by al-Ramahurmuzi (d. 360). The next major contribution was *Ma'rifah 'Ulum al-Hadith*, by al-Hakim (d. 405), which covered fifty classifications of hadith but still left some points untouched; Abu Nu'aym al-Isbahani (d. 430) completed some of the missing parts in this work. After that came *Al-Kifayah fi 'Ilm al-Riwayah*, by al-Khatib al-Baghdadi (d. 463) and another work on the manner of teaching and studying hadith; later scholars were considered to have been greatly indebted to al-Khatib's work.

After further contributions by Qadi 'Iyad al-Yahsubi (d. 544) and Abu Hafs al-Mayanji (d. 580), among others, came a work that, although modest in size, was so comprehensive in its excellent treatment of the subject that it came to be seen as the standard reference for thousands of hadith scholars and students to come, over many centuries, until the present day: *'Ulum al-Hadith*, by Abu 'Amr 'Uthman Ibn al-Salah (d. 643), commonly known as the *Muqaddimah of Ibn al-Salah*, compiled while he taught in the hadith colleges (*dar al-hadith*) of several cities in Syria.

The numerous later works based on that of Ibn al-Salah include the following: an abridgment of *Muqaddimah*, *Al-Irshad* by al-Nawawi (d. 676), which he later summarized in his *Taqrib*; *Tadrib al-Rawi*, a valuable commentary on the latter by al-Suyuti (d. 911); *Ikhtisar 'Ulum al-Hadith,* by Ibn Kathir (d. 774), *Al-Khulasah,* by al-Tibi (d. 743), *Al-Minhal,* by Badr al-Din ibn Jama'ah (d. 733), *Al-Muqni',* by Ibn al-Mulaqqin (d. 802), and *Mahasin al-Istilah,* by al-Bulqini (d. 805), all of which are abridgments of the *Muqaddimah* of Ibn al-Salah; *Al-Nukat,* by al-Zarkashi (d. 794), *Al-Taqyid wa al-Idah,* by al-'Iraqi (d. 806), and *Al-Nukat,* by Ibn Hajar al-'Asqalani (d. 852), all of which are further notes on the points made by Ibn al-Salah; *Alfiyyah al-Hadith,* by al-'Iraqi, a rewriting of the *Muqaddimah* in the form of a lengthy poem, which became the subject of several commentaries, including two (one long, one short) by the author himself; and *Fath al-Mughith,* by al-Sakhawi (d. 903), *Qatar al-Durar,* by al-Suyuti, and *Fath al-Baqi,* by Shaykh Zakariyya al-Ansari (d. 928).[18]

Hadith criticism, as Ibn Khaldun summarized in the aforementioned citation, was guided by some principles. However, these principles are scattered in the classical literature. Below I tried to codify these principles to make them easily accessible to the modern reader. These principles have their roots in our daily experience with reported speech and narrative. They developed gradually, gained considerable acceptance in the hadith community, and constrained the narrative actions of narrators. These metastructural features combined will give us an idea about the culturally operative measures used in the hadith literature to determine the relative reliability of ahadith and the identity of narrators.

The first principle the hadith critic uses concerns the number of ties to the source in the chain of narration: the fewer the ties, the more reliable the chain (fig. 2.3). This may be seen as the primary principle in the critique of the narrative chain. It is common sense that each addition in the narrative chain increases the possibility of distortion and reduces the level of authenticity and reliability. Hadith scholars turned this familiar rule into a guiding principle and systematically employed it in the critique of hadith. The shortness of a chain is a relative measure and can be determined only in comparison to other chains. When the lengths of two chains are compared, the one with fewer nodes is termed "high" (*'ali*), while the one with relatively more nodes is called "lower" (*nazil*). Particularly prior to the spread of the canonical compilations, ahadith had been compared to each other by examining the length of their chains. Aspiring students traveled to remote lands to obtain shorter chains of narrative from prominent teachers. However, after the general acceptance of the canonical texts, the emphasis on the shortest chains increas-

LENGTH OF CHAINS

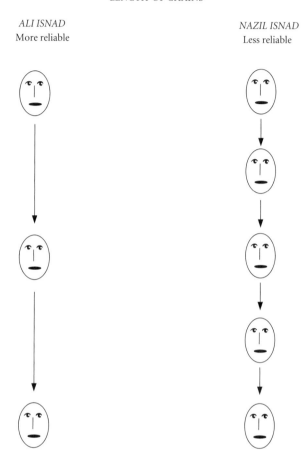

The lesser the number of ties in a chain, the better the chain is.

FIG. 2.3. First Principle of Hadith Criticism

ingly lost its importance. Jurists prefer ahadith with shorter chains of narrative in case of contradiction.

The second principle adopted by the hadith critic is the number of corroborative or parallel chains for a narrative. Briefly put, the more parallel chains a narrative has, the more reliable the narrative is (fig. 2.4). We may see this rule as the second major principle of hadith critique. Again, it is common sense that

NUMBER OF CHAINS

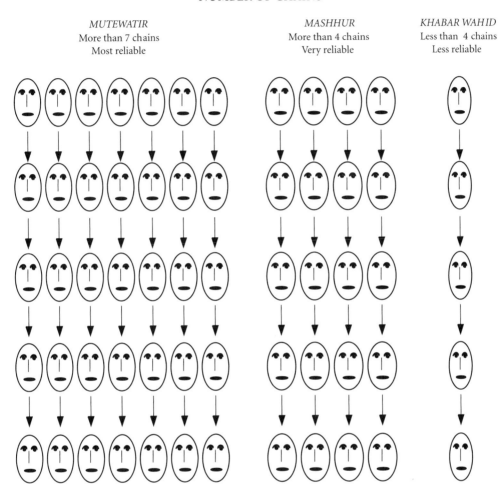

MUTEWATIR
More than 7 chains
Most reliable

MASHHUR
More than 4 chains
Very reliable

KHABAR WAHID
Less than 4 chains
Less reliable

The more chains a hadith has, the better the hadith is.

FIG. 2.4. Second Principle of Hadith Criticism

the narrative with the higher number of parallel chains is more assuring to the audience, compared to the one with fewer parallel chains. Hadith critique extrapolated a general principle from this common notion and employed it in determining the relative reliability of contesting narratives. Jurists give priority to a hadith with more parallel chains because it is considered more reliable.

CONTINUITY OF CHAINS

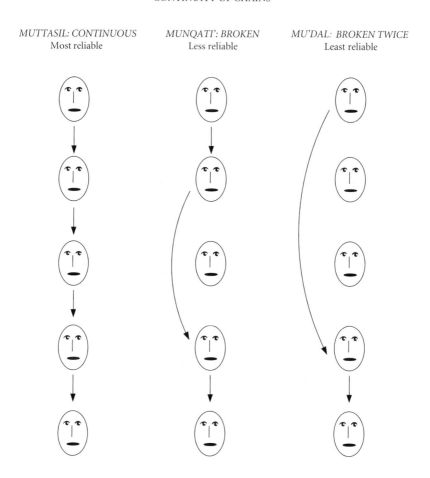

The more continuous the ties in a chain, the better the chain is.

FIG. 2.5. Third Principle of Hadith Criticism

The third major principle used in hadith critique can be identified as the principle of continuity of the chain: the fewer the indirect ties, the better the chain (fig. 2.5). In other words, the less broken, the better the chain, or the more completely recorded the ties in a chain, the more reliable the chain. In a reported speech, one of the first features we examine is the possibility of tracing the chain to the source without any interruption. Each node and each relationship must be verifiable. This is required to prove that the chain of narrative is reliable and the content is true. Yet sometimes it is not easy to determine the exact information about each node and relation. In such a case, we have to rely on what is available to us at the moment. From this perspective, each chain has a relative reliability, the unbroken being the most reliable. The resulting typology includes the following categories: *muttasil,* "unbroken," a continuous chain; *mu'allaq,* "suspended," a chain that lacks the names of one or more narrators in the chain; *munqati',* "broken," a chain in which several narrators are unknown; and *mursal,* "loose," a chain in which the name of the Companion is not mentioned.

The fourth main principle used by hadith critics can be identified as that of the reputations of the narrators in the chain. Thus the fourth principle can be stipulated as follows: the more prominent the narrators in a chain, the more reliable the chain (fig. 2.6). This principle can also be traced back to our daily experience with reported speech. The report that comes with the authority of respectable and well-known narrators is usually more assuring to us. By contrast, unknown and obscure narrators or reporters could not possibly command equal trust and reliability. The systematic application of this principle produced three types of chain: *ma'ruf,* "renowned," which means a chain of narration with all well-known narrators; *shadhdh,* "rare," which indicates a narrative chain with one or more obscure figures in it; and *mudallas,* "intentionally corrupted," which means a suspicious chain of narration, with narrators either unmentioned or mentioned in a misleading manner that gives the impression that they are well known and reliable though the truth of the matter is otherwise.

The fifth principle concerns the type of narration, relation, or tie between teacher and student. Hadith critics examine the strength of narrators' ties to each other to judge their relative reliability, which is determined by methods of narration: the more adequate the methods of narration, the more reliable the chain (fig. 2.7). Eight types of narration are identified by hadith narrators, and they also demonstrate how the teacher-student relationship is established among hadith scholars: (1) *Sama'* and *imla*: verbal narration with or without dictation by the mentor; (2) *Qira'a* and *'Ard*: student reading back to the mentor what is initially narrated by the mentor; (3) *Ijaza*: permission of the teacher to the student to narrate his narratives; (4) *Munawala*: student obtaining a copy

PROMINENCE OF NARRATORS IN THE CHAIN

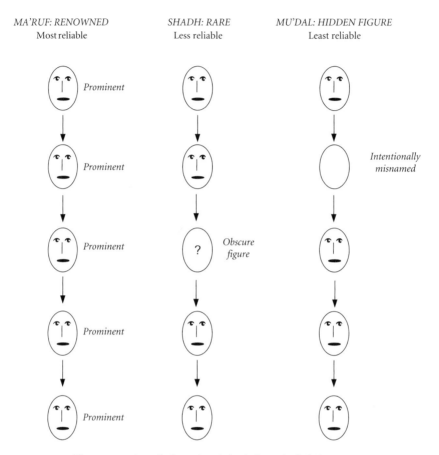

The more prominent the figures in a chain, the better the chain is.

FIG. 2.6. Fourth Principle of Hadith Criticism

of a compilation by the mentor; (5) *Mukataba*: student receiving the traditions of the mentor in writing, through correspondence; (6) *I'lam*: narration by a mentor to a student, without the mentor's giving the student permission to narrate; (7) *Wasiyya*: student obtaining the collection of a teacher by his will; and (8) *Wijada*: student finding the collection of a mentor.

The sixth general principle of hadith critique concentrates on the academic competence of narrators (*zabt*), which is demonstrated by the relative strength

TYPES OF NARRATION

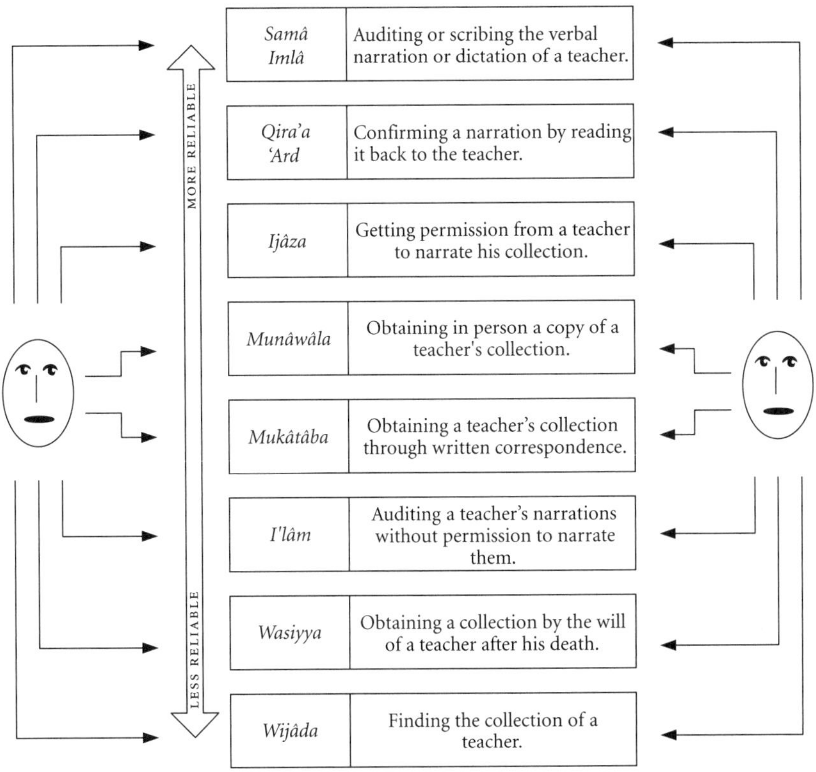

	Samâ Imlâ	Auditing or scribing the verbal narration or dictation of a teacher.
	Qira'a 'Ard	Confirming a narration by reading it back to the teacher.
	Ijâza	Getting permission from a teacher to narrate his collection.
	Munâwâla	Obtaining in person a copy of a teacher's collection.
	Mukâtâba	Obtaining a teacher's collection through written correspondence.
	I'lâm	Auditing a teacher's narrations without permission to narrate them.
	Wasiyya	Obtaining a collection by the will of a teacher after his death.
	Wijâda	Finding the collection of a teacher.

The more adequate the methods of narration, the better the chain is.

FIG. 2.7. Fifth Principle of Hadith Criticism

of their memories. Thus, the principle goes, the stronger the memories of the narrators, the more reliable the chain (fig. 2.8). According to this principle, the strength of the memory of each narrator in the chain is required for the reliability of narrative. Therefore, one must make sure that the following five defects do not exist in the narrators: *Su' al-hifz*, unreliable memory; *kathrat al-ghalat*, excessive mistakes; *wahm*, persistent uncertainty; *fart al-ghafla*, absentmindedness; *mukhalafat al-thiqat*, contradicting the most reliable authorities. If one of these attributes is found in a narrator, he is no longer considered reliable.

The seventh principle on which hadith critics focus concerns the character

TYPES OF ACADEMIC DEFECTS

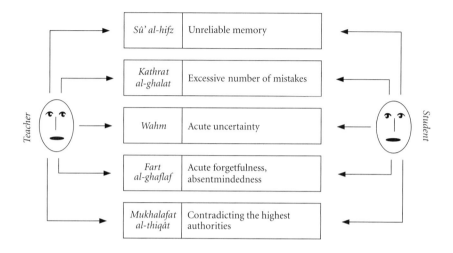

Sû' al-hifz	Unreliable memory
Kathrat al-ghalat	Excessive number of mistakes
Wahm	Acute uncertainty
Fart al-ghaflaf	Acute forgetfulness, absentmindedness
Mukhalafat al-thiqât	Contradicting the highest authorities

The more competent the narrators, the more reliable the chain is.

FIG. 2.8. Sixth Principle of Hadith Criticism

TYPES OF ETHICAL DEFECTS

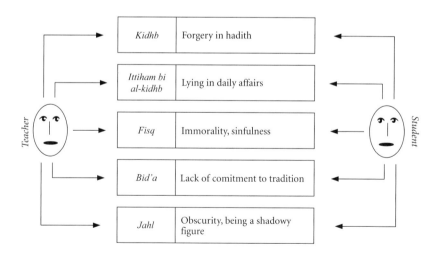

Kidhb	Forgery in hadith
Ittiham bi al-kidhb	Lying in daily affairs
Fisq	Immorality, sinfulness
Bid'a	Lack of comitment to tradition
Jahl	Obscurity, being a shadowy figure

The higher the character of the narrators, the more reliable the chain is.

FIG. 2.9. Seventh Principle of Hadith Criticism

TABLE 2.1

Classification of Narratives according to Five Criteria

The value of a chain is equal to its weakest link		
Criterion	Type	Brief definition
Length of chain	'Âli	Continuous *isnad* with relatively fewer transmitters
	Nâzil	Continuous *isnad* with relatively more transmitters
Number of chains	Mutawâtir	*Isnad* with abundant chains, so that forgery can reasonably be ruled out
	Mashhur	*Isnad* with several chains, but not enough to establish perfect certainty
	Âhad	*Isnad* with fewer parallel chains
Continuity of chain	Muttasil	Continuous
	Mu'allaq	Suspended chain: one or more names missing
	Munqati'	Broken chain: more than one node (other than the Companion) missing, but not two in a row
	Mursal	Chain with the Companion's name missing
Prominence of transmitter	Ma'ruf	*Isnad* with all prominent figures
	Shadh	*Isnad* with an obscure name
	Mudallas	*Isnad* with a misnamed narrator
Validity of hadith	Sahih	Perfectly reliable
	Da'if	Relatively less reliable
	Hasan	Reliable
	Mawdu'	Unreliable

and morality (*'adl*) of narrators: the better the character of the narrators, the more reliable the chain (fig. 2.9). This may be seen as the seventh major principle of the hadith critique. A narrator's character is required to be free from five defects: *kidhb*, forging a hadith; *ittiham bi al-kidhb*, lying in daily affairs; *fisq*, violating ethical and religious principles; *bid'a*, heresy; and *jahl*, obscurity. The existence of these defects in a narrator of hadith is unacceptable and disqualifies him from the profession.

Operationalization of these concepts gave rise to a sophisticated, multi-dimensional, or multifactor, evaluation system (see table 2.1). Some narratives are denied the authority that others enjoy. Ahadith are classified in accordance with authority attributed to them by scholars as follows: (1) *Sahih*: reliable, sound; (2) *Hasan*: good, acceptable; (3) *Da'if*: weak; (4) *Mawdu'*: fabricated. This classification is not universal; one can find more refined classifications, too.

Narrators' self-reflection focuses more on transmission structure than on content. This orientation drew criticism from those who wanted more focus on texts. The principles of hadith critique, which are used in coordination, appear to exhaust all aspects of the system of narration: types of chains, narrators, and narration. It is generally accepted that the value of a chain is equal to its weakest link. Regarding content, it is generally stipulated that inconsistency with empirically proved facts provides sufficient ground to dismiss a narrative as forged. Otherwise, hadith critique must strictly focus on narrative process, narrators, and relations.

The stratification of narrative is consequential because Islamic theology relies only on the perfectly *sahih* ahadith (*mutawatir*); Islamic law uses the first two categories; some schools of law, history (*seerah*), and mysticism (*tasawwuf*) on moral lessons may use weak (*Da'if*) ahadith as well. A legal or theological principle can be derived only from a sound (*sahih*) hadith—a concept variously defined. I can, therefore, confidently claim that each religious science (hadith, law, theology, mysticism, and history) developed a distinctive metanarrative about hadith for the different purposes for which they put it to use. Yet a detailed comparative analysis of these approaches is beyond the purpose of this study.

Below are two examples of hadith criticism. These examples show how the above rather abstract principles and concepts are put into play in context.

> "Knowledge is only by learning." ["Innama al-'Ilm bi al-Ta'allum."]
>
> Al-Tabarani related it in *al-Kabir*. Abu Nuaym and al-Askari also related it from Abu al-Darda' who reported it from the Prophet with the following phrases: "Knowledge comes only through learning; insight comes only through persistent study. Only those who search for the good will be given it. Only those who want to protect themselves will be protected. Those who cast lots (or seek an oracle from the deity), see evil omens in (or believe that they are dispelled by) a bird that makes them give up their travel plans, will not reach the high levels—and I do not say to you only in Paradise."
>
> Muhammad bin al-Hasan al-Hamadani, one of the authorities in the chain, is a liar. Yet al-Bayhaqi related it in *al-Madkhal* on the authority of Abu al-Darda as a *mawquf* hadith. It is also reported in a narration from al-Tabarani. Similarly, al-Bayhaqi related it from Abu al-Darda with the addition, after his word "he is protected," "whoever has the following three qualities will not reach high levels—and I do not say to you only in Paradise: those who make prophesy, or cast lots, or gave up a journey because of an evil omen." Al-Askari also related it from Anas as a *marfu* hadith, and also from Muawiya as a *marfu* hadith but with the phrase "O People! Knowledge

comes only through learning; understanding comes only through persevering investigation. If God wishes good for someone, He gives him a comprehensive understanding in religion. Among the servants of God, only those who have knowledge really honor Him."

Likewise, al-Tabarani related it in *al-Kabir* and Ibn Abi Asim in *al-Ilm* also from Muawiya. Al-Bukhari related it with an expression that indicates certainty as he said in one of the chapter headings: "The Prophet, May God bless him and give him peace, said: If God wishes good about someone, He gives him a comprehensive understanding in religion." He also said, "Knowledge comes only through learning."

Al-Daraqutni narrated it in *al-Afrad,* from [illegible] and al-Khatib from Abu Hurayra on the authority of Abu al-Darda with the phrase "Knowledge comes only through learning; insight comes only through persistent study. Only those who search for the good will be given it. Only those who want to protect themselves will be protected."

Abu Nuaym also related it from Shaddad bin Aws with the phrase "A man said, 'O the Messenger of God! What increases knowledge?' He said, 'Learning.'" In its chain of authorities, there is a liar. He is Umar bin Subayh.

Al-Bazzaz also related it as part of a long narrative whose chain of authorities consists of the reliable narrators on the authority of Ibn Masud as a *marfu* hadith, which stated: "He used to say: Hold on to this Qur'an because it is the counter [or dining table] of God. Whoever, among you, can take from the counter of God must do so because knowledge comes only through learning."

Al-Bayhaqi related in *al-Madkhal,* and al-Askari related in *al-Amthal,* both from Abu al-Ahwas, that the Prophet said: "A man is not born as a scholar. Knowledge comes only through learning."

Al-Askari also narrated from Hamid al-Tawil that al-Hasan used to say: "If you are not insightful, try to become so. If you are not a scholar, study. If one tries to imitate a group, he usually becomes one of them."

Al-Askari also narrated through a different chain of authorities on the authority of Amr al-Bajili that al-Hasan said: "Pay attention! Even if you are dressed with the dress of a scholar, the one who is dressed with the dress of insight is better than you. If you did not have insight, I would not deal with you. So do your best to gain insight, for whoever tries to become like a group eventually joins them" [al-Jarrahi 1932, 215–16].

Here is another example of hadith critique.

"What God created first is the Pen" ["Awwalu ma khalaqa Allah al-qalam"].

Ahmad narrated it. Tirmidhi narrated and acknowledged its authenticity on the authority of Ubada bin al-Samit as a *marfu* hadith with the following addition: "And

He said to it: 'Write.' The Pen said: 'O my Lord! What should I write?' He said: 'Write the measure of everything.'"

Ibn Hajar said in *al-Fatawa al-Hadithiyya*: "This hadith reached us and authentically reached us through several chains."

In another narration, "God created the Throne and prevailed on it; then He created the Pen and ordered it to draw with his permission. The Pen said: 'O my Lord! What should I draw?' He said: 'What I am going to create and what is going to be in my Creation, from rain or plants or living or the different ways of life or food to the time of death.' And the Pen drew what is going to be until the end of the world." Its men [that is, narrators] are reliable except for al-Dahhak bin Muzahim. Ibn Hibban honored him and said he did not hear from Ibn Abbas, yet a large group of scholars considered him weak.

It reached us on the authority of Ibn Abbas, may God bless both of them, as a *marfu* hadith up to him, that "the first thing God created was the Pen. He ordered it to write everything." Its men are reliable.

In another narration for Ibn al-Asakir as a *marfu* hadith that "the first thing God created was the Pen; then He created *nun*, that is, the inkpot. Afterwards, He told it, 'Write what will happen or what will exist . . . until the end of the hadith.'"

Ibn Jarir also narrated that the Prophet, may God bless him and give him peace, said: "'By the Inkpot! By the Pen and what they inscribe [Qur'an LXVIII, 1–2]!' He said a tablet from light and a pen from light which inscribes what will happen until the doomsday." The hadith ended here.

In *al-Nujum,* and by al-Tirmidhi, on the authority of Abu Hurayra, it is narrated that "the first thing God created was the Pen. Afterwards, He created the *nun,* which is the inkpot, and said to it: 'Write.' It said: 'What should I write?' He said: 'Write what happened and what will happen until the doomsday.' This is the word of God 'by the inkpot! By the Pen and what they inscribe [Qur'an LXVIII, 1–2]!' After that, he sealed the mouth of the Pen, as a result of which it did not speak and it will not speak until doomsday. Then God created the intellect, and said, 'By my power and glory, I will perfect you in those I love, and I will leave you imperfect in those I anger.'"

Al-Laqqani said in his *Jawhara,* "The Pen is a being from the light of God. He created it and ordered it to inscribe what happened and what will happen until the Last Day." He stayed away from defining its real nature. In some reports the first thing God created was the Pen, and he ordered it to inscribe everything. In one narration, the first thing the Pen wrote is 'I am a repenter. I repent on behalf of those who repent.'" The hadith ended [al-Jarrahi 1932, 263–64].

The metanarrative stipulations outlined above, and their historical implementations, are important for two reasons. First, they shed light on the logic of strategic investment in ties and thus on social power in the hadith transmission network. Second, they explain how ahadith and narrators were perceived by their public, especially students of hadith and jurists. Below I will present more examples from two more metanarrative genres, the biographical dictionary and the methodology of jurisprudence, to further illustrate the aforementioned principles of hadith critique, with the purpose of demonstrating how various metanarratives actually work.

Methodology of Jurisprudence: Usul al-Fiqh

Another genre, which illustrates the play of metanarrative, is the methodology of Islamic law, variously defined by different schools of law. Operating in the context of the assumptions already described, and following the guidelines provided by the methodology of law, jurists critically examine the structure of the transmission network and the text of the hadith before they grant a hadith the status of legal evidence (Coulson 1964, 36–73; Schacht 1964, 28–36; Kamali 1991, 44–85).

Jurists developed distinctive metanarratives on hadith, and each school of law also created its own metanarrative, expressed in its methodology of law. In this connection, different metanarratives developed, and a line was drawn between the "People of Hadith" and the "People of Opinion," with resulting conflicts that are observable among Sunnis as well as Shiites. The People of Hadith claimed to be more faithful to the legacy of the Prophet and accused the People of Opinion of limiting the role of hadith in Islamic law. Both sides developed distinct methodologies of hadith and law, on which, because of further differentiation, numerous schools of Islamic law were founded. Only four of these schools survived the test of time: Hanafi, Shafii, Maliki, and Hanbali.[19]

The debates about the hadith on marriage without permission of one's guardian illustrate the process of extracting rulings from hadith. Narrative has it that the Prophet said, "The marriage contract [for a minor girl] without the permission of a guardian is invalid" (Darimi, *Sunan*, Chapter on *Nikah*, Hadith no: 11). Among the four major Sunni schools of Islamic law (the Shiites also have a different understanding of hadith), the Hanafi jurists did not grant this hadith the status of legal evidence. They argued that this hadith was an *ahad* ("lone," or "unique") hadith, a hadith with insufficient parallel chains. Also,

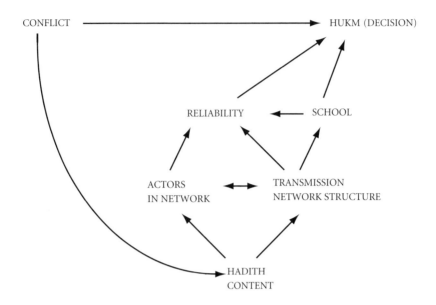

FIG. 2.10. Hadith in Islamic Legal Reasoning

they argued, one of the narrators, Aisha, wife of the Prophet, went against her own narrative by allowing the marriage of her niece while her father was away on a business trip. This also showed that she did not think this was a binding legal rule.[20] (See fig. 2.10.)

Jurists almost unanimously view the *isnad* as a source of conjectural knowledge (*dhann*), with varying degrees of certainty regarding the authenticity and denotation of the hadith. Theirs is the task of dealing with a dual uncertainty: first, varying reliability of the sources of knowledge, and, second, varying explicitness of the meaning of the narrative. The outcome, which is legal decision (*ijtihad*), is also conjectural and binding only on those who accept it. Thus, as Berman (1983) has documented for the Western legal tradition,[21] Islamic legal tradition also developed out of narrative, primarily the Qur'an and, supplementary to it, the hadith. In primary and secondary oral cultures, narrative remained the best way to store legal knowledge (Ong 1982, 139–55) for easy dissemination, memorization, and recall. Around the tenth century, in Iceland, among oral traditions, law occupied a distinct place: "The second oral tradition was the law, one third of which was recited from memory at the Parliament on each of three years by an elected . . . lawspeaker" (Scholes and Kellogg 1966, 44; see also Yates 1966; Eickelman 1992).

Commentaries on Hadith Compilations

Every well-known hadith compilation has at least several commentaries (*shuruh,* the plural of *sharh*) on it. This literature constitutes an important part of hadith studies and helps the public in the interpretation of hadith texts as well as the chains of hadith. Commentaries analyze the chain and the text of the hadith. For instance, al-Ayni's huge twenty-volume commentary on Bukhari's seven-volume compilation systematically discusses the significance of chapter headings, the relationship between the hadith and the chapter heading under which it is narrated, analysis of the chain of authorities, comparison with other sources where the same narration is related, various versions of the narrative in the broader hadith literature, explanation of the vocabulary in the text of the narrative, grammatical analysis of the text, literary art in the text (if there is any), legal analysis and consequences, and debates arising from the narrative.

Biographical Dictionaries: Science of People and Their Layers

Biographical dictionaries (*tabaqat* and *tarikh*) constitute a metanarrative genre on hadith with a particular focus on the network connections between narrators. The knowledge about the biographies, teachers, and students of narrators constitutes the subject matter of a particular discipline, the science of people, *'ilm al-rijal,* which is also called the science of layers, *'ilm al-tabaqat.*[22] In Islamic scholarship, there had developed biographical dictionary literature in all fields of scholarship, from law to poetry. None of these is as rich as the one on the scholars of hadith.

Biographical dictionary literature, as I will discuss in the following section, presents a rich variety in its scope. For instance, some biographical dictionaries provide information only about the transmitters of a particular book or from a particular city. Also, the narrators of al-Bukhari's *hadith* collection, *The Reliable Hadith Collection of Bukhari,* became the subjects of a few biographical studies. In Bukhari's collection, there are 7,275 chains and around 4,000 texts, with a total number of 1,525 transmitters (Ayni 1972). The most renowned among these is the one by the famous Kalabazi (363–398 AH), who compiled a two-volume biographical dictionary on the lives and network connections of the narrators who appeared in Bukhari's work, *Rijal Sahih al-Bukhari* (The People of Bukhari's Authentic Book).[23]

Biographical dictionaries about hadith transmitters, the primary source with which to reconstruct the network of transmitters, provide biographical information about each figure, which may include the name of the person, father and grandfathers, birth date and place, death date and place, teachers, students, travels, scholarly works, and the comments of other authorities about him or her. What follows is a brief example of a transmitter from the fifth layer whose name was Bakr and who lived between 102 and 174 AH:

> 215. Bakr son of Mudhirr son of Muhammad son of Hakim son of Sulaiman, the father of Muhammad, the Egyptian. He narrated from Muhammad son of Ajlan, and Yazid son of the father of Habib. Narrating from him were the son of Wahb, Qutaiba, and al-Walid son of Muslim. He was reliable, honest and pious. He was born in 102 and died in 174 on the day of *arafa*, a day before the festival of *eid* [Suyuti 1984, 108].

Dhahabi's *Tarikh al-Islam* (History of Islam), with only thirty-eight volumes that could yet be published, contains around 40,000 biographies of important figures in Islamic history, from the time of the Prophet Muhammad until Dhahabi's time. This magnificent study is the mother of several other small and more specialized biographical dictionaries, two of which are very well known among specialists in their field: *Tadhkirah al-Huffaz* (Biographical Dictionary of Elite Hadith Narrators) and *Biographical Dictionary of Elite Reciters of the Qur'an, etc.*

The following record is taken from Dhahabi's biographical dictionary of prominent narrators (huffaz). The way the narrator strategically built his network as a student, and the criteria by which the narrator is judged, are striking. I will add relevant points to the text references to the above-mentioned meta-narrative criteria. I will also add "H" to indicate those who are hafiz in the network.

> 178. 25/5 [meaning 25th narrator from layer 5] A ["A" after the number of the narrators is used by Dhahabi to indicate that the narratives through his chain were accepted by the authors of the "six most reliable collections"] Abdurrahman son of Yazid son of Jabir. The outstanding scholar, jurist, and prominent narrator of hadith [principle 4], father of Utaybah of Azd, from Damascus and Daran. He took narra-

tive from the father of Salam Mamtur, [H] Makhul, the father of al-Ash'ath of Sana, Abdullah son of Amir of Yahsin, and [H] Zuhri as well as from a great number of other narrators [principle 2]. He traveled to Mansur when he wanted to take narrative from him. He was well respected and was from the outstanding scholars of Damascus [principle 4]. The son of Ma'in and the father of Hatim confirmed his reliability [principle 7]. The best word of his is what Walid son of Muslim heard from him, "Do not write down knowledge [narrative] from anyone except from those who truly know the quest for knowledge" [principles 5, 6]. He met some of the elderly Companions, and I have not come across any narrative he reported from the young Companions [principle 1]. During the rule of Walid, son of Abdulmalik, he underwent oppression along with his father [principle 7]. His narrative is accepted by the Six [most reliable] Books. Son of Mushir said, "I saw him." He passed away in 153 [after Hijrah]. [H] Son of Mubarak, [H] Walid son of Muslim, [H] Muhammad son of Shu'ayb son of Shabur, Umar son of Abdulwahid, and [H] Husayn of Ja'f as well as many other narrators related from him [principle 2]. May God bless him.

We learn from this biographical narrative that Abdurrahman was a figure of high repute, with several renowned teachers and students.[24] Having met with some of the Companions, disciples of the Prophet, he increased his status, but since he did not report narrative from them, his social ties are not definitive of his position. Thus he is placed in the subsequent generation, layer 5, for position in the network is determined only by narrative ties but not by other kinds of social ties. He also got good reviews from the critics. Hence there is not much controversy about his reliability and identity as a hafiz.[25]

The above account helps us visualize who was a hadith narrator, *muhaddith*, and what it took for a scholar to gain authority to get his narratives accepted. The titles mentioned in the beginning of the record, al-Hafiz, *al-Imam, al-Allamah, al-Hujjah*, are used in the community of scholars to indicate position in the social stratum. These titles had been assigned by the consensus of the intellectual community but not by a formal institution or the state, so they are different from the titles given by the church and from the diplomas and titles given by universities. Acknowledgment of one's title and position does not make one immune to scholarly criticism.

The group is differentiated from the general community of scholars by the name *muhaddith*, which serves as a social identity. It is gained through the rituals of obtaining a diploma, *ijazah*, from the master. One can also acquire more than one diploma from various mentors. Yet within the group, internal competition leads to social stratification, which eventually determines whose narrative will gain acceptance and survive. The stratification of narrative that we discussed above must be analyzed in conjunction with the stratification of its holders, the narrators of hadith. Here are the strata of hadith scholars:

1. *Talib*: student, apprentice
2. *Musnid*: one who can report a hadith, with its chain of authorities
3. *Muhaddith*: scholar of hadith[26]
4. *Hafiz*: distinguished scholar of hadith
5. *Imam*: leading scholar of hadith
6. *Hujjah*: scholar whose word is accepted as evidence
7. *Shaykh al-Islam*:[27] leader of all Muslims in knowledge[28]

The title *shaykh al-Islam* was reserved for very few scholars, those with the greatest merits. Sakhawi defines it as follows: "The term *shaykh al-Islam*, as inferred from its use as a term among the authorities, is a title attributed to that follower of the book of Allah Most High, and the example of His messenger, who possesses the knowledge of the principles of the science [of religion], has plunged deep into the different views of the scholars, has become able to extract legal evidence from the texts, and has understood the rational and the transmitted proofs at a satisfactory level" (al-Sakhawi 1986b, 14).

There were not many scholars known as *shaykh al-Islam*. According to Sakhawi, the title was used for the following scholars: (1) Abu Isma'il al-Harawi (d. 481 AH); (2) Abu 'Ali Hassan ibn Said al-Mani'i al-Shafi'i; (3) Abu al-Hassan al-Hakkari; (4) Abu Sa'id al-Khalil ibn Ahmad ibn Muhammad ibn al-Khalil al-Sijzi, who died after 370 AH; (5) Abu al-Qasim Yunus ibn Tahir ibn Muhammad ibn Yunus al-Basri (d. 411 AH); (6) Abu al-Hasan Ali ibn al-Husayn ibn Muhammad al-Sughdi (d. 461 AH)—also called *rukn al-Islam* (pillar of Islam); (7) Abu Nasr Ahmad ibn Muhammad ibn Sa'id al-Sa'idi (d. 482 AH); (8) Ali ibn Muhammad ibn Ismail ibn Ali al-Isbijabi (d. 535); (9) his student, Burhan al-Din Ali ibn Abu Bakr 'Abd al-Jalil al-Farghani (d. 593 AH); (10) Muhammad ibn Muhammad ibn Muhammad al-Halabi (d. 817); (11) al-'Imad Mas'ud ibn Shaybah ibn al-Husayn al-Sindi; (12) Abu Sa'd al-Mutahhar ibn Sulayman al-Zanjani; (13) Sadid ibn Muhammad al-Hannati; (14) Abu 'Uthman Isma'il ibn 'Abd al-Rahman ibn Ahmad al-Sabuni al-Shafi'i (d. 449 AH); (15) Taj al-Din al-

Firkah; (16) Ibn 'Abd al-Salam; (17) Abu al-Faraj (Shams al-Din) ibn Abi 'Umar; (18) Ibn Daqiq al-'Iyd (d. 702 AH); (19) Ibn Taymiyya; (20) Siraj al-Din al-Bulqini (Ibn Hajar's shaykh); (21) Ibn Hajar (al-Sakhawi 1986b, 14–21). This list, although it may not be exhaustive, demonstrates how limited was the number of scholars regarded as *shaykh al-Islam.*

Yet the lines that distinguish the strata of scholars are fuzzy. There has been engaging debate among the scholars for centuries about the definition of each title. Since different critics have different ideas about the merits of a scholar, scholars may be classified differently. The opinions of critics on the merits of scholars are reflected in their works, usually in the format of a biographical dictionary.

The principles for the critique of scholars are the subject matter of a branch of the sciences of hadith known as *Jarh wa Ta'dil* (Wounding and Honoring; see al-Subki 1984). The vast literature on the subject is beyond our scope here because in this study we limit ourselves to the group of huffaz. The aforementioned principles 6 and 7 also shed light on the ranks of scholars on the basis of their scholarly achievement and ethics.

Age Structure of Learning: A Fortuitous Aspect

In the hadith transmission network, patron and client narrators came from generationally unequal positions, thereby creating a historical example of clientelism. The exchange, as Makdisi demonstrates concerning the institution of the diploma obtained from a teacher but not from a school, is interpersonal and between nonequals (Makdisi 1981; Graham 1993). The concept of a diploma from a school as a corporate body is foreign to traditional Islam. According to Makdisi (1981, 271), "Islamic education, like Islamic law, is basically individualistic, personalist."[29]

There is a fortuitous aspect to this individualistic process of learning and stratification, which manifests itself in two ways: choice of the most prominent and the oldest teachers at a young age, and longevity after maturity. Thus the fortuitous aspect characterizes the beginning and the final stages of a prominent scholar's career, in the former while he is a student and in the latter while he is a mentor.

TABLE 2.2

Age Structure of Learning: Birth-Death Dates and Longevity of the Scholars

Layer	Longevity of layer in years (latest death–earliest birth)	Date of earliest death	Date of latest death	Date of earliest birth	Date of latest birth	Minimum longevity in layer	Maximum longevity in layer	Average longevity in layer	Sum of longevity for all scholars reported	Count of reported longevity in layer	Count of reported birth dates in layer	Count of reported death dates in layer
1	63	11	11	-52	-52	63	63	63	63	1	1	1
2	140	13	90	-50	-3	38	100	73	1245	17	17	23
3	177	32	105	-72	22	65	131	101	1513	15	15	42
4	103	90	117	14	52	40	101	73	1174	16	17	29
5	118	100	151	33	89	36	103	76	2200	29	29	58
6	110	144	180	70	107	54	86	73	2278	31	31	78
7	111	174	206	95	129	60	98	79	4197	53	51	81
8	124	191	230	106	150	54	100	82	5818	71	71	106
9	125	213	264	139	174	50	100	81	6942	86	86	129
10	122	239	292	170	204	49	102	81	5279	65	65	105
11	138	264	318	180	240	55	123	84	6081	72	72	116
12	130	305	348	218	271	45	99	82	4082	50	52	77
13	138	304	388	250	306	46	100	83	3738	45	45	79
14	150	360	441	291	363	47	94	76	3422	45	45	74
15	125	427	486	361	409	56	95	80	1840	23	23	31
16	136	468	540	404	467	42	89	70	2743	39	39	46
17	118	542	581	463	506	56	101	76	1218	16	16	18
18	125	575	619	494	548	36	87	70	1680	24	24	25
19	116	611	662	546	584	47	93	70	1812	26	26	26
20	100	630	680	580	605	37	83	63	695	11	11	12
21	116	667	708	592	631	45	92	73	728	10	10	10
22	118	672	742	624	661	26	88	66	396	6	6	7
Sum	2703					1047	2128	1676.23	59144	751	752	1173
Average	122.9					49.86	101.33	79.82	2816.38	35.76	35.81	55.86

One must begin one's hadith education at a young age in order for one's chain of authorities to be shorter than those of one's colleagues because one's chances later in life as a teacher will depend on how short one's chain of authorities is. Bulliet (1983, 109) observes that "typical students had begun their education by the time they reached the age range 4.8–10.2." Yet a pupil cannot plan his own education, because he is too young and inexperienced to do that. If he became prominent later in life because he had prominent teachers in his network when he was very young, then his parents, or accidents, must have guided him to the right teachers as a child, without his own control and planning. Even if a student made decisions about his education at a young age, he could hardly be expected to know all the consequences involved in choosing a particular mentor. Rational planning in education by a student can begin only after a certain age (Merton 1973).

The fortuitous aspect becomes even clearer when we look at the longevity of scholars. A hafiz died on average at the age of 79.82. This observation derives from reports, primarily by Dhahabi, about a population that consists of 1,177 scholars over twenty-two generations.[30] The sources used in this study report birth dates for 751 figures, death dates for 752 figures, and longevity for 1,173 figures. It is evident that the sources are less careful about reporting birth and death dates than longevity. As table 2.2 shows, the figures for average longevity vary by layer.

A scholar of hadith had to outlive his peers—a circumstance over which he had no control—for his chain of authorities to be comparatively shorter and thus attract students. If the narrative string of a scholar was longer than the string of other existing teachers, then students would not seek him out. Furthermore, teaching hadith to students when there was someone else with shorter chains would not have been considered ethical in the hadith culture because it was not in the best interest of the students and might have been seen as gulling them. Bulliet's observation also confirms that scholars had to wait a few decades after completing their education before they could commence teaching hadith.

If the typical teacher died between the ages of 75 and 93 at the end of a teaching career of twenty-two years, then 53–71 should be the age range for the commencement of a career in hadith transmission. Taking into account the high standard deviation associated with the estimate of twenty-two years, a plausible conclusion is that while it was not out of the question for a person to begin transmitting hadith when he was as young as 40, it was more likely that he would be over 50 if not over 60 years old (Bulliet 1983, 112).

Changing Modes of Narration and Networking

Tension and diachronic switching (White 1995a) between various modes of narration affect narrative social structure. Switching from eyewitness narrative to reported narrative is a crucial change in narrative social structure. Eyewitness narrative empowers those who can provide it. In the narrative chain, distance from eyewitness narrative means a decrease in the social value of the narrative and thus in the prestige of its holders. Most of the activity in the hadith transmission network (measured by the degree of connectedness between its layers) takes place between nonadjacent layers, which means less activity between adjacent layers and even less activity within a single layer, because of the attempts of narrators to get as close as possible to the stratum of eyewitness narrators by reducing network distance[31] (recall principle 1, above).

The impact of changing literary structures on social structure is also observable in the switching from eyewitness narrative to reported narrative, which is demonstrated in the lexica: the lexicon of the Companions in reporting narrative is different from the lexicon of later layers. The lexica and structures used by eyewitness narrators and by those of later generations, who merely reported speech (Lucy 1993; Hickman 1993), illustrate how the switch in language from participative to reportorial mode paralleled the shift in network domains from Companions to Successors[32] (White 1995b; Scholes and Kellogg 1966, 256–65). Structures such as "in the presence of the Prophet I did . . . ," "while we were sitting . . . ," "I saw," "I asked," "I heard" were replaced, as the Companions disappeared, by structures such as "'A' told us that," "from 'A'," "I heard 'A' telling." The first set of words is participatory and emphatic: these words indicate either actual participation in or witnessing of an event (Morson and Emerson 1989, 127–30). (Note how narrators report the speech from different layers in the above hadith.) The second set of structures does not indicate participation but indicates reporting. Thus none of the structures used by later narrators to de note some eight modes of transmission[33] (Siddiqi 1993, 86) applies to the Companions.

One of the explicit impacts of switching from oral to written mode (Abbott 1957–72) was the decrease in the number of narrators who memorized a substantial amount of narrative. In the beginning, the pure oral tradition, hence memorizing, was valued more than the written tradition. This led an increasing number of narrators to memorize narratives. However, later on, certain contextual changes, such as institutionalization of education, which contributed to the spread of literacy, and canonization of certain texts, considerably helped written narration triumph over oral narration. In the beginning, literacy was an aid to orality; later, orality became an aid to literacy.

The question this system served to answer was whose narrative would gain the power to survive in the competition for authority. But how? The remainder of this study will attempt to provide an answer to this question. Prior to looking more deeply into the structural features of the hadith transmission network in subsequent chapters, in the next chapter I will explore the contesting theoretical approaches in sociology and humanities to the relationship between social narrative and social structure.

CHAPTER THREE

The Ceaseless Synergy between Literary
and Social Structures

Robinson Crusoe did not need a language. Disconnected completely from human society on an isolated island, he lived for a while a solitary life and functioned without speech. Nor did Adam need a language. As the first and only man, he had no one to talk to. The image of social actor in traditional social theory resembles that of Crusoe or Adam, for it strips social actor, action, and organization away from language. Traditional social theory conceives speech as a peripheral phenomenon, if not merely an epiphenomenon, that sociologists can do without.

Yet we are neither Crusoe nor Adam. If we eliminate speech from our day-to-day life, no social organization, from the family to the state, can survive. "A social system in the present sense is not possible without language" (Parsons 1964, 34). Furthermore, by uncoupling discursive and social processes, traditional social theory created a big gap between two mutually dependent social planes as well as a discrepancy between our day-to-day social experience and thought.

Coupling literary and social patterns through a reciprocal process provides a solution to the question of the relationship between speech and action. The reciprocal model does not annihilate the dialectic between words and deeds and maintains the tension between the two. The dialectic between words and deeds is a fundamental and long-established one in literary and social theory. Yet there are different responses as to how these two relate to each other. Traditionally, either they are treated in complete isolation from each other or one is reduced or conflated with the other. Recent alternatives to these one-sided theories explore their relationship without reducing or conflating one with the other. From this perspective, a reciprocal or circular causal model to explain the interplay between literary and social patterns replaces nonreciprocal causal models. One of the leading advocates of this new approach is Andrew Abbott (Abbott 1984; Abbott 1988a; Abbott 1998b; Abbott and Hrycak 1990a; Abbott and Hrycak 1990b; Abbott 1992a; Abbott 1992b; Abbott 1995).

Harrison White's recent work marks a fundamental shift in social theory in this direction (1992, 1995b), which aims to bring language back in. He explores how social ties and narratives are mutually constructed through language use, and he couples long-divorced linguistic and social patterns. By doing so, he breaks away not only from the traditional social theory represented by Marx, Weber, Durkheim, and Simmel but also from the social constructionist approach originally formulated by Berger and Luckman. The constitutive approach to language, which characterizes White's work, is fundamentally different from the social constructionist approach, which originated in the work of Berger and Luckman. The concern of the latter is to explain how our concepts and symbolic structures are historically and socially constructed, which also suggests a nonreciprocal model. Furthermore, it is grounded in the conventional referential approach to language as a symbolic means of expression. White's attempt, by contrast, is to tie language in to social action through a circular model in which language and action are inseparably intertwined.[1]

Taking the issue on a broader plane, I claim that views of the relationships between language use, narrative, and social structure are founded on a particular concept of language, whether it is reflective or constitutive of social action. The first is based on the referential approach to language that concentrates on how language is used solely as a system of signification and communication.[2] The latter, however, is based on awareness that language, in addition to its referential role, serves in establishing and maintaining interpersonal relations and constructing social networks. Recent literary and social theory, as I will outline below, have moved gradually in this direction (Culler 1988).

Language use, and thus narrative and metanarrative, from this perspective, are reflective but, most important, constitutive of social actions, relations, and structures. Social ties constitute social structures, yet discourse and stories shape ties and bestow meaning upon them. From the interaction of the two, metanarrative emerges. From this integrated perspective, narrative and social networks, intricately related to each other in both subtle and unstable ways, constitute a narrative social structure.

Following the prevailing perspectives, one can analyze the structures of narrative and social relations separately. However, my purpose here is to explore their mutual relationship more fully. I subscribe to structural realism and do not in any way conceptualize social structures as mere narratives. Instead, my purpose here is to explore the problematic of the multilayer complex relationship between the content and the configuration of a social network.

Instead of adopting nonreciprocal models that attempt to reduce narrative to social structure or vice versa, I will use a causally reciprocal model that will allow me to demonstrate the interplay between narrative and social structure. At the same time, this model facilitates transitions between macro and micro levels as well as between qualitative and quantitative aspects of social structure. On the micro level, actors are the attributed agency that finds its expression in various forms of narratives created, modified, or selectively conveyed by them as well as in metanarrative activity. The reciprocal model allows us to view both structure and narrative as well as configuration and content and thus to explore more fully what is going on in a network.

Structuralism has several strains rather than a unified and homogeneous outlook. Common to all these strains is the idea that there exists a structure to signification, which can be discerned and explained with the same tools in social and cultural contexts. Consequently, structuralism extends methodological models initially developed by structural linguistics to all aspects of culture and society (Saussure; Culler 1975; Culler 1988, 17; Lefkovitz 1989, 60–80). Speaking of the explanatory model used by structuralism, Culler (1975, 255) writes, "As the example of a 'scientific' discipline, it suggested to critics that the desire to be rigorous and systematic did not necessarily entail attempts at causal explanation. An element could be explained by its place in a network of relations rather than in a chain of cause and effect." Although they share an interpretive framework, there is a gap between literary and social structuralism that needs to be bridged. Yet this gap cannot be bridged, I argue, unless the underlying referential concept of language is replaced by a constitutive approach to language (see fig. 3.1).

The present gap between the two strands of structuralism and the nonreciprocal models therefrom is a result of the referential approach to language. This

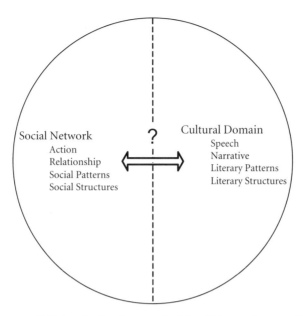

F I G . 3 . 1 . Bridging the Gap between Social and Literary Structuralism

is because the referential approach can produce only nonreciprocal models that privilege action over speech. Once the referential approach is replaced by a constitutive approach to language, most of the problems blocking the way of social theory in coupling literary and social processes will be solved.

How Does Narrative Relate to Social Structure?

I will first critically review the nonreciprocal, deterministic, and reductionist models before turning to the mutually causal models that I advocate on the theoretical level and implement on the empirical level. I will also show how each model is founded on a particular concept of language. More concretely, I will outline how nonreciprocal models are based on a referential image of language, while reciprocal models are rooted in a constitutive image of language. The exemplary models that I will discuss below demonstrate the long quest among scholars from a broad range of disciplines for an interpretive framework that will account for the relationship between literary and social phenomena. The puzzle, however, has yet to be solved.

Nonreciprocal Models: Referential Language

The referential approach allows us only to produce nonreciprocal models. From this perspective, language refers to "reality" and thus is only secondary to it in importance. What one-sided theories do can be summarized as follows: first, they uncouple language use from social actions and relations; second, they reduce one to the other or conflate it with the other. Classical structuralism, both in the social and the human sciences, is characterized by the referential approach to language. As a reaction to this approach, which downplays the role of language, speech act theory, with the purpose of elevating language to the level of action, conflated speech with action and reconceptualized speech as action (Austin 1962).

Among the striking examples of nonreciprocal models, narratology has a special place. Its central question with respect to how things are ordered on the social and literary planes—mimesis (telling) versus diegesis (showing)—can be traced back to Aristotle and Plato (Chatman 1978, 32). Classical structuralism isolates language from social relations and thus suggests a self-contained system.

In contrast, speech act theory and deconstructionism can be seen as two renowned forms of reaction against this isolated and ahistorical classical approach to language. Nevertheless, deconstructionism conflates language with extralinguistic phenomena by turning everything extratextual into a text. Speech act theory, on the other hand, with the purpose of emphasizing the importance of speech and elevating it to a level equal to that of social action, defines speech as an act that requires reducing speech to acts. In contradiction, Baker (1990) argues the opposite. For him, social patterns can be reduced to discursive patterns.

The referential approach problematizes the relationship between referent and language, sign and signified. The way the referent is conceived by this approach, as the given and the fixed entity to which speech refers, poses problems because it is not easy to build a picture of social organization without including speech. This approach produces a rather Newtonian mechanistic image of social structure in a two-dimensional space.

A more sociologically oriented referential approach problematizes the relationship between context and speech, but it takes them as given, without looking at how they emerge in the first place. It also treats them as fixed entities. Yet neither the referent nor the context can be taken as a given or fixed entity, because both are unstable and unfinished relational constructs. Neither the referent nor speech is a fixed entity, nor is the meaning that is believed to be stored in symbolic acts.

Narrative without Social Organization

The study of narrative, or *narratology* (the term is the English translation of a French neologism, *narratologie*), which claims that the study of narrative texts constitutes a new science (Bal 1985), can be seen as a prime example of isolating narrative from its social context. Bal defines narratology as "the theory of narrative texts" (Bal 1985, 3). For her, a narrative text is "a text in which an agent relates a narrative" (Bal 1985, 5).

This isolationism is founded on a referential approach to language that is determined by "truth value," which denotes "the 'reality' of the actants within the actantial structure" (Bal 1985, 34–36). Bal argues that events in narrative and outside narrative follow the same rules, yet she completely disregards the significance of this connection in her approach to narrative. "Structuralists," claims Bal, "often work from the assumption that the series of events that is presented in a story must answer to the same rules as those controlling human behavior, since a narrative text would otherwise be impossible to understand" (Bal 1985, 6). The ancient Greeks referred to this as *mimesis,* that is, imitation of reality, or merely telling what happened.

Scholes and Kellogg (1966, 4, 240) also contend that for a narrative to exist, there must be two requisites, a story and a storyteller. Valid as this may be, from their perspective, this approach ignores the narrative social structure in which the story, the listener, and the storyteller are embedded. From their perspective, the sole concern of narrative is to discover the patterns in the series of events (beginning, middle, and end). Bal summarizes this approach as follows: "Once we have decided which facts can be considered events, we can then describe the relationships which connect one event to the other: the *structure* of the series of events" (Bal 1985, 18).[3]

Current studies of narrative from the perspective outlined above merely concentrate on the text and aim to determine two things: (1) how faithful it is to the "reality" it imitates, and (2) how the events in the text are connected to each other, which must also imitate the way they are interconnected in the outside world. Both purposes are evidently rooted in a referential understanding of language.

Social Organization without Narrative

The referential approach in the social and human sciences sees language as a representation of the *real* and thus as secondary in importance to it. From this perspective, speech is seen as either completely irrelevant to social organization or, at most, as its symbolic representation. The referent, the social, on the other hand, is variably constructed by divergent strands of social and literary theory. The outcome is either complete isolation or conflation of the literary with the social (Archer 1989). Hence the image of a social actor resembling Adam or Crusoe, divorced from the discursive dimension.

This approach rightly emphasizes the way discourse and narrative are socially constructed but completely ignores how social structures are in turn narratively constructed. The result is a nonreciprocal causal model, and reductionist. Narrative, from this perspective, is a symptom, and real meaning lies elsewhere. The task of the analyst is to debunk the narrative and discover the real meaning. Even as a referential system, language is not straightforward; it functions indirectly. This approach can be traced back to Marx, if not to an earlier period. Marx conceived literature as superstructure produced by infrastructure, and he thereby privileged the latter over the former.

By contrast with the founding fathers of sociology—such as Weber, Durkheim, and Simmel, who, quite curiously, remain almost completely silent on the issue of language, discourse, and narrative—Marx, in a few tangential comments, at least acknowledges a place for language in the workings of society. For Marx, language and thought are dependent variables; neither thoughts nor language in themselves form a realm of their own, and they are only *manifestations* of actual life. In *The German Ideology,* Marx and Engels write:

> Language is as old as consciousness, language *is* practical consciousness that exists also for other men, and for that reason alone it really exists for me personally as well; language, like consciousness, only arises from the need, the necessity, or intercourse with other men. Where there exists a relationship, it exists for me: the animal does

not enter into *"relations"* with anything, it does not enter into any relation at all. For the animal, its relation to others does not exist as a relation. Consciousness is, therefore, a social product from the very beginning and remains one as long as men exist at all (Tucker 1978, 158).

Literary theorists who subscribe to classical Marxism still see language as a superstructure, and literary structures as representations of a real phenomenon, that is, social relations (Jameson 1981, 145–48):[4]

> We would therefore propose the following revised formulation: that history is *not* a text, not a narrative, master or otherwise, but that, as an absent cause, it is inaccessible to us except in textual form, and that our approach to it and to the Real itself necessarily passes through its prior textualization, its narrativization in the political unconscious [Jameson 1981, 35].

Jameson calls narrative a "socially symbolic act," reminding us of Burke, who also called language "symbolic action" (Burke 1966). What Jameson means by this is the act of interpretation of the text (1981, 10): "Interpretation is here construed as an essentially allegoric act, which consists in rewriting a given text in terms of a particular interpretive master code." Interpretation is an inevitable act because we cannot confront texts immediately; hence metacommentary, the interpretive master code or political ideology, that determines the way we variably carry on the socially symbolic act of interpretation.

Theory's task should, then, be to expose the implicit master code by deconstructing the dominant metacommentary. In this connection, Derrida's work, which represents a sophisticated obliteration of the literary in favor of the social, comes to mind. His work shows how he reduces the social to the textual by applying to the social a terminology originally developed for the textual. For him "there is nothing outside [the] text," and social acts also must be treated as texts whose referents are power relations. Derrida's approach reduces the text to the extratextual by turning everything extratextual into text, and texts into representations (Anderson 1989; Ellis 1989; Kamuf 1991, 8–19).

At a later date, Parsons went further than the epiphenomenalism of Marx in recognizing the necessity of incorporating language into social theory, yet he did not seriously pursue this tangent interest. "Language," he writes, "as that concept is generally understood, is not an isolated phenomenon" (Parsons 1967, 356). For Parsons, learning language, which is a necessary condition of becoming part of society, is impossible without entering into social relations. Parsons writes:

> We know quite definitely that the individual does not develop language sponta-
> neously without undergoing a socially structured learning process in relation to oth-
> ers. It is quite definite that this process must be part of a system of social relations
> which is orderly within certain limits, however difficult it may be to specify the lim-
> its in detail. It is altogether probable that many protohuman groups failed to make
> the transition to the human sociocultural level of action because of failure to fulfill
> the prerequisites of the emergence of language or of some other functionally essen-
> tial aspects of culture [Parsons 1964, 34].

Furthermore, a social system, Parson suggests, is impossible without language. Nor is it possible to reproduce and maintain the social system without the help of language:

> Thus a social system in the present sense is not possible without language, and with-
> out certain patterns of culture, such as empirical knowledge necessary to cope with
> situational exigencies, and sufficiently integrated patterns of expressive symbolism
> and of value orientation. A social system which leads to too drastic disruption of its
> culture, for example through blocking the processes of its acquisition, would be ex-
> posed to social as well as cultural disintegration [Parsons 1964, 34].

Although Parsons acknowledged the vital importance of language for the construction and maintenance of a social system, and although he refuted the traditional image of social structure uncoupled from literary structure, his concept of language was still heavily influenced by the prevailing referential approach to language. The primary social function of language(s), for him, was transmitting meaning: "The use of language is a process of emitting and transmitting messages, combinations of linguistic components that have specific reference to particular situations" (Parsons 1967, 357). Since Parsons did not seriously pursue his interest to its logical ends, the task of conjoining literary and social practices, as I will show in the remainder of this chapter, was left to future generations of social and human scientists.

One of the first serious attempts to add this missing dimension—that is language—to social theory was made by Habermas, who suggested the need to "linguistify" social action. Habermas attempts, in *The Theory of Communicative Action,* to append the linguistic dimension to the works of the founding fathers of sociology by cross-fertilizing and retooling them from a contemporary perspective. His project is to reconstruct the concept of society as "an ideal communication community," founded on a conceptual framework of "normatively regulated" and "linguistically mediated" social interactions. He borrows the latter two concepts from Mead and Durkheim, respectively, in order to overcome the limitations of Weber's purposive activity and rationality. This, he suggests, can happen through "taking as our guide the idea of 'linguistification'" (Habermas 1984–87, 2:2).

Another prominent example of foregrounding the role of language in social life is offered by the work of Foucault. Yet his work is also characterized by a referential approach to language, and he conflated the literary with the social at different stages of his career. Since he was of different minds at different times, it is daunting to treat Foucault's work as a coherent body. Archer writes:

> In his earlier work, where "discourse" was presented as an abstract structure of thought, it was also viewed as uninfluenced by nondiscursive elements like interests and power. Consequently at this stage he had to emphasize the *arbitrariness of discursive changes*, which was effectively to conclude that cultural dynamics can be described but cannot be grasped theoretically. In his later work he switched his stress to the other side of the divide and overemphasized the role of power in constituting knowledge, which now became *relative to* Socio-Cultural contingencies. However, such contingencies were viewed as patternless processes where domination was confronted by a recalcitrant "agonism," a sort of inveterate thirst for struggle, independent of particular conditions. Consequently, the later work endorses the *arbitrariness of Socio-Cultural interaction* because no account is given of why, when, or how people do struggle [Archer 1989, xviii].

The above survey demonstrated that the referential approach to language would allow only nonreciprocal and reductionist explanatory models of the relationship between literary and social patterns. The nonreciprocal model can be achieved only if violence is done both to linguistic and social structures. For the most part, they reflect the bias against speech and language, and they conflate literary phenomena with social phenomena or reduce the former to the latter, or they attempt to treat social phenomena in terms created initially for literary phenomena. None of these models can sufficiently capture the interplay between literary and social structures. The recent orientation of this quest, however, moves rightfully toward a reciprocal model based on a constitutive concept of language, which I will discuss next.

Reciprocal Models: Constitutive Language

One can see from the above survey that nonreciprocal frameworks marked an important developmental stage in the way we perceive the relationship between language and social organization. Regardless of their reductionism, these frameworks increasingly stressed the importance of language and its place in social life, which had been a nonissue in the classical period of social theory. They may even be considered to have prepared the ground for the arrival of reciprocal models because they did half the task by drawing a causal line from the social to the literary, complemented by another causal line from the literary to the social. These stages can be seen as different phases in the quest for an answer to the question of the relationship between words and deeds.

The ceaseless synergy between words and deeds, as we have recently come to know, can be demonstrated only if we apply a constitutive outlook on language. This uninterrupted interplay between narrative and social structure is best demonstrated by a reciprocally causal model of culture and social structure. Saussure, the founder of modern structural linguistics, can be considered to be the first to have noticed this strong connection, although he did not elaborate on it, and his views on this issue have not been appreciated until recently. However, as I will demonstrate, social scientists, literary theorists, and linguists increasingly adopt the constitutive view and reciprocal model.

Social and human scientists alike, in increasing numbers, have come to accept a constitutive view of language and to explain the relationship between language and social action through reciprocal models. In the reciprocal model, causality works both ways. Traditional nonreciprocal models, on the other hand, suggest a one-way causality. I will show below, just by way of example, that in the social sciences White, Sewell, Abrahamson and Fombrun, Somers, and Emirbayer and Goodwin have suggested such a model in their own terms. Culler also provides a survey of scholars from various disciplines who have adopted this approach (Culler 1988, 15). There are others whose names would be difficult to enumerate here, nor is it necessary to provide a catalog of them.

Literary theorists and linguists also increasingly acknowledge the relationship between literary and social phenomena. A common interest runs through contemporary literary theory in its various strains: "connecting the literary and the non-literary" (Culler 1988, 23). The linguists I will discuss below, because their work is crucial to the present study, include Silverstein and Lucy on metalanguage, and in particular on reported speech. Ong's work on orality and literacy will also be discussed in this connection because it will be used to identify oscillating modes of narrative between the verbal and the written in the history of the hadith transmission network.

Saussure on the Relationship between Society and Language

If Saussure was the first architect of structuralism in the modern sense, then he was also the first to acknowledge the relationship between social and literary processes. More important, Saussure, unlike his contemporaries, rejected the reduction of one to the other. To his credit, he demonstrated that society and language cannot be imagined separately, nor can they be reduced to each other. Yet as a linguist, he concentrated on "language as a social institution," and his primary concern was linguistic patterns. Consequently, he did not fully address the mechanisms that connect these two inseparable and mutually dependent planes. This was left to future generations.

Saussure's image of language and the community of speakers is best illustrated by a graph he included in his book (Saussure 1966, 78; Saussure 1993, 101a–102a). This graph is reproduced here (see fig. 3.2).

As figure 3.2 illustrates, the connecting mechanism between language and the community of speakers, according to Saussure, is time: "Language is no

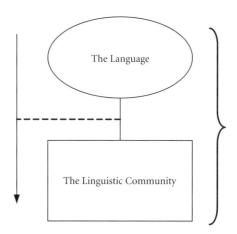

FIG. 3.2. Language, Time, and the Community of Speakers. Source: Saussure (1994, 78).

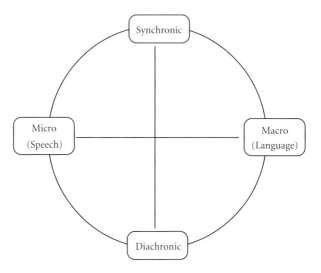

FIG. 3.3. Map of Saussure's Query for Structures

longer free, for time will allow the social forces at work on it to carry out their effects" (Saussure 1966, 78). Change and continuity are jointly produced by the interaction of language and the community of speakers, which are connected through time. Saussure continues, "This brings us back to the principle of continuity, which cancels freedom. But continuity necessarily implies change, varying degrees of shifts in the relationship between the signified and the signifier" (Saussure 1966, 78).

It is evident that Saussure recognizes a dynamic mutual dependence between language and the discourse community without conflating one with the other or reducing one to the other. Saussure discusses and rejects reductionist views. For Saussure, literary and social mechanisms are so intrinsically coupled that the whole field of language can be subsumed under the rubric of sociology.

He asks (Saussure 1966, 6), "But must linguistics then be combined with sociology?" However, he concludes, this would not be correct, because it would lead to reductionism. Language, for Saussure, is a "social fact," a term possibly borrowed from Durkheim and jointly owned by all the social sciences, yet it cannot be reduced only to a "social fact," either. Likewise, speech is a social act and requires at least a dyad or the "speaking circuit," as Saussure calls it, to take place. Saussure claims, "The act [speech] requires at least two persons; that is the minimum number necessary to complete the circuit" (Saussure 1966, 11). Language, Saussure argues, belongs to the individual (micro structures) and to society (macro structures); therefore, it must be studied on both planes. Saussure calls the former "speech" (*langage, parole*) and the latter "language" (*langue*).[5] Similarly, there are diachronic and synchronic structures on both the micro and macro levels. It is possible to map Saussure's query for structures as shown in figure 3.3.

Literary Theorists on Narrative and Social Action

Building on Saussure's vision, literary critics expanded structuralist query in two ways: first, in the direction of everyday narrative, by emphasizing the similarity between the structures of literary and nonliterary texts; and, second, in the direction of social life, by emphasizing the interplay between social and literary processes. These two developments are interrelated. Once literary theory had successfully claimed everyday language use, it became possible to investigate its relationship with daily life from a literary perspective. This expansion in focus gave unprecedented primacy to language in the interpretation of social action.

Literary theorists employ a constitutive approach to language, and they aim to demonstrate the crucial role of language in the construction and regeneration of social identities, control mechanisms, and structures. Reciprocal causality is used as a method for connecting literary and social mechanisms. Culler examines the work of a group of literary theorists who subscribe to the notion of a reciprocal mode in the relationship between literary and social phenomena.

Thanks to this redefinition of their paradigm, the influence of literary theorists expanded into areas that traditionally had been left to such other disciplines as history, anthropology, political science, sociology, and psychology. Increasing numbers of scholars from these disciplines revised the conventional approach that neglected the role of language and began to problematize the relationship between their own subject matter and language use.

Barthes argues that "narrative's function is not to represent, it is to constitute a spectacle."[6] For Barthes, the coherence, unity, and naturalness of the text out of sequence are "myths" to be denied by the critic whose task is to ceaselessly break and interrupt the narrative text and disregard its seemingly natural divisions (Barthes 1974, 13–16; Barthes 1988, 95–150).[7] Barthes's tool in doing that is semiology.[8]

Saussure postulated semiology (*sémiologie,* from the Greek *semion,* sign) as that which would study "the life of signs within society" (Saussure 1966, 16). Saussure envisioned that linguistics should remain only as a part of semiology, and he acknowledged that the success of his linguistics was due to this approach. The project was to be taken up later by Barthes. Semiology is not primarily concerned with content, thus the referential dimension, as such but with the forms that enable sounds, images, gestures, and so on, to function as signs (Moriarty 1991, 23).

Barthes questions the referential approach not only to language but also to all social signs, and he problematizes what this approach assumes as natural. Like Bakhtin, he stresses the communal structure needed in order for language and meaning to be possible. Moreover, Barthes sees the role of listener, or reader, as more important than that of teller, or author. Barthes proclaimed "the death of the author" in an article he wrote in 1968 by shifting the authority for meaning from the author to the reader through reversing the traditional image of the way in which meaning is produced:

> Classical criticism has never paid any attention to the reader; for it, the writer is the only person in literature. We are now beginning to let ourselves be fooled no longer by the arrogant antiphrastical recriminations of good society in favour of the very thing it sets aside, ignores, smothers, or destroys; we know that to give writing its future, it is necessary to overthrow the myth: the birth of the reader must be at the cost of the death of the Author [Barthes 1977, 148].

Denial of the complete authority that the author and the sign/word traditionally enjoyed is necessary to a more complete understanding of the way in which the system of social signs, a part of which is language, operates in producing and reproducing the social system. Nothing in these processes should be seen as natural, and everything in them, especially claims of authority, must be subjected to critical inquiry:

> Thus is revealed the total existence of writing: a text is made of multiple writings, drawn from many cultures and entering into mutual relations of dialogue, parody, contestation, but there is one place where this multiplicity is focused and that place is the reader, not, as was hitherto said, the author. The reader is the space on which

all the quotations that make up a writing are inscribed without any of them being lost; a text's unity lies not in its origin but in its destination. Yet this destination cannot any longer be personal: the reader is without history, biography, psychology; he is simply that *someone* who holds together in a single field all the traces by which the written text is constituted [Barthes 1977, 148].

Linguists on Discourse and Social Action

Like literary theorists, an increasing number of linguists also problematize the relationship between patterns in discourse and social action. Discourse analysis and pragmatics are particularly concerned with the ways language constructs and is constructed by social organization. In this connection, the works of Silverstein, Lucy, and Ong are especially important for the concerns of the present study.

Silverstein: Reflexive Language and Reported Speech

The recent attempt to foreground metalinguistic activity and the reflexive aspect of natural or ordinary language is significant not only for studies of language structure and use but also for all research in the human and social sciences with an interest in discourse as well (Lucy 1993, 1–4). This new orientation departs from and elaborates further on the constitutive role of language. Most of our talk is about talk, others or ours, past or future, which is called *reflexive language* or *metalanguage*. If our language did not have the reflexive capacity it has now, we would not be able to comment on other talk and, consequently, our daily life would be impaired. "This [language] use depends in crucial ways on the reflexive capacity of language, that is, the capacity of language to represent its own structure and use, including everyday metalinguistic activities of reporting, characterizing, and commenting on speech" (Lucy 1993, 1).

Reported speech, unique to the human language (Hockett 1963, 13; Lyons 1977; Silverstein 1976, 16; Lucy 1993, 9; Gombert 1992), is a crucial metalinguistic activity. "Among the most important of such explicitly reflexive activities is *reported speech,* speech which purportedly re-presents another specific speech event" (Lucy 1993, 2). Thus the patterns in reported speech present a special interest for social network analysts. Reported speech, as I will show below, has an extremely important role in the way social networks are constructed and maintained. Reported speech is also especially important in building indirect ties with those who are in a time and space different from those of the social actors. Sociologists, using methods from social network analysis and metalinguistics, can show the parallelism between the uniqueness of human language and the uniqueness of human social organization.

The reflexive power of language and its various uses in everyday life are currently explored from three perspectives: (1) the logico-linguistic tradition, which, from a referential approach to language, makes a distinction between language that refers to objects (object language) and that which refers to other language events (metalanguage); (2) the semiotic-functional tradition, which emphasizes the centrality of the metacommunicative framing of all language use; and (3) the literary performance approach, which foregrounds the use and power of reflexive speech in transforming exciting contexts, especially in the verbal arts.

Silverstein's work on metapragmatics aims to delineate the patterns and structures involved in this newly discovered plane as well as metapatterns emerging from its relationship to (mere) pragmatics and its object, whether it is the same, a different, or a fictive speech event. Silverstein argues that social/discursive interaction is contingent upon concurrent operation of the three planes: ordinary speech, pragmatics, and metapragmatics. Indexicals, which serve as pragmatic and metapragmatic signals, tie these planes to each other and to the social context in which speech event occurs. Each interaction, from this perspective, creates an "interactional" and a "denotational" text:

> But DISCURSIVE INTERACTION—to name the social happening that language use indexically constitutes—does, indeed, seem to have a coherence as a dynamic event that maps presupposed cause onto entailed effect. And this coherence seems to require a modeling in terms of real-time durational phases during which the discursive interactional "work" is accomplished in the medium of indexical signaling (which, it should be recalled, is nothing more than the signal-form-centered projection of presupposed/entailed context). That is, the "event" model of discursive interaction, with whatever internal serial stages and hierarchical relationships, is already a *meta*pragmatic representation of the facts of indexicality, attributing to them a COHESIVE STRUCTURE that orders discursive interaction as some INTERACTIONAL TEXT with event-relevant sequentiality, accomplishable or achievable purposivity, etc.
>
> To achieve or accomplish the laying down of (at least one) interactional text in

and by discursive interaction thus requires that, in addition to the paired indexical semiotic functions of presupposition and entailment, the functional modality of pragmatics that discursive interaction literally consists of, there be simultaneously in play another functional modality, that of metapragmatics—here, the metapragmatic *function* of occurring sign-forms—that at least implicitly models the indexical-sign-in-context relationships as event-segments of interactional text. Without metapragmatic function simultaneously in play with whatever pragmatic function(s) that may be in discursive interaction, there is no possibility of interactional coherence, since there is no framework of structure—here, interactional text structure—in which indexical origins or centerings are relatable one to another as aggregated contributions to some segmentable, accomplishable event(s). In effect, metapragmatic functions serve to regiment indexicals into interpretable event(s) of such-and-such type that the use of language in interaction constitutes (consists of). Understanding discursive interaction as events of such-and-such type is, precisely, having a model of interactional text [Silverstein 1993, 36–37].

Silverstein defines his concept of denotational text as follows:

Referring-and-predicating in the usual construal of these are, from this point of view, purposively accomplishable or achievable event-types central to which is a special kind of mapping that we will term here the DENOTATIONAL TEXT. Such a text, which many theorists tend to identify incorrectly with interactional text, has seeming concreteness to the extent that referring-and-predicating are understood as the central, or even exclusive, purposive functions of discursive interaction (cf. most information-processing or logical views of the coherence of discursive interaction) [Silverstein 1993, 37].

Silverstein's analysis employs a constitutive approach to language and metalanguage to demonstrate the sophisticated operation of language on several planes in continuous interaction with each other as well as with the social context. In the process, both the social and the linguistic, which make each other possible in the first place, are mutually produced and reproduced.

As Silverstein perceives them, linguistic phenomena are multilayered. There are language and metalanguage, pragmatics and metapragmatics. The interrelationship between these levels, in addition to their relationship to social action, is the new problematic that Silverstein brings to linguistics. Silvestein tries to show how these levels are differentiated from each other and how they dynamically interact in social processes. In this work, I also adopt such a multilayered image of language, which opens up new possibilities that the classical unilayered approach to language does not afford. Employing such an image, I will argue below that the interplay between discursive and social patterns is better demonstrated on the level of metalanguage.

Ong: Changing Modes of Narrative between Orality and Literacy

Silverstein's work sheds light on micro-level interactions between language and social action. Macro-level interactions, and the historical processes derived therefrom, still beg an explanation. I can say that Ong's work on macro-level analysis of interactions between changing modes of discourse and social change complements Silverstein's micro-level analysis.

It is well known to social scientists that changing modes of production affect social structure. What about changing modes of discourse? Ong undertakes the task of exploring the transition to writing, and to its sequel, print. He attempts to unearth the origins and consequences of changing modes of discourse in social life. The media and technology used in the production and marketing/dissemination of narrative underwent historical changes, from oral conversation to writing, from writing to print, and from print to electronic media. What are the correlates of these changes of discursive production in social life, their origins, and their consequences?

> To say that a great many changes in the psyche and in culture connect with the passage from orality to writing is not to make writing (and/or its sequel, print) the sole cause of all the changes. The connection is not a matter of reductionism but of relationism. The shift from orality to writing intimately interrelates with more psychic and social developments than we have yet noted. Developments in food production, in trade, in political organization, in religious institutions, in technological skills, in educational practices, in means of transportation, in family organization, and in other areas of human life all play their own distinctive roles. But most of these developments, and indeed very likely every one of them, have themselves being affected, often at great depth, by the shift from orality to literacy and beyond, as many of them have in turn affected this shift [Ong 1982, 175].

The macro-level analysis of interaction between discursive and social patterns will probably gain more interest as we move now into a new stage, with the advent of computers and the Internet. We already observe how communities emerge in cyberspace, how they conflict with each other, and how they strive for control. They even commit crimes. For example, Dibbell (1993) describes how a rape took place on the Internet and how the community reacted, after long debate, with capital punishment. Of course, both the crime and the punishment were virtual, as was the community itself, consisting of people miles away from one another communicating via computer:

> I have come to believe that they [the author's experiences in the virtual community where the rape and reactions occurred] announce the final stages of our decades-long passage into the Information Age, a paradigm shift that the classic liberal firewall between word and deed (itself a product of an earlier paradigm shift commonly known as the Enlightenment) is not likely to survive intact . . . the commands you type into a computer are a kind of speech that doesn't so much communicate as make things happen, directly and ineluctably, the same way pulling a trigger does. They are incantations, in other words, and anyone at all attuned to the technosocial megatrends of the moment—from the growing dependence of economies on the global flow of intensely fetishized words and numbers to the burgeoning ability of bioengineers to speak the spells written in the four-letter text of DNA—knows that the logic of the incantation is rapidly permeating the fabric of our lives [Dibbell 1993, 42].

The author's experiences shook, if they did not completely change, his political views about freedom of speech and the liberal distinction between speech and action—a remarkable example of the far-reaching ramifications of changing modes of discourse. "The more seriously I took the notion of virtual rape, the less seriously I was able to take the notion of freedom of speech with its tidy division of the world into the symbolic and real" (Dibbell 1993, 43).

> I can no longer convince myself that our wishful insulation of language from the realm of action has ever been anything but a valuable kludge, a philosophically damaged stopgap against oppression that would just have to do till something truer and more elegant came along. Am I wrong to think this truer, more elegant thing can be found on LambdaMOO [the name of the text-based virtual community where the aforementioned database is saved]? Perhaps I continue to seek it there, sensing its presence just beneath the surface of every interaction [Dibbell 1993, 42].

Yet old modes of discourse never completely recede before the advent of new technologies of discourse. Just as the invention of the automobile did not make the bicycle disappear, electronic media–based discourse will not completely replace other modes of discourse. Computers have not replaced pen and paper, nor did writing become a substitute for verbal conversation. Perhaps the electronic media, just like writing and printing, will open new possibilities for social organization by reproducing it, and by being reproduced by it.

Social Scientists on Language and Social Organization

An increasing number of social scientists, as I mentioned earlier, apply a mutually causal model to the relationship between literary and social patterns. The scholars whose works are reviewed below should be seen only as examples because the purpose is not to provide a catalog of names of those who subscribe to this view but rather to map a recent orientation among social scientists from various disciplines. I will briefly review the views of Sewell, Emirbayer and Goodwin, Abrahamson and Fombrun, Somers, Steinmetz and Hart, and finally White.

In contradiction to Baker's nonreciprocal model, Sewell develops a causally reciprocal model concerning the relationship between culture and structure. For him, "symbolic activity both shapes and is shaped by phenomena not reducible to symbolic meaning—for example, interpersonal communication networks. . . . Texts should be seen as social products that have social consequences" (Sewell 1994, 32). He explains his model in the following way: "They are linked to extratextual realities both through their authors, who creatively use existing linguistic conventions to carry out their socially formed intentions, and by readers, who are influenced by texts but also interpret them—again, creatively—in terms of their own socially specific identities and interests" (Sewell 1994, 37). Sewell's perspective is an important indication of departure from reductionism toward a reciprocal model (Sewell 1992).

Emirbayer and Goodwin also suggest a reciprocally causal model in order to account for the "multiplicity of structures—societal as well as cultural—within which actors are situated in any given moment." They propose that network analysts "would do well also to thematize the complex ways in which actors' identities are culturally and normatively, as well as societally, determined—the empirical interpenetration, in other words, of those cultural and social structures." They try to develop "a truly synthetic account of social processes and transformations that takes into consideration not only structural but also cultural and discursive factors" (Emirbayer and Goodwin 1994).

Abrahamson and Fombrun explain the relationship between culture and social structure by a "circular influence process." "Most importantly," they write, "we specified a circular influence process between value-added networks and macrocultural homogeneity: Interorganizational cooperative and competitive interdependence both shape macroculture and are stabilized and perpetuated by the macroculture they engender" (Abrahamson and Fombrun 1994, 750).

Somers, Steinmetz, and Hart also subscribe to causal reciprocity, although in varying terms. Sewell, analyzing their work, writes, "Steinmetz addresses the . . . question of how narratives shape lived history—the question of what Margaret Somers calls 'ontological narrativity' and Steinmetz himself calls 'social narratives.' The premise of these articles is that narrative has what Janet Hart calls a 'dual role': it is not only a means of representing life, used self-consciously by historians, novelists, and storytellers, but a fundamental cultural constituent of the lives represented" (Sewell 1992, 482–83).

White: Mutual Construction of Ties and Stories

For White, whose model I will be using in this study, narrative reflects and constitutes ties, while ties presuppose and generate stories. White explores the intricate ways identities, ties, and stories interact to produce a social structure. His emphasis is on attempts to control and on how these attempts relate to identities, stories, and ties. "Stories," White says (1992), "are essential vehicles for elaborating networks" (67); stories "describe the ties in networks" (65) for actors and onlookers (69) and constitute them; a tie "becomes constituted with story, which defines a social time by its narrative of ties" (67); stories "come from and become a medium for control efforts: that is the core" (68).

Control efforts, for White (1992, 3–64, 312–16), result from and develop into multiple and multilevel identities intermeshing with each other to form a social organization. Identity, embedded within a broader social organization, is a relational concept different from "self" and "personality." Contentions and contingencies produce identities in social action, while identities generate action. "Identity," as White defines it (1992, 6), "is any source of action not explicable from biophysical regularities, and to which observers can attribute meaning." Identities, like ties, are narratively constructed. They are multiple and multileveled, each accompanied by a set of stories, again exhibiting interplay between the literary and the social. Identities remain as sites of conflict and can survive only if "they fall into [a] self-reproducing [configuration] . . . which inducts as it embeds an identity into still further social organization" (White 1992, 23).[9]

White stresses that switching language is the key process for demonstrating the interdependence between, and the coevolution of, social and discursive structures. In the process of switching talk, social actors and their ties remain the same, though modified by the newly added content, whereas stories and the way they are told undergo change. Stories, or, more clearly, accounts of what happened, are continuously and selectively altered through reflexive accountings:

> Ties of a type are both network and domain, both relation and talk. It is talk that switches, not tie—and certainly not persons, they being deposits and byproducts of the process. The substance of a tie lies in what reflexive accountings are accepted in that network domain as warranties, and in what are the presuppositions and entailments. These can all together be approximated as a particular set of accepted stories. Thus, within a particular microhistorical setting, the tie is also a boundary, which comes as the envelope of a joint selection process across story set [White 1995a, 1042].

White aims to extend discursive reflexivity, discussed earlier, to social interaction and then firmly tie them to each other. For him, reflexivity characterizes both discourse and social interaction; hence the challenge of managing our accounts and ties via careful and/or spontaneous switchings, a process that produces a greater challenge: that of managing ambiguity in discourse and social relations in the presence of onlookers (the public):

> In continuing reflexive processes of mutual perception, the switchings to publics being negotiated may not appear abrupt or even be marked, either by those relations that go along in that switch or by those that do not. At least at a micro scale of dyad, there can be many realizations of publics that are strategic. But publics may sustain censoring among fellow temporary inhabitants, censoring which accords with some culturewide code of politeness rather than the concerns of the specific network domain [White 1995a, 1056].

Switching between networks, as this work demonstrates, may be synchronic or diachronic. Switching between the former, as White argues, is necessary for the rise of language registers. Narrative, on the other hand, as this study aims to show, comes from and survives through diachronic switchings between the network domains to which it gives life in the first place. Discursive patterns, as White emphasizes, "evolves in mutual accommodation with some form of dominance order" (White 1995a, 1039). I will also use both synchronic and di-achronic switching of language and network to shed light on the structure of dominance, or power/authority, in a narratively constructed social network that I will introduce in greater detail in the following chapter.

I outlined above how the quest to account for the relationship between words and deeds has taken various turns. The examples I have reviewed in this connection are far from exhaustive. There are many other researchers, such as Geertz, Bruner, Tilly, Bearman, and Shotter, among others from divergent disciplines contributing to the reciprocal model as an alternative to the linear model, whose work I cannot discuss here because of space constraints.

The above survey demonstrated that the advocates of literary and social structuralism from different academic disciplines increasingly appreciate the importance of the relationship between literary and social patterns. These movements in different disciplines increasingly reinforce each other. Consequently, a growing number of scholars from diverse fields have recently come to acknowledge that neither narrative and discourse nor action and speech can be uncoupled. Instead, they attempt to couple them through a circular model. Labov (1984, xiii) formulates this interpretive framework succinctly: language use "defines and is defined by social organization."

How to Bridge the Gap between Literary and Social Structuralism?

"What does one gain, what does one perceive by moving through these layers of comprehension? Patterns of patterns—metapatterns" (Volk 1995, 1). Metapatterns produce metastructures. Literary and social patterns, brought to bear upon each other, jointly produce metapatterns. Human social organization is a metastructure conjoined by speech and action. Speech is perceived to be a distinctive capability of humans, which has its undeniable role in their social actions and relations, and which distinguishes human social organization from that of animals (White 1992). Social organization divorced from language is not human. What is gained by coupling literary and social processes as metapatterns is this distinctive nature of human social organization.

Such an image can be created by bringing literary and social structuralism to bear upon each other, which would replace the rather mechanistic and non-reciprocal models of social process (Abbott). In recent decades, structuralism has made considerable advances in the social and literary fields. These rather isolated attempts produce a segmented understanding of language and society, which recent studies try to integrate to construct a more comprehensive image of social and literary processes. Yet there is still a gap between social and literary structuralism.

Social and Discursive Authority

One example of how such an integrated approach can enhance our understanding involves the issue of social power. Although social and discursive power always come together, the common practice today in the human and social sciences is to use one, from a linear causal perspective, to explain the other. Since they always exist together, it is easy to advocate both models: social power leading to discursive authority, or discursive power leading to social authority.

Yet, as I will argue in the following chapters, network centrality and discursive power are contingent upon each other. Baker (1990, 4–5) also writes that "political authority is, in this view, essentially a matter of linguistic authority." In order to demonstrate this, however, we cannot rely on the traditional non-reciprocal models of the relationship between discursive and social power.

Each social network is at the same time a cultural domain (White 1995a). In other words, the borders of a discourse community overlap with the borders of a social network. Conventionally, the question of power has been treated separately on both planes, a practice that has led to reductionist interpretations. The sociological problem, from this perspective, has been to determine which has primacy over the other. Some have argued that the social plane has supremacy, while others have argued the opposite. In contrast, from the integrated perspective outlined above, we can expect new questions to emerge. For instance, how do social and discursive power/order mutually produce and reproduce each other? Why do social actors with social authority have discursive authority as well?

Coupling Literary and Social Patterns

The above critical survey showed, however, that there is a large-scale movement in the human and social sciences toward bridging the gap between the various strands of structural query. This new orientation adopts a constitutive approach to language, as opposed to the traditional referential approach. It also adopts a nonlinear image of social process, as opposed to conventional non-reciprocal models. Equipped with these constitutive approaches to language and with a reciprocal model for the interplay between literary and social processes, rapprochement grows between the two lines of structural query.

Sociologists have long internalized the referential approach to language that resulted in the privileging of action over speech. Yet social action is impossible to imagine without speech. However, the referential approach blocked the way of establishing the connection between language use and social process without reducing or conflating one to or with the other. But the recent constitutive approach to language, as I showed above, allows us to show the synergy between action and speech, to construct and reconstruct social structures.

The above account also demonstrates that the relationship between words and deeds—and, more specifically, between narrative and social structure—should not be taken as a binary dichotomy but rather as a mutually productive and constitutive dialectic. It became clear that there are problems in establishing and maintaining such a dichotomy because speech can be perceived as act and act can be perceived as speech, given the fuzzy border between them. Yet the dialectic and the tension should be maintained while the difference between the two is exploited in establishing a constitutive approach to language, which, in turn, would allow us a better understanding of social action and relations.

The fallacy of conflation holds no more, giving way to the recognition of the relative autonomy of, and interdependence between, literary and social structures. The Crusoe- or Adam-like image of the social actor in literary and social theory is increasingly being replaced by an image more able to stand up to everyday experience.

CHAPTER FOUR

Reconstructing the Hadith Transmission Network

Narratives into Networks

Narrative both reflects and reconstructs networks of social relations. It thus reproduces them on the social and literary levels. The following account may be seen as a historical example of our preceding theoretical discussion on the mutual relationship between narrative and social structure. It illustrates how narrative reproduces diachronic networks at each generation; how retelling stories reactivates our ties and expands our networks retrospectively. This view helps us better appreciate why scholars of hadith were extremely attentive to their past networks, embodied in the biographies of their mentors across generations. The existence of an independent discipline, the "science of people and layers" (*'ilm al-rijal wa al-tabaqat*), attests to the extraordinary care they showed for documenting their past ties. This particular discipline has focused on the study of scholars and their networks through time.

This chapter expands our earlier discussion of the biographical dictionary literature, which I see as a major hadith metanarrative. The traditional science of people and layers has been far from monolithic. Instead, it has different genres, each one focusing on a particular range or scale in the hadith transmission network. Furthermore, each new generation of scholars has continuously updated and appended this body of literature, adding new information about the most recent layers, without interruption, over centuries.

Hadith scholars cared more than any other intellectual community about their network because they were aware that it alone gave them their identity, status, authority, and social capital. It helped them not only in establishing their own reliability and the authenticity of ahadith but also in competing against their colleagues for more and better students. Even if it was possible for a student to acquire from other sources the narrative that a scholar of hadith offered, it was impossible for the student to gain access to the network for which the scholar alone had the authority to link students, simply because the scholar represented the final and possibly sole available link to the chain. A written text alone did not suffice to provide the student what he sought; instead, it was a particular position in the network that the student stood to inherit from his master and that he could leverage as social capital later in his academic life.

While conducting this research, I reorganized the information gleaned from numerous historical sources in the form of an electronic data set, which allowed me to use modern tools to analyze the networks of huffaz. Statistical analysis requires transformation of scattered historical records, in the form of narratives, into measurable variables. Below, I describe my sources of information about the networks of huffaz and the way I unearthed data from them and reconstructed the time-honored network of hadith transmission.

The historical sources of the networks of Muslim scholars can be grouped according to four levels on a spectrum ranging from the microscopic to the macroscopic levels. The first and most narrowly circumscribed level is that of a single chain for a single narrative. These single chains can be found abundantly in such hadith compilations as those by Bukhari and Muslim. The second level is that of the individual narrator, which consists of network autobiographical works of scholars, such as those by Ibn Hajar, Dhahabi, and Suyuti. The third level is the local level, which consists of city histories. Examples of this genre are works on the history of Nishapur and Baghdad. The fourth level consists of general biographical dictionaries and history books. These represent, hierarchically, the most macroscopic and inclusive source of data.

Classical Sources about Scholarly Networks

The present study makes comparative use of the information derived from works anchored at these four levels. In particular, the famous biographical dictionaries of Dhahabi and Suyuti about prominent hadith scholars have served as the two main sources of this work. Furthermore, the micro-level data derived from the compilation of Bukhari have also been used to contrast and complement the network data derived from the other sources. Before I discuss the particular historical works from which data have been derived for this study,[1] it would be appropriate to provide an overview of these genres.

The above-mentioned four levels of network data about prominent scholars from the medieval period are based on various genres of historiography among Muslim historians who recognized the significance of personal connections and social networks in history and society. History, *tarikh,* meant for them primarily interrelations of individual social actors over time. The individual as a historical actor is not an abstract force; instead, the individual is the focus of analysis. The references to aggregate social actors, nations, groups, tribes, and the like, are secondary in these writings. The city, for instance, was an aggregate entity that was conceived as the web of personal relations woven over centuries. Similarly, schools of law and theology have also been seen as networks through time. The following brief review will make clear the remarkable emphasis on social networks on the part of classical Muslim historians.

Network Autobiographies

It should be noted at the outset that the concept of autobiography among hadith scholars was different from ours today. The focus of their autobiographical works was on their relations with colleagues and especially mentors, following the custom and literary genres of autobiography prevalent in their time. These genres include *mashyakhah,* which literally means a list of mentors, and *mu'jam,* which literally means a biographical dictionary of mentors. Below, I will briefly introduce both types of literature.

The first and the most common autobiographical genre, *mashyakhah,* is a work of personal academic history in which a scholar provides a list of the teachers from whom he obtained a formal diploma, *ijazah.* Biographical information and the content of the relationship are also provided. (Recall in this connection the eight types of relation between a teacher and a student, discussed in chapter 2).

In particular, works in this genre record the type of *ijazah* a disciple obtained from a master. This genre can be considered the first level of historiography because the works comprising it provide firsthand information about networks of scholars. The limitation inherent in this type of source is imposed by the confidence we can invest in a writer's appraisal of his own academic accomplishments. However, there are ways to cross-check this information from other sources, especially from the *mashyakhah* of scholars whose names are mentioned in one's writing as one's own teachers and students.

At times, students went even further. They listed all or some of the ahadith they received from each of their teachers, to preclude any future confusion. This gave rise to a literary genre called *mu'jam* (the plural is *ma'ajim*). This genre was not used exclusively for hadith. In fact, there were two kinds of *mu'jam*: the *mu'jam* of hadith, exclusively dedicated to hadith teachers, and the *mu'jam* of teachers, inclusive of all teachers from various branches of the traditional disciplines. Occasionally the term *mu'jam* of hadith was interchangeably used with the term *mashyakhah*.

These genres prevailed in the eastern part of the medieval Muslim world. Scholars in the western part—in Andalusia, Islamic Spain—developed their own style, however, when they recorded their academic network. They created *fihris* (the plural is *faharis*) or *mufahras* and *barnamaj* (the plural is *baramij*), borrowing both words from Persian. Compared to their colleagues in the east, scholars in Andalusia put a relatively high importance on preparing a list of their teachers in the form of a *fihris* or *barnamaj*. An interesting example is that of Shaykh al-Tayyib ibn Muhammad al-Fasi (d. 1113 AH), who composed his *fihris* in the form of a 618-line ode (Kettani 1994, 280).

Only a very few of these works have been published. Hundreds of them, written in classical Arabic, remain in manuscript form in scattered libraries around the world.[2] Some of these works are alphabetically ordered—most *ma'ajim* follow this pattern—while some are chronologically ordered. The number of teachers reported in these works may be two thousand or only a few hundred. Below is a brief description of the *mashyakhah*s of Dhahabi, Ibn al-Hajar (773–852 AH), and Suyuti, whose works are used in this study.

Dhahabi, who belongs to layer 21, wrote three *mashyakhas*—one long, one medium, and one short. They appeared in several editions. The long one is called *Al-Mu'jam al-Kabir*, the medium one is called *Al-Mu'jam al-Latif* (or *Al-Mu'jam al-Saghir*)—according to this work, Dhahabi's first hearing of hadith took place in 694 AH— and the short one is called *Al-Mu'jam al-Mukhtass bi al-Muhaddithin*.

Ibn Hajar, who belongs to layer 24, compiled two books about his academic connections. One is called *Al-Mu'jam al-Mufahras* and is chronologically ordered. It provides information about the chains he established via audition (*sama'*) and reading back to the mentor (*qiraah*). Later in his life, he ordered this work alphabetically and divided it into two sections: one section for teachers who taught him disciplines concerning solely the narrative sciences (*riwayah*), and the other for teachers who taught him interpretation of narrative and other rational sciences (*dirayah*). He composed his work over a period of twenty-six years, from 806 to 832 AH (Kettani 1994, 286). Sakhawi (831–906 AH), who was a student of Ibn Hajar, wrote a great biographical work in two volumes about the life and work of his teacher, *Al-Jawahir wa al-Durar fi Tarjamah Shaykh al-Islam Ibn Hajar*.[3] In this work, Sakhawi listed an extensive number of Ibn Hajar's teachers.

Al-Suyuti, who was a student of Ibn al-Hajar,[4] collected the names of his own teachers from whom he obtained diplomas in his autobiographical work titled *Al-Munajjam fi al-Mu'jam*. Another work by him on the same subject is called *Al-Mu'jam al-Kabir Hatib al-Layl wa Jarif al-Sayl*.

Writing a *mu'jam* or *mashyakhah* seems to have been a common practice of recordkeeping about one's teachers. Usually such works were for the private use and reference of scholars. Yet, later on, the works of prestigious figures were occasionally copied by aspiring students and have survived to the present day. This tradition gave rise to a very rich literature that can be used now for reconstructing the networks of scholars on the basis of firsthand information from their own writings. Today this genre is drawing increasing attention; consequently, there is a growing number of *mashyakhah* manuscripts being discovered and published throughout the world.

City Histories

Scholars from major cities collected information about the cultural legacies of their cities, information that was based on biographies and that came via connections with other scholars who were their countrymen. This genre must have increased the prestige of the cities as well as of the scholars who studied and resided in them. The number of works in this vein reaches the hundreds. The cities that were subject to extensive attention by hadith scholars include Baghdad, Damascus, Isphahan, Nishapur, Mecca, Medina, Marw, and Cairo (Kettani 1994, 263–70). These works, one can easily assume, were usually based on the *mashyakhah* genre. Earlier works survive through later works that update them (Frye 1965, 7). Local history as a biographical dictionary of scholars, with emphasis on their networks, was a new style brought about by hadith scholarship.

An interesting example is provided by the data about Nishapur, analyzed by Bulliet (1972), who derived them from *Al-Muntakhab min al-Siyaq* or *Muntakhab min Kitab al-Siyaq li Tarikh Nishabur* (Frye 1965; al-Mahmudi 1403 AH)[5] by al-Sarifayni (581–641 AH). The work, which is in Arabic and arranged alphabetically, includes biographical and network information about 1,678 scholars, including the author himself. This work includes 202 of the most prominent scholars. *Al-Muntakhab* is an abbreviation and extension of an earlier work, *Al-Siyaq li Tarikh Nisabur,* by Abdulghafir al-Farisi (451–529 AH). Al-Farisi's work is also an abbreviation and updating of the work of the famous hafiz al-Hakim al-Bayyi' (d. 405 AH/1014 CE). Al-Kattani reports that Dhahabi also abbreviated the work of al-Hakim (Kettani 1994, 267). There is an abridged version in Persian as well, *Kitab Ahwal Nisabur,* by al-Khalifa al-Nisaburi, organized into six layers. The evolution or updating of the data on the intellectual history of Nishapur in the hands of scholars from subsequent generations illustrates how these data have been gathered and compiled over centuries.

General Biographical Dictionaries

Al-Hakim's work on the Nishapur scholars was also used by famous historians who composed more inclusive and general biographical dictionaries about scholars, regardless of their regional origins. For instance, Sam'ani, Yakut, Subki, and al-Baghdadi made extensive citations from al-Hakim's work (Frye 1965, 10; Rosenthal 1968, 39). This illustrates how authors of general history (*tarikh* literature) and biographical dictionaries (*tabaqat* literature) derived their data from local histories as they built the network of scholars through the generations. The genre of history thus constitutes another level of Islamic historiography. Here, what is meant by history is *tarikh* (the plural is *tawarikh*) literature. The literary genre that came to be known as *tarikh* differs in crucial respects from what we describe by that term today. It is founded on a distinct historical approach that emphasizes both the role of individual social actors and the social networks in which they are embedded. Since for our purposes here the difference between the *tarikh* and *tabaqat* genres is not significant, I will refer to both genres as biographical dictionary literature, bearing in mind at the same time that these works served as general histories in classical Islamic culture.

Besides local histories, the encyclopedic works about particular generations must also have helped the authors of biographical dictionaries in collecting their data. For instance, there are numerous encyclopedic works exclusively dedicated to the Companions, who constitute the layer 1 (Kettani 1994, 254–59). Three of the most outstanding examples of this rich genre are the following works, in chronological order: (1) *Al-Isti'ab fi ma'rifah al-Ashab*, by Ibn Abd al-Barr al-Qurtubi (d. 463 AH/1071 CE), which includes biographical and network information about 3,500 Companions; (2) *Usd al-Ghabah fi Tamyiz al-Sahabah*, by Ibn al-Athir al-Jazari (d. 630 AH/1233 CE), which includes around 8,000 entries, with the last volume exclusively dedicated to the women Companions; and (3) *Al-Isabah fi Tamyiz al-Sahabah*, by Ibn Hajar al-'Asqalani (d. 852 AH/1448 CE), which is the largest encyclopedic work in the field and provides information about 12,279 Companions. All three of these works are ordered alphabetically.

Al-Dhahabi also authored such a general history. Apparently he wanted his work to be the greatest of his time, for he called it *Tarikh al-Islam wa Wafayat al-Mashahir wa al-A'lam* (The History of Islam and the Death Dates of the Famous and the Prominent). This work was said to consist of twenty huge volumes in manuscript form. So far, none of the efforts to publish it in its entirety has succeeded. Ma'ruf's critical edition, in progress since 1977, has already reached thirty-eight large volumes and still does not appear to be near completion. The finished work is expected to include around 40,000 entries about eminent men and women, organized into seventy layers, each layer consisting of people who died within the same decade. If one adds those who are not registered as separate entries, the number goes much higher. If we take into consideration that the history of al-Bukhari, who lived long before al-Dhahabi, also included around 40,000 hadith narrators, this number would still look small compared to the data that were available to Dhahabi in his time.

The History of Islam, briefly called, is the main source of several other books that al-Dhahabi authored later in his career. These works include *Kitab al-Duwal* (The Book of States); *Nukhabat al-A'lam bi Tarikh Dawlah al-Islam* (Selected Passages on Prominent Figures in the History of the Islamic State); *Duwal al-Islam* (The States of Islam); *Al-'Ibar fi Khabar man 'Abar* (Lessons from the News of Those Who Have Passed Away); *Siyar A'lam al-Nubala'* (Biographies of Eminent Celebrities); and *Tadhkirah al-Huffaz* or *Tabaqat al-Huffaz* (The Biographical Dictionary of Prominent Hadith Narrators). The latter is the primary source from which data were collected for this study.

Dhahabi composed another encyclopedic work exclusively on the "weak" and the "abandoned." He named this book *Diwan al-Du'afa wa al-Matrukin* (The Register of Weak and Abandoned [Hadith Narrators]). This work, among many other, similar studies with an exclusive focus on "weak" scholars, provides crucial insight into the critical process among scholars in the hadith transmission network. The work is ordered alphabetically in two volumes and includes brief information about 5,099 scholars up to the time of Dhahabi who were accused of incompetent scholarship. The level of weakness, however, varied for each scholar. In the introduction to a recent edition, the editor names twenty types of weakness used in the work by al-Dhahabi (El-Mis 1988). Examples include *da'a'fahu ba'duhum* (criticized by some), *laysa bi thiqah* (unreliable), *matruk* (abandoned), *takallamu fih* (they questioned his reliability), and the like.

Almost all the works of al-Dhahabi gained remarkable acceptance within the scholarly community; they have been appended by scholars of subsequent generations. Abu al-Mahasin al-Husayni (715–765 AH) wrote *Al-Tanbih wa al-Iyqadh li ma fi Zuyul Tadhkirah al-Huffaz*. Taqiyyuddin al-Makki (787–871 AH) wrote *Lahz al-Alhaz bi Zayl Tabaqat al-Huffaz*. The famous polymath al-Suyuti (849–911 AH) also updated the work up to his own time, with an appendix titled *Zayl Tabaqat al-Huffaz li al-Dhahabi*. All these works are also published along with the main text. An interesting work on *Tadhkirah al-Huffaz* was produced by Ismail ibn Muhammad ibn Bardis (720–786 AH), who recomposed the work as a long poem with the title *Nazm Tadhkirah al-Huffaz al-I'lam fi Wafayat al-A'lam*. This work is preserved in manuscript form in Istanbul (Kettani 1994, 272).

Hadith Compilations

There is yet another literary genre in Islamic culture, in fact the most important, intricate, and challenging one, which was not meant to be an encyclopedic source for the lives and relations of scholars—namely, the hadith compilation literature. A requirement incumbent upon the hadith scholar was to provide the chain of authorities through whom a narrative had passed before reaching him. These data could very well be used to reconstruct the network of scholars until the time of the hadith compiler. The only drawback is that data of this kind are based solely on the connections of individual hadith scholars. On the other hand, these data are closer to the empirical world because the connections are extracted from actual chains of narration, *isnad*. Most important, the network connections derived from the chain of authorities, which comes before the text of the narrative, enable readers to see what kind of information has passed through this channel as part of a particular scholarly contact.

The most outstanding and best-received hadith compilation is that of al-Bukhari (d. 656 AH), which includes 7,563 ahadith based on a recent edition (Bukhari 1995). It should be noted that Bukhari belongs to the ninth generation, according to the stratification of al-Dhahabi. According to al-Kalabazi (333–398 AH), who composed a biographical dictionary exclusively about the narrators in al-Bukhari's hadith compilation, the total number of hadith narrators whose names pass in the network of al-Bukhari is 1,525. This number does not seem very precise, because during my research it became noticeable that al-Kalabazi had failed to include all the names. For instance, the names of Yahya ibn Sa'id ibn Ferruh Abu Sa'id al-Kattan al-Ahwal al-Basri, Hisham ibn Hassan Abu Abdillah al-Firdawsi al-Azdi al-Basri, and Yahya ibn Hammad Abu Bakr al-Shaybani al-Basri are missing from al-Kalabazi's work.

Reconstructing the social network of scholars from hadith compilations is quite difficult because a considerable number of the scholars were known according to pen names that were similar to or even identical with one another. Therefore, it is a most daunting task to figure out who is who in the network. This difficulty is multiplied by the use of the shortest abbreviations in the chains, to make them as brief as possible.

One drawback of these data is their limited scope, which is to say that they are confined to the network of the author of the immediate compilation. Even then, the data are still incomplete because the scholar under investigation may have authored other works as well. Reconstructing Bukhari's network on the basis of his hadith compilation can provide only a partial picture because Bukhari alone is reported to have had no fewer than 1,000 teachers to whom he was directly connected. Yet the total number of narrators in the whole hadith compilation, which includes Bukhari's second step (the teachers of his teachers), his third step (the teachers of his teachers' teachers), and his fourth step (the teachers of his teachers' teachers' teachers), is less than 1,600. Consequently, one needs to incorporate all the works of al-Bukhari in order to reproduce a reasonably complete picture of his network.

Besides the famous compilation of al-Bukhari, there are many other well-known hadith compilations that can be used for a complete reconstruction of the hadith transmission network. In addition to the Six Reliable Hadith Books, Ibn Hanbal's hadith compilation, *Al-Musnad,* must be mentioned. Equally important are the compilations of multiply transmitted (*mutawatir*) hadith—for instance, those by Suyuti and Zabidi.[6] All these works, along with countless others not mentioned here, provide information about the social networks of scholars over time.

A Closer Look at the Two Major Sources

I used historical texts to reconstruct the hadith transmission network. The data mainly came from two biographical dictionaries. The first, *Tadhkirah al-Huffaz,* by Dhahabi (d. 1348 CE/784 AH), includes 1,176 entries; the second, *Tabaqat al-Huffaz,* by Suyuti (d. 1505 CE /911 AH), includes 1,188 entries. The biographical dictionary of Muhammad ibn Hibban (d. 965 CE/354 AH), which includes 1,602 entries, was used for determining geographical distribution. Hadith compilations, in particular that of al-Bukhari, which includes 7,275 ahadith, were also used to tie information obtained from biographical dictionaries to actual narratives and chains of authorities. These sources, along with innumerable auxiliary sources that I will discuss below in greater detail, afforded information about the biographies and networks of narrators from 610 to 1505. These classical sources, as mentioned earlier, are the collective work of scholars from successive generations who appended the works of the earlier authors. I processed this information to establish an electronic database with 1,226 social actors, organized in twenty-six layers, with a total of 13,712 connections. The total number of connections is symmetrically divided in half, as teacher and student connections, because each connection is both a teacher connection and a student connection. Therefore, the total number of student connections and teacher connections is 6,856.

This study reconstructed the network of eminent hadith narrators up to the

TABLE 4.1

Comparison of Layers from Dhahabi's Tadhkirah and Suyuti's Tabaqat

Layer	Population (Dhahabi)	Number (Dhahabi)	Population (Suyuti)	Number (Suyuti)	Variation
1	23	1–23	23	1–23	0
2	42	24–65	40	24–63	2
3	30	66–95	30	64–93	0
4	58	96–153	55	94–148	3
5	78	154–231	71	149–219	7
6	81	232–312	81	220–300	0
7	106	313–418	99	301–399	7
8	130	419–548	127	400–526	3
9	107	549–655	105	527–631	2
10	116	656–771	112	632–742	4
11	77	772–848	75	743–817	2
12	79	849–927	78	818–895	1
13	48 + 26 = 74	928–1001	71	896–966	3
14	31	1002–1032	31	967–997	0
15	46	1033–1078	46	998–1042	0
16	18	1079–1096	18	1043–1060	0
17	25	1097–1121	25	1061–1084	0
18	26	1222–1147	27	1085–1111	1
19	12	1148–1159	12	1112–1123	0
20	10	1160–1169	10	1124–1133	0
21	7	1170–1176	23	1134–1156	15
22			11	1157–1167	
23			9	1168–1176	
24			11	1177–1190	

time of al-Dhahabi on the basis of his *Tadhkirah al-Huffaz* (Dictionary of Huffaz). In addition, Suyuti's *Tabaqat al-Huffaz* (Layers of Huffaz) provided more data, to extend the network up to his time, namely, the sixteenth century. The latter work appends and updates the first. The two works mostly converge on information regarding the names and numbers of huffaz. However, there are differences as well (see table 4.1). I primarily relied on Dhahabi's work, which is more detailed and more respected as an authority on the period it covers.

Besides these differences in numbers of scholars in different layers, the style and size of the two works are also different. Suyuti's work is only one volume and thus very brief, although it covers a longer period than Dhahabi's work, which is four volumes and more detailed. Furthermore, Dhahabi presents an actual hadith that was transmitted to him through the chain of the scholar whose life he discusses.

TABLE 4.2
Overlapping Duration of Layers

No.	Hijra Calendar			CE Calendar		
	Beginning	End	Duration	Beginning	End	Duration
1	13 BH[a]	10	23	610	632	22
2	13 BH[a]	90	90	622	708	86
3	14[b]	105	91	635	723	88
4	34	117	83	654	735	81
5	46	151	105	666	768	102
6	70	180	110	689	796	107
7	100	206	106	718	821	103
8	106	230	124	724	844	120
9	139	264	125	756	877	121
10	170	292	122	786	904	118
11	180	318	138	796	930	134
12	218	348	130	833	956	123
13	250	388	138	864	998	134
14	291	441	150	903	1049	146
15	361	486	125	971	1093	122
16	404	540	136	1013	1145	132
17	463	581	118	1070	1185	115
18	494	619	125	1100	1222	122
19	546	662	116	1151	1263	112
20	580	680	100	1184	1281	97
21	592	708	116	1195	1308	113
22	624	742	118	1226	1341	115

[a]BH: Before Hijrah. The spread of Islam began 13 years before the flight of the Prophet Muhammad from Mecca to Medina, in 622 CE, the beginning of the Hijrah calendar.
[b]In the present study, the birth date of the first hafiz from a generation marks the beginning of that layer, and the death date of the last hafiz from the same layer marks its end. These dates may not converge with the death and birth dates of the broad population from each generation.

Table 4.2 illustrates the way I reconstructed the layers for this study by revising the classical system used by Dhahabi and Suyuti. The birth of the first hafiz marks the beginning of a layer, and the death of the last hafiz marks its end. One should bear in mind that these dates may not be the same if we look at the entire population of the generations instead of focusing exclusively on huffaz, which is the usual practice in many historical works. I also consider the time of the Prophet Muhammad a separate layer because of the peculiar structural features of that period regarding the dissemination of hadith, enough to set it apart from the following period. The fact that the Prophet was alive in that period means that the production of narrative continued along with its dissemination, and that to determine the authenticity of a hadith, one could simply ask the Prophet himself. Yet the production of narrative concluded after the demise of the Prophet; activity was then concentrated on dissemination alone, and new methods had to be developed for ascertaining the reliability of a narrative.

Distilling and Processing Data from Textual Sources

I have already presented two brief examples of entries in biographical dictionaries (chapter 2). I would like to present additional and more detailed accounts from al-Dhahabi's *Tadhkirah*. These accounts can in fact be very lengthy. For instance, Dhahabi developed some of them as separate works and published them individually.

Using these examples, I will display the method I used to extract network data from biographical dictionaries and the steps I followed to construct my database. The first step was to read the record of the scholar from the source text. The second step was to extract the relevant biographical and network information, concrete birth and death dates and places, and names of teachers and students. The third step was to make an exhaustive list of teachers and students by making a thorough survey of records of all scholars from previous and future layers who might have had a connection with the scholar under investigation. Since a connection is mentioned, for the most part, only once, either in the record of the teacher or the student, one cannot rely only on the network information provided in the entry about a scholar. The fourth step was cross-checking with names and dates to eliminate elusive mistakes. The fifth step was to process the data in order to build an electronic database by entering the information into HADITHNET, the data storage and retrieval program I designed for manipulating cross-temporal network data as well as for linking them to the narratives from which the ties come.[7] The sixth and the final step entailed producing a sociomatrix in HADITHNET and exporting it to the analytical software used to perform the intended analyses.

The first example is the entry about the most famous hadith scholar, al-Bukhari:

578 (IX: 30) al-Bukhari

The highest world authority in Islamic knowledge [*shaykh al-Islam*], and the leader of huffaz [*imam al-huffaz*], Abu Abdullah Muhammad son of Ismail son of

Ibrahim grandson of al-Mughira son of Bardazbah, from the tribe of Ja'f, their former client [*mawlahum*], al-Bukhari. The author of *Al-Sahih* [The Authentic] and many other books. His birth was in the month of Shawwal in 190 AH.

His first auditing of hadith took place in 205 AH. He memorized the compilations of Ibn al-Mubarak when he was just a little boy. He grew up an orphan and traveled with his mother and brother in 210 AH after he audited entirely the narratives of his country from Muhammad ibn Salam, al-Musnadi, and Muhammad ibn Yusuf al-Baykandi.

He heard from [studied hadith under] Makki ibn Ibrahim in Balkh, from Affan in Baghdad, from al-Muqri' in Mecca, from Abu Asim and al-Ansari in Basra, from Ubaydullah bin Musa in Kufa, from Abu al-Mughira, and al-Firyabi in Syria, from Adam in Asqalan, from Abu al-Yaman in Humus, and from Abu Mushir in Damascus.

He traveled extensively, authored books, and narrated hadith even before his beard had grown. He was the leader in intelligence, knowledge, piety, and worship of God.

Those who narrated from him include al-Tirmidhi, Muhammad bin Nasr al-Marwazi the Jurist, Salih bin Muhammad Jazirah, Mutayyan, Ibn Khuzaymah, Abu Quraysh Muhammad bin Jumru'ah, Ibn Sa'id, Ibn Abi Dawud, Abdullah al-Farabri, Abu Hamid ibn al-Sharqi, Mansur bin Muhammad al-Bazdawi, Abu Abdillah al-Mahamili, and a multitude of other people. He was a skinny old man, neither tall nor short, with a skin color approaching brown.

He used to say, "When I completed collecting hadith at the age of eighteen, I began writing books on the legal decisions of the Companions and the Successors, and their opinions in the time of Ubaydullah bin Musa. I wrote *Al-Tarikh* [The History] at that time by the gravesite of the Messenger of God, may God bless him and his family and give them peace, on the moonlit nights." He is also reported as saying, "I wrote hadith from over one thousand masters."

Regarding the accounts of his merits, his scribe Muhammad bin Ali Hatem said, "I heard Hashid bin Ismail and another person saying: 'Bukhari used to attend hadith audition sessions with us while he was still a young boy. Yet he was not writing down the hadith he was hearing. This continued like that for many days. We used to advise him on that. Finally, he said: "You went too far in insisting! Bring me what you wrote down." We brought him our notes. That proved that he had committed to memory over fifteen thousand hadith from the sessions he attended with us, which was more than what we could write down, and read them all from his heart. Then, we began verifying our notebooks from his memory. At the end, he said, "Do you think I am wondering in vain and wasting my days?" We realized that no one can surpass him.'"

Muhammad ibn Khumayruyah said, "I heard al-Bukhari saying, 'I carry in my memory a hundred thousand authentic hadith, and I also carry in my memory two hundred thousand inauthentic hadith.'" Ibn Khuzaymah said, "I have not seen under the sky anyone more knowledgeable than Bukhari in hadith."

I [al-Dhahabi] say: I authored a large volume exclusively on the biography and merits of this leading scholar, which includes astonishing facts.

According to al-Maqdisi, Bukhari, Muslim, Abu Dawud, and al-Tirmidhi are among the scholars of the fifth generation, out of forty layers.

He died on the night of the Festival of the Breaking Fast at the end of Ramadan in 256 AH, in which al-Zubayr bin Bakkar, Ali bin al-Mundhir al-Tariqi, Muhammad ibn Abi Abdirrahman, Abdullah ibn Yazid al-Muqri, and Muhammad ibn Uthman ibn Karamah, may God be merciful to them all, also died.

I [al-Dhahabi] read to Ismail bin al-Farra, Yusuf bin al-Sharqawi, Muhammad bin Bayan, and a multitude of other scholars who were told by al-Husayn ibn al-Zubaydi that Abu al-Waqt told us that al-Dawardi told us that ibn Hamuyah told us that Ibn Matar told us that al-Bukhari told us that Ubaydullah bin Musa told us on the authority of al-A'mash, on the authority of Shaqiq who said: "I was with Abdullah and Musa. They both said, 'The messenger of God, may God bless him and his family and give them peace, said, "Before the end of this world comes, ignorance will prevail and knowledge will disappear. In that time anarchy—killing—will increase."'"

The narrator Muslim also related the same hadith. Apparently Abu al-Waqt heard it from Muslim as well [al-Dhahabi 1968, 2:555–57].

The structure of the entries in the biographical dictionary follows more or less the same pattern for all the scholars. At the very outset al-Dhahabi gives the short name by which the scholar is known. He also identifies to which layer he belongs and what number he has assigned to him. After that come the titles the scholar was given in the scholarly community, which show his rank. We also learn about his upbringing, his family, and even his physical features. Then he provides the complete name of the scholar, which is not familiar in the modern name structure we are accustomed to. Below, I will discuss the structure of Arabic names in more detail. The biographical information includes birth and death dates and places as well as the date of the scholar's first audition of hadith. This information is important for scholars of hadith in determining the possibility of connection with alleged teachers and students. For the same purpose, Dhahabi provides information about the cities a scholar traveled to and the masters he met in those cities.

We also learn about the works of a scholar and the time when he commenced publishing his works as well as the conditions under which he worked. After reporting on the masters and how the scholar met them, Dhahabi provides a brief list of prominent students while warning the reader that his list is far from complete. Since he refers us to the monograph he authored on al-Bukhari, he does not go into detail.

Dhahabi relates anecdotes about the scholar in question that were told by him or by the scholars closely associated with him. These accounts may not always be favorable. He also reports the opinions of scholars from later generations about the master whose life is the subject of the entry, to show how public opinion has formed about him. In the following example, concerning the famous al-Tabarani, these features will become even more evident. At the end of each entry, Dhahabi reports an actual hadith related by the scholar under investigation through a chain of authorities in which Dhahabi himself is the latest node. By doing so, Dhahabi displays the wealth of his own narratives and connections.

Having concluded this brief elucidation of the structure of an entry in Dhahabi's biographical dictionary, I now want to present another example, to show how I proceeded to dissect the record for the scholars whose network I analyzed:

Al-Tabarani (XII: 27) 875: al-Hafiz, al-Imam [the leader of scholars], al-Allamah [the most knowledgeable], al-Hujjah [the authority], the father of al-Qasim, Sulayman the son of Ahmad the son of Ayyub the son of Mutir, affiliated with Lakhm, with Damascus, and with Tabaran, the narrator of the world. Born in 260 AH. Began auditing hadith in 273 AH in Syria, Mecca, Medina, Yemen, Egypt, Baghdad, Kufah, Basra, Isphahan, the Arabian Peninsula, and many other places. He narrated hadith from one thousand or more teachers.

Tabarani compiled *Al-Mujam al-Kabir* [The Grand Lexicon]. It is a *musnad* [a compilation of hadith organized according to the name of the first authority in the chain of narration, the Companion, and containing all the ahadith narrated by the Companions listed] except for Abu Hurayra because, apparently, he wrote exclusively a volume on his narratives. Tabarani also compiled *Al-Mu'jam al-Awsat* [The Medium Lexicon], which is six huge volumes on the narratives of his teachers, where he reported their uncommon or unique narratives. It is similar to *Kitab al-Afrad* [The Book of Unique Narratives] by al-Daraqutni. In this work, Tabarani introduced his teachers and explained their merits and the vastness of their knowledge in narration. He is reported to have said, "This is the book of my soul," because he exhausted all his energy working on this book. There are excellent, valuable, and refutable narratives in the book. Tabarani also compiled *Al-Mu'jam al-Saghir* [The Small Lexicon], which contains only a single hadith from each teacher he studied under. He authored many other books as well.

He was one of the knights of this discipline, with sincerity and reliability. He audited narratives from Ibn Murthad al-Tabarani, Abu Zur'ah al-Thaqafi, Ishaq al-Dabri, Idris al-Attar, Bishr bin Musa, Hafs bin Umar Sinjah, Ali bin Abdilaziz al-Baghawi, Miqdam bin Dawud al-Ru'ayni, Yahya ibn Ayyub al-Allaf, Abu Abdirrahman al-Nasai, Abdullah ibn Muhammad ibn Sa'id ibn Abi Maryam, and others like them. His father paid the utmost attention to his education in his youth and accompanied him on his journeys for knowledge. His father was also narrating from Duhaym and the like. The birth of Tabarani was in Akka in the lunar month of Safar in the year 260 AH. His mother was from Akka.

His works also include *Kitab al-Dua'* [The Book of Prayers], in a big volume; *Kitab al-Manasik* [Book on Pilgrimage]; *Kitab 'Ishrat al-Nisa* [The Book of Etiquette of Interaction with Women]; *Kitab al-Sunnah* [The Book of Prophetic Customs]; *Kitab al-Tiwalat* [The Book of the Lengthy Ahadith]; *Kitab al-Nawadir* [The Book of the Rare Ahadith]; *Kitab Dalail al-Nubuwwa* [The Book of the Proofs of Prophethood]; *Kitab Musnad Shu'bah* [The Book of the Narratives of Shu'bah]; *Kitab Musnad Sufyan* [The Book of the Narratives of Sufyan]; and *'Amal Asanid Jama'ah min al-Kibar* [Narrative Chains of a Group of Great Scholars]. He is also the author of *Kitab Hadith al-Shamiyyin* [The Book of the Narratives of the Syrians]; *Kitab al-Awail* [The Book of the First]; and *Kitab al-Ramy* [The Book of the Aging]. He is the author of *Tafsir al-Kabir* [Grand Commentary on the Qur'an] and many other things you have not come across.

Those who narrated from him include Abu Khalifah al-Jumahiand Ibn 'Uqda, Ahmad bin Muhammad al-Sahhaf (who were at the same time his teachers), Abu Bakr bin Marduyah, the jurist Abu Amr Muhammad ibn Al-Husayn al-Bistami, al-Husayn ibn Ahmad ibn Al-Marziyan, Abu Bakr ibn Abi Ali al-Dhakwani, Abu al-Fadl Muhammad bin Ahmad al-Jarudi, Abu Nu'aym the Hafiz, Abu al-Husayn ibn Fadshah, Muhammad bin 'Ubaydillah bin Shahriyar, Abdirrahman bin Ahmad al-Saffar, and Abu Bakr bin Riydha, the last of his students to die. His student Abdurrahman ibn al-Dhakwani lived two years more than he, yet he could narrate only through *ijazah*.

Yahya bin Manda listed the works of Tabarani without actually seeing most of them: his *Al-Mu'jam al-Kabir* [The Grand Lexicon], in two hundred volumes; *Al-Mu'jam al-Awsat* [The Medium Lexicon], bound as three volumes; *Al-Mu'jam al-Saghir* [The Small Lexicon], bound as one volume; *Musnad al-Ashara* [Narrative of the Ten], thirty volumes; *Musnad al-Shamiyyin* [Narratives of the Syrians], several volumes; *Al-Nawadir* [The Rare], one volume; *Marifa al-Sahaba* [Knowledge of the Companions], one volume, and its sequel, ten volumes; *Musnad Abi Hurayra* [Narratives of Abu Hurayra], one huge volume; *Musnad Aisha* [Narratives of Aisha]; *Tafsir al-Kabir* [Grand Commentary on the Qur'an]; Dalail al-Nubuwwa [*Proofs of Prophethood*], one volume; *Al-Dua* [The Prayer]; *Al-Sunna* [The Prophetic Customs], one volume; *Al-Tiwalat* [The Lengthy], one volume; *Hadith al-Shu'ba* [Hadith of Shu'bah], one volume; *Hadith al-A'mash* [Hadith of al-A'mash], one volume; *Hadith al-Awza'i* [Hadith of al-Awza'i], one volume; *Shiban,* one volume; *Ayyub,* one volume; *'Ishrat al-Nisa* [Friendship with Women], one volume; *Musnad Abi Dhar* [Narratives of Abu Dhar], two volumes; *Al-Ru'yah* [The Dream], one volume; *Al-Jud* [Generosity], one volume; *[Al-Ilm] Al-wiyah* [The Commanders], one volume; *Fadl Ramadan* [Merits of Ramadan], one volume; *Al-Faraid* [The Obligatory Duties], one volume; *Al-Radd ala al-Mu'tazila* [The Refutation of the Mutazila School], one volume; *Al-Radd ala al-Jahmiyya* [The Refutation of the Jahmiyya School], one volume; *Makarim al-Akhlaq al-Uzza'* [Superior Morality of Saints]; *Al-Salah ala al-Rasul Sallallahu Alayhi wa Sallam* [Greeting the Messenger of God, May God Bless Him and Give Him Peace], one volume; *Al-Ma'mun* [The Ma'mun], one volume; *Al-Ghusl* [The Ritual Bath], one volume; *Fadl al-Ilm* [Virtues of Knowledge], one volume; *Dhamm al-Ra'y* [Critique of Speculation], one volume; *Tafsir al-Hasan* [Qur'anic Commentary of Hasan], two volumes; *Al-Zuhri an Anas* [Narratives of al-Zuhri from Anas], two volumes; *Ibn al-Munkadir an Jabir* [Narratives of Ibn al-Munkadir from Jabir], one volume; *Musnad Abi Ishaq al-Sabi'i* [Narratives of Abi Ishaq from al-Sabi'i]; *Hadith Yahya bin Abi Kathir* [Narratives of Yahya bin Abi Kathir]; *Hadith Malik bin Dinar* [Narratives of Malik bin Dinar]; *Ma Rawa al-Hasan an Anas* [What Hasan Narrated from Anas]; *Hadith Rabi'ah* [Narratives of Rabi'ah]; *Hadith Hamza al-Zayyat* [Narratives of Hamza al-Zayyat]; *Hadith Mus'ir* [Narratives of Mus'ir]; *Hadith Abi Sa'd al-Baqqal* [Narratives of Abi Sa'd al-Baqqal]; *Turuq Hadith Man Kadhdhaba 'Alayya* [Paths of the Hadith of "Whoever Slanders Me . . . "], one volume; *Al-Nuh* [Noah], one volume; *Musnad ibn Hajada* [Narratives of ibn Hajada]; *Man Ismuh Abbad* [Those Who Carry the Name Abbad]; *Man Ismuh 'Ata* [Those Who Carry the Name 'Ata]; *Man Ismuh Shu'bah* [Those Who Carry the Name Shu'bah]; *Akhbar Umar bin Abdilaziz* [The News of Umar bin Abdilaziz]; *Abdilaziz bin Rafi*; *Musnad Ruh bin al-Qasim* [Narratives of Ruh bin al-Qasim]; *Fadl 'Ikrimah* [Merits of 'Ikrimah]; *Ummuhat al-Nabiy Sallallahu Alayhi wa Sallam* [Mothers of the Messenger of God, May Allah Bless Him and Give Him Peace]; *Musnad Ammarah bin Ghazya, Talha bin Musarrif wa Jama'ah* [Narratives of Ammarah bin Ghazya, Talha bin Musarrif, and Others]; *Musnad al-'Abadilah* [Narratives of the Abdullahs], one huge volume; *Ahadith Abi Umar ibn al-'Ala* [Narratives of Abu Umar ibn al-'Ala]; *Gharaib Malik* [Peculiar Narratives of Malik], one volume; *Aban ibn Tha'lab,* one volume; *Hadith ibn Abi Matar* [Narratives of Abu Matar]; *Wasiyya Abi Hurayra* [The Will of Abu Hurayra]; *Musnad al-Harith al-'Akli* [Narratives of Harith al-'Akli]; *Fadail al-Arba'a al-Rashidin* [Virtues of the Four Rightly Guided Caliphs], two volumes; *Musnad ibn 'Ajlan* [Narratives of ibn 'Ajlan]; *Kitab al-Ashriba* [The Book of Drinks]; *Kitab al-Tahara* [The Book of Ritual Cleansing]; *Kitab al-Imara* [The Book of Governance]; *Musnad Abi Ayyub al-Ifriki* [Narratives of Abi Ayyub the African]; *Musnad Ziyad al-Jassas* [Narratives of Ziyad al-Jassas]; *Musnad Zafir* [Narratives of Zafir]; and many others.

Al-Dhakwani said that when al-Tabarani was questioned for the high number of his reports, he responded by saying, "I slept on horses for thirty years" [referring to his academic journeys day and night]. Abu Nu'aym said, "Tabarani came to Isphahan in 290, listened to the scholars, and traveled. Later, he came back and resided there for sixty years." Ibn Marduya said, "Al-Tabarani came in 310. The governor, Abu Ali ibn Rustam, met him, took him into his circle, and sponsored him by assigning him a salary from the House of Revenues [*Dar al-Kharaj*]. He used to receive it until he died." Abu Umar bin Abdilwahhab al-Sulami said, "I heard al-Tabarani saying, 'Upon his return from Faris, Ibn Rustam gave me five hundred silver coins [*dirham*], but toward the end of his career, he started speaking against Abu Bakr and Umar, may Allah bless both of them, on a few small matters. I left him and never turned back again.'"

Ibn Faris, author of the *Dictionary*, said that he heard the master Ibn al-'Amid saying, "I used to think that there was nothing in the world more enjoyable than being a vizier or a leader, which I had enjoyed until I witnessed a debate between al-Tabarani and Abu Bakr al-Ju'ani in my presence. Al-Tabarani was defeating him with his vast memory, and Abu Bakr was defeating al-Tabarani with his wit. The debate continued until their voices raised to a level where al-Ju'ani said, 'I have a hadith, nobody has it in the world except me.' Tabarani said, 'Narrate it.' Al-Ju'ani said, 'Abu Khalifa narrated from Sulayman ibn Ayyub who narrated from . . .' until he had finished reporting the hadith. Al-Tabarani responded by saying, 'Sulayman narrated this hadith to me, and Abu Khalifa heard it from me. And listen from me to the same hadith through even a shorter chain.' He defeated al-Ju'ani. I wished I had not had the position of vizier and, instead, were al-Tabarani so that I had the contentment he had."

Ja'far bin Abi al-Sirri said, "I asked Ibn 'Uqda to repeat to me what I had missed, and insisted on it. He said, 'Where are you from?' I said, 'From Isphahan.' He said, 'Evil!' I said, 'Don't say that about them. There are jurists and supporters among them.' He said, 'Supporters of Mu'awiya.' I said, 'No, supporters of Ali, may God bless him. There is nobody there except those who like Ali more than their eyes and families.' He repeated what I had missed and then said, 'Have you heard Sulayman ibn

Ahmad al-Lakhmi [meaning al-Tabarani]?' I said, 'I do not know him.' He said, 'Glorified is my Lord! Abu al-Qasim [al-Tabarani] is in your town, and you do not study under him and give me all these problems. I do not know anyone equal to him.'

"He also said, 'Do you know Ibrahim ibn Muhammad ibn Hamza?' I said, 'Yes.' He said, 'I have not seen anyone equal to him in memory. Ibn Manda said, "Al-Tabarani is one of the noted huffaz, narrated from Ahmad ibn Abdirrahim al-Barqi. Why does he indiscriminately narrate everything he comes across with?" I said: 'Yes, but he did not want him, nor did he mean to narrate from him except that he narrated from Abdirrahim al-Barqi the *Seerah* [narratives on the biography of the Prophet], and the like. He also made a mistake in his name and named him with the name of his brother, without any doubt. Pitfalls in this vocation are easy to fall in. Al-Hafiz Abu al-Abbas Ahmad bin Mansur al-Shirazi warned against that because he said, "I wrote from al-Tabarani three hundred thousand hadith. He is extremely reliable with one exception. In Egypt, he studied under a master who had a brother. Tabarani unknowingly confused the name of his teacher with the name of his brother."''"

Sulayman bin Ibrahim, the hafiz, said that al-Batirqani said, "Ibn Marduya's opinion on al-Tabarani was negative." Then Sulayman said, "Abu Nu'aym said to him, 'How many narratives did you write from him?' And he pointed to Hazm. Abu Nu'aym said, 'Who saw someone equal to him?' He could not say anything. Then Hafiz al-Diya said, 'Ibn Marduya mentioned al-Tabarani in his *History* without criticizing him. I say: He used this as evidence that it became clear for Ibn Marduya that al-Tabarani was reliable.' Abu Nu'aym said, 'Al-Tabarani died two nights before the end of the month of Dhu al-Qa'da, in the year 360 AH.'" I [al-Dhahabi] say: He completed a hundred years and ten months. His hadith filled the world because in the time of the Hafiz Ismail ibn Muhammad al-Taymi he was in demand—students listened to hadith from him; then, in the time of Ibn Nasir and Abu 'Ala' al-Hamadani, his market was extremely active—they heard from him in big numbers, and then, in the time of Abu Musa al-Madini, he was considered to be the highest [the one with shortest path to the Prophet] to be heard. In that time al-Hafiz Abdulghani audited and learned from him *The Grand Lexicon*. Afterward, Ibn Khalil traveled to study under him; Dhiya and others competed with each other to listen to his narratives. In the year 606, As'ad bin Sa'id [who was a "grandstudent" of al-Tabarani] became the single world authority with the shortest chain of narratives, as a result of which the works on hadith and criticism became full of Tabarani's narratives.

It is related to me [al-Dhahabi] in writing by Ibn Abi al-Khayr and a large group of other masters from Abu Ja'far Muhammad bin Ahmad the Pharmacist who said that Fatimah the daughter of Abdillah told them that Ibn Riydha reported to her from Abu al-Qasim al-Tabarani who reported from Abdullah ibn Muhammad ibn Abi

Maryam al-Firyabi who reported from Israil who reported from Sammak bin Harb who reported from ʿAlqama bin Wail who reported from his father that "in the time of the Prophet, may God bless him and his family and give them peace, a woman left her home with the intention of joining in the congregational prayers. On the way, a man met her and satisfied his desire from her. The woman screamed and the man escaped. They caught a man passing by on her way. [Upon questioning], she said, 'This is the man who did to me such and such.' They arrested this man she accused. They asked her, 'Are you sure? Is this the one?' She said, 'Yes, this is he.' They brought him to the Prophet, may God bless him and his family. When he ordered him punished, his friend, who actually had raped the woman, stood up and confessed: 'I am the one who assaulted her.' The Prophet said to him: 'Come closer, to be sure, God has forgiven you.' He also said good words to the other [innocent] man. They said, 'Are we going to stone him?' The Prophet said, 'He repented from his sin so much that if he repented for all the sins of the residents of Medina it would have been accepted for them, too.'" This is an inauthentic hadith, despite its clean narrative chain. Al-Tirmizi accepted it as authentic and narrated it from al-Zuhali who narrated from Muhammad bin Yunus. We [al-Dhahabi] have, instead, a shorter alternative chain.

I chose to present the preceding selection in its entirety to give readers a sense of the nature of the historical data. The selection offers the portrait of a leading hadith scholar. More important, it demonstrates how the genre of biography is constructed. We also observe how Dhahabi makes critical use of previous sources that are available to him. A significant point to which Dhahabi draws our attention is that al-Tabarani became renowned through a student of one of his students, Asʾad bin Saʾid, because he was the mentor whom students sought out the most in that time, because of the brevity of Tabarani's chain of narration, in which he was merely the third link.

Structure of Names in Medieval Arabic

The examples we have so far examined have demonstrated that there is a peculiar structure to medieval Arabic names, which is quite different from the way we structure our names today. There is not only one name by which a scholar is always referred to. There are also short names, medium-short names, and complete long names. The structure of the name is closely related to the multiple social identities in existence during the medieval period. They also reflect some of the social and cultural characteristics of medieval Islamic society.

Short names were usually derived from the name of the city, the tribe, or school of thought to which one belonged. However, since there are usually many scholars with similar affiliations, it is not easy to differentiate them and determine who is who. It is easy to note that "al-Tabarani," "of Tabaran," or "Tabaranian" is the shortest and most commonly used name for our scholar. Tabaran is the name of a city in central Asia famous for its scholars.

His long and complete name is "Abu al-Qasim Sulayman bin Ahmad bin Ayyub bin Mutayyar al-Lakhmi al-Shami al-Tabarani." The words "abu" (father) and "ibn/bin" (son) are used to denote genealogy. The name would translate to English as "the father of al-Qasim, Sulayman the son of Ahmad the son of Ayyub the son of Mutir, affiliated with Lakhm, name of a famous tribe, with Damascus, and with Tabaran." This served as a very helpful device not only for knowing the person's family and genealogy but also, and more important, for distinguishing people from each other. Furthermore, the name includes information about the tribe and the city to which a person is affiliated. From his name, we recognize that al-Tabarani did not spend his entire life only in Tabaran but also in Damascus. The name structure helps bring together the familial, genealogical, and scholarly networks. Thus the name, which is constituted by the *ism,* the *kunya,* and the *nisba,* stands out as an invaluable source of information for historians and sociologists:[8]

> Arabic names, whether borne by ethnic Arabs or by non-Arabs, were typically composed of several distinct parts: (1) the *ism* or first name, which was given at birth, (2) the *kunya,* a name beginning with Abu, meaning "father of," or Umm, meaning "mother of," which was theoretically acquired after one had become a parent but which was very frequently given at birth for euphonic or other reasons unrelated to potential parenthood, (3) the *nasab* or genealogy, which was a series of isms, kunyas, or other names strung together with the word *ibn,* "son of," or *bint,* "daughter of," (4) the *nisba,* a name most frequently ending in *-i,* which signified some sort of an affiliation (for example, al-Baghdadi = person from Baghdad) and often served for several generations as a family surname, and (5) the *laqab* or honorific name, under which may conveniently be lumped all sorts of honorary titles, nicknames, and epithets. An example of a medieval Arabic name using all these parts in the order of laqab, kunya, ism, nasab, nisba would be Burhan ad-Din Abu Ahmad Muhammad ibn Yusuf ibn Al-Hasan al-Misri [Bulliet 1979, 10].

Some names are very commonly used, such as Muhammad, Abdullah, and Hasan. In this case, it would be a daunting task to determine who is who. Which Muhammad, Abdullah, or Hasan is the one we are after among hundreds of them? Certain methods are used to eliminate impossible options and narrow the search: (1) lifetimes must converge; (2) the father's, grandfather's, and great-grandfather's names must match; (3) affiliations (geographical, tribal, intellectual) must match; (4) names of sons or daughters, if mentioned, must match; (5) nicknames, if any, must match. These methods are used for each scholar in checking the reliability of reported connections.

The following simple example illustrates this process. Bashshal, a hafiz from layer 10, is reported to have a teacher with the name Sulayman bin Ahmad (Sulayman son of Ahmad)—both the name of Tabarani and the name of his father. One might easily be misled into thinking that this person is the same as our scholar because the name and the father's name match. However, these names do not refer to the same people because (1) the *kunya* "al-Tabarani" is not mentioned (note that in the list above, his name is never mentioned without his *kunya*), (2) a scholar from layer 10 does not usually take hadith from a 12th-layer scholar, and (3) al-Tabarani is listed among this person's students (al-Tabarani was the student of Bashshal but not his teacher).

Furthermore, one cannot rely solely on the entry about a particular scholar in the biographical dictionaries in order to determine his entire network of academic relations, because the connections of scholars are only partly mentioned in the entries under their names. Therefore, an extensive and painstaking search must be conducted to determine the entire network. Moreover, not all the connections that are recorded in the entries are to other huffaz; instead, as the following example demonstrates, the proportion of Tabarani's ties to huffaz was significantly less than his connections to less prominent scholars.

For instance, the names of the mentors of Tabarani who are listed in the entry about him are as follows (the numbers following some names are HADITHNET codes unrelated to numbers found in the original sources): (1) Hashim ibn Marthad al-Tabarani, (2) Abu Zur'ah al-Thaqafi, (3) Ishaq al-Dabri, (4) Idris al-'Attar, (5) Bishr ibn Musa (637), (6) Hafs ibn Umar Sinjah, (7) Ali ibn Abdilaziz al-Baghawi (650), (8) Miqdam ibn Dawud al-Ru'ayni, (9) Yahya b Ayyub al-'Allaf, (10) Abu Abdirrahman al-Nasa'i (564), and (11) Abdullah ibn Muhammad ibn Sa'id ibn Abi Maryam. The majority of these students, eight of them, are non-hafiz (1, 2, 3, 4, 6, 8, 9, 11). Only three of them are huffaz (5, 7, 10). The non-hafiz teachers are not included in our database because of the exclusive focus of the present study on hafiz scholars. Therefore, connections to the scholars who did not gain reputations as hafiz are not accounted for in the network of al-Tabari. The exclusion of the non-huffaz is a necessary limitation of this study.

Likewise, the students of Tabarani who are listed in the entry about him reflect the same features as the list of mentors in that they are incomplete and include figures who are less prominent. The following names are included: (1) Abu Khalifah al-Jumahi (691), (2) Ibn 'Uqdah (821), (3) Ahmad ibn Muhammad al-Sahhaf, (4) Abu Bakr ibn Marduyah (966), (5) Abu Umar Muhammad ibn al-Husayn al-Bistami, (6) al-Husayn ibn Ahmad ibn al-Marzuban, (7) Abu Bakr ibn Abi Ali al-Dhakwani, (8) Abu al-Fadl Muhammad ibn Ahmad al-Jarudi (816), (9) Abu Nu'aym al-Hafiz (994), (10) Abu al-Husayn ibn Fadishah, (11) Muhammad ibn 'Ubaydillah ibn Shahriyar, (12) Abdurrahman ibn Ahmad al-Saffar, and (13) Abu Bakr ibn Ridhah. The majority of these students, eight of them, are non-hafiz (3, 5, 6, 7, 10, 11, 12, 13). Only five of them are huffaz (1, 2, 4, 8, 9). Students who are not recognized as hafiz are not included in the data. Consequently, connections to them will not be accounted for in the analysis, another unavoidable limitation of this study.

To judge from the entry under his name in the biographical dictionary, al-Tabarani had twenty-four connections: eleven to his mentors, and thirteen to his students. Among these were only eight connections to huffaz: three hafiz teachers, and five hafiz students. Had I based my analysis only on the information provided in the biographical record of al-Tabarani, I would have reconstructed his network inaccurately because the above names are far from an exhaustive list of teachers and students. With the purpose of avoiding repetition, Dhahabi recorded connections only once, either in the record of teachers or in the record of students.

After a thorough search for the connections of Abu al-Qasim al-Tabarani, I came to the conclusion that he had forty-two teachers and nine students. Teachers can be grouped according to the layers they belong to: (1) from layer 9: 637, 648, 650, 652 (four scholars); (2) from layer 10: 674, 681, 682, 683, 684, 685, 688, 690, 691, 693, 705, 709, 710, 712, 720, 729, 737, 740, 741, 742, 745, 747, 752, 754, 760, 761 (twenty-six scholars); (3) from layer 11: 773, 777, 787, 788, 798, 799, 801, 819, 821 (nine scholars). His students can also be grouped according to the layers they belonged to: (1) from layer 12: 691, 821, 966, 816, 994 (five scholars); (2) from layer 13: 943, 969, 976 (three scholars). One can easily observe that there is

TABLE 4.3

Interlayer Connections

	L1[a]	L2	L3	L4	L5	L6	L7	L8	L9	L10	L11
L0	23	0	0	0	0	0	0	0	0	0	0
L1	16	156	103	56	1	0	0	0	0	0	0
L2	1	5	33	115	6	0	0	0	1	0	0
L3	0	0	1	132	115	2	0	0	0	0	0
L4	0	1	1	22	274	264	41	1	0	0	0
L5	0	0	0	6	63	174	409	126	1	1	0
L6	0	0	0	3	20	18	41	599	52	3	0
L7	0	0	0	0	2	6	15	196	553	39	0
L8	0	0	0	0	0	2	85	29	288	608	80
L9	0	0	0	0	0	0	27	5	46	206	229
L10	0	0	0	0	0	0	1	2	15	31	91
L11	0	0	0	0	0	0	0	0	0	10	3
L12	0	0	0	0	0	0	0	0	0	3	5
L13	0	0	0	0	0	0	0	0	0	0	5
L14	0	0	0	0	0	0	0	0	0	0	0
L15	0	0	0	0	0	0	0	0	0	0	0
L16	0	0	0	0	0	0	0	0	0	0	0
L17	0	0	0	0	0	0	0	0	0	0	0
L18	0	0	0	0	0	0	0	0	0	0	0
L19	0	0	0	0	0	0	0	0	0	0	0
L20	0	0	0	0	0	0	0	0	0	0	0
L21	0	0	0	0	0	0	0	0	0	0	0
sum	40	162	138	334	481	466	619	958	956	901	413

[a]L stands for layer. The columns include the total number of teachers, while the rows include the total number of students for scholars from a layer.

a striking difference between the number of teachers and the number of students. This is not so common, although in general the number of teachers tends to be higher than the number of students. The number of in-layer connections is also unusually high.

Constructing Measurable Variables from Historical Narratives

I repeated the process described above for all the huffaz whose networks are analyzed in this study. After I collected all the information about the ties of the scholars, I still had to perform one last step to produce the data set required by our analysis, one with measurable categories and variables. I constructed several types of data to use in this study: link data (on macro and micro levels),

L12	L13	L14	L15	L16	L17	L18	L19	L20	L21	sum
0	0	0	0	0	0	0	0	0	0	23
0	0	0	0	0	0	0	0	0	0	332
0	0	0	0	0	0	0	0	0	0	161
0	0	0	0	0	0	0	0	0	0	250
0	0	0	0	0	0	0	0	0	0	604
3	0	0	0	0	0	0	0	0	0	783
0	0	0	0	0	0	0	0	0	0	736
1	0	0	0	0	0	0	0	0	0	812
3	1	0	0	0	0	0	0	0	0	1096
42	2	0	1	0	0	0	0	0	0	558
361	21	1	0	0	0	0	0	0	0	523
134	57	2	0	0	0	0	0	0	0	206
31	143	4	1	1	0	0	0	0	0	188
6	69	63	13	4	3	1	0	0	0	164
0	2	16	58	2	0	0	0	0	0	78
0	1	5	44	42	11	0	0	0	0	103
0	0	1	4	16	29	4	1	0	0	55
0	1	0	0	1	10	51	4	1	0	68
0	0	0	0	0	1	18	3	11	2	35
0	0	0	0	0	1	2	3	9	2	17
0	0	0	0	0	0	3	3	2	4	12
0	0	0	0	0	0	0	0	0	0	0
581	297	92	121	66	55	79	14	23	8	6804

node data, and qualitative data. To express this element of the study more clearly, the data that were used can be categorized into five sets: (1) macro-link data about the connections between generations; (2) micro-link data about the connections between individual scholars; (3) macro-node data (information about each layer); (4) micro-node data (information about each scholar); (5) and qualitative historical data.

I constructed a number of variables that I will introduce here along with the notations I used for them. The capital letter L stands for "layer" (a generation of hadith narrators). A layer had student and teacher connections within itself as well as connections to earlier and later layers. The capital letter S stands for a student connection, and the capital letter T stands for a teacher connection.

Table 4.3 demonstrates the connections between layers, without showing type and direction. A still more detailed approach would require differentiating teacher connections from student connections. From this perspective, as ex-

plained previously, in connection with figure 1.3, the connections are distributed in six categories based on (1) direction (whether the tie is a student tie or
a teacher tie), (2) origin and destination (whether it is within the same layer or
goes to upper or lower layers), and (3) distance (the generation difference between students and teachers). The distance between generations is indicated by
"Up1" (ties to 1 upper/earlier generation), "Up2" (ties to a 2-step earlier generation), and "Up3" (ties to a 3-step earlier generation). For instance, while connections from layer 4 to layer 4 are considered under the category "In," connections from layer 4 to layer 3 are considered under the category "Up1";
connections from layer 4 to layer 2 are designated "Up2"; and connections from
layer 4 to layer 1 are designated "Up3."

Various combinations of these categories were used to construct measures
that were operationalized in the research. For instance, in-layer connections are
further divided as "Sin" (student ties within a layer) and as "Tin" (teacher ties
within a layer). Upward and downward connections are also further subdivided
according to whether they represent student or teacher ties. "Sup" stands for
student ties to upper or earlier layers; "Sdown" stands for student ties to lower
or later layers. The same distinction applies to teacher ties. "Tup" stands for
teacher ties to upper layers, and "Tdown" stands for teacher ties to lower layers.
One important point must be made here about the numbering of layers.

Reliability and Limitations of Sources and Data

It has been a daunting task to reconstruct the hadith transmission network.
The information is scattered in classical historical sources. Most troublesome
was the question of differentiating scholars who not only had identical names
but who also had fathers and even grandfathers with the same names. Since
scholars are usually briefly referred to by their various types of short names
(*ism, kunya, nisba*, or *laqab*), misidentifications and confusion are bound to
arise in determining who scholars really are. Instances of misidentification, if
any remain at this point, need to be eliminated when they are detected, and that
is an endless process.

I tried to overcome this problem by using several techniques. If I encountered several scholars with the same name, the first thing to do was to look at
the names of their ancestors (fathers, grandfathers, and great-grandfathers).
When the confusion could not be resolved, the next step was to check the re-

gions and tribes to which the scholars belonged. If this also did not resolve the issue, I checked the layers that the scholars belonged to as well as their birth and death dates.

Death dates are more readily available than birth dates. Curiously, classical Islamic historians put more emphasis on death dates than on birth dates, for reasons that are not clear to a modern reader. Perhaps it was because the early years of a scholar's life, a period usually spent in obscurity as a child and student, were not as important as his later years. Dhahabi, following the custom of his colleagues, reports death dates for a great majority of the narrators. This is less often the case when it comes to birth dates. Additional classical sources have also been used to obtain information about birth dates, which Dhahabi neglected.[9] This attempt greatly increased the number of scholars for whom birth and death dates are available. (Some death dates and especially dates of birth are missing for a very small and tolerable proportion of the scholars.)

An exclusive focus on connections between huffaz is another limitation of this study. Non-hafiz scholars and connections to them are excluded from the analysis because including them would have expanded the data beyond any reasonable hope of control. Neither collecting such quantities of data nor analyzing them would have been feasible within the study's established limits, even though the network configuration of non-hafiz scholars would have provided a contrast case.

Nevertheless, I checked the reliability of the data over twenty-six generations, using two methods. First, data concerning each layer were contrasted with data from other layers, for the purpose of detecting biases either inherent in the data themselves or attributable to selectivity on the part of the authors of the biographical dictionaries. Second, the data obtained from Dhahabi's work were compared with the data obtained from Suyuti's work. (The information for layers 22 to 26 was gathered from Suyuti's biographical dictionary, and it was assumed that if there was any inherent bias in the data, or any selectivity bias on the part of the authors, it would be detected through comparison of the layers within the network, or through comparison of different sources.) In addition, as an informal check, the data obtained from biographical dictionaries were occasionally linked and contrasted, in the course of discussion, with the data from actual chains of narration, *al-asanid,* biographical and autobiographical literature.

Using the first test, I looked at the values for different layers and compared them. I did not observe any abrupt changes in the data concerning different layers. Using the second test, I looked at the data from Dhahabi's work and the data from Suyuti's work; because I did not see any abrupt changes or striking inconsistencies in the reported values between these two sources, we can safely assume that the data are not biased. Furthermore, I made occasional references to the chains of narration, biographies, and autobiographies to compare them with biographical dictionaries. This exercise does not demonstrate any inconsistency in the way the network of hadith transmission is described over centuries by different genres of Islamic history. Instead, the various branches of historical literature confirm each other.

The historical network data posed new challenges, but to begin with the assumption that historical sources are less reliable than present-day sources would be to oversimplify the issue. Reliability testing is a common issue in studies that involve both historical and contemporary data. Neither historical nor contemporary data can be considered inherently reliable outright; tedious effort is required in order to demonstrate the reliability of both types of data.

Yet there are some advantages that can be offered only by historical data. Social network data collected through interviews are generally used to construct synchronic and cross-sectional social networks. By contrast, social network data gathered from historical sources can be used to reconstruct historical networks over a span of time or within a single period. The structure of the data from within any single period shows variations by comparison to data compiled over a long period of time. Only diachronic data make possible the analysis of social structures over time.

From this perspective, the data that were used in this study to unearth the structure of the hadith transmission network over time represent just a tiny sample, less than the tip of the iceberg in the vast ocean of available data concerning the networks of scholars in Islamic civilization. Current tools of social network analysis, especially network analysis software, do not come up to the level of what is required for rigorous processing of so much data over time. Moreover, given the various types of sources, it is not easy to do justice to data that require enormous amounts of time and energy to sift through and analyze. The larger picture remains incomplete.

Yet, even with these limitations, the application of social network analysis methods offers a fresh look at data that have appeared to be in limited use among conventional historians operating with traditional concepts. For example, the historian who prepared a facsimile edition of the above-mentioned works on the history of Nishapur writes, "Most of the city or local chronicles in Arabic or Persian are rather tedious catalogues of prominent inhabitants with emphasis on their pious deeds, pronouncements, or writings" (Frye 1965, 7). Note that Frye completely disregards the social network dimension of the data he is dealing with. He continues, "As such, they provide valuable information for the specialist on biography, but for the general historian of the Islamic world their worth seems small." No doubt Frye would have thought otherwise if he had considered the possibilities for structural analysis opening up to researchers who could approach classical material from the perspective of social networks. But, given his rather narrow perspective, which reflects the view common to many historians of Islamic civilization, he concludes, "It is not surprising, then, that many local chronicles remain unpublished." Nevertheless, the perspective of network analysis has the potential to broaden this narrow approach by making better use of the biographical dictionary literature, which once seemed almost useless to our predecessors in the field of history. This change is made possible by paving the way from narratives to networks, and vice versa.

CHAPTER FIVE

From Synchronic to Diachronic Methods

Temporal Constraints on Action

Narrative is by definition diachronic, since it involves sequential events. So is social life, which also comprises events in sequential order. The sequential nature of narrative has drawn the attention of scholars since Aristotle. Social scientists, however, have paid little attention to the diachronic dimension of social structure. From the very beginning, they have erroneously conceptualized social structure as above and beyond time and constituted only by synchronic relations. Yet since Ferdinand de Saussure there have been attempts to embed social structure in diachronic time. However, this is not a simple issue that can be so easily resolved; it requires recasting our concept of social structure.

"The fact that time intervenes to change a language does not at first seem to be a very momentous fact or to have important consequences for the conditions governing linguistics. Few linguists are inclined to believe that the question of time gives rise to special questions. Few treat it as a central crossroads, at which you have to decide whether to follow time or step outside it," writes Saussure (1993, 102a). The claim applies to sociologists today as well. The major methodological problems in a study of a structure through time, such as this one, stem from the embryonic state of diachronic analytical tools in the social sciences. At the turn of the last century, Saussure proposed a concurrently diachronic and synchronic structural inquiry.

Yet in the social sciences, with the exception of econometrics, the query for structures has remained synchronic in focus, thereby creating a gap between diachronic and synchronic analysis of structures. A cross-temporal structure is produced by the enduring patterns of diachronic social relations between social actors who are differentiated from each other by virtue of time. Sociological research has concentrated for the most part on the structures produced by the enduring relations between social actors who are differentiated from each other, and thus stratified into different groups, by virtue of economic, social, and cultural attributes.

However, structural analysis of social relations cannot reach its full potential without developing methods to explore cross-temporal structures. Any analysis that ignores the passage of time and the temporal constraints arising from it produces hypothetical and inauthentic images of social and discursive process.

> But here the historical reality of time intervenes. If you had time without the body of speakers, perhaps there would be no external effect <(of change)>. The body of speakers without time: we have just seen that the social forces of the language will not act unless time is brought in. <We come to complete reality with this schema, that is to say by adding the axis of time:> <From that point on> the language is not free because, even *a priori,* time will provide the opportunity for the social forces affecting the language to take effect through countless ties with previous ages [Saussure 1993, 101a–102a].

Saussure pointed out that bringing social forces to bear upon language requires taking the passage of time into account. As a sociologist, I should add that it will also allow discursive forces to be brought to bear upon society. Furthermore, it will also expose the constraints that the passage of time imposes on us.

White's work on the structure of opportunity (White 1979), Mullins's work on academic networks (Mullins 1973), and Zuckerman's work on the "scientific elite" (Zuckerman 1977) are among the few examples of genuine social network studies of cross-temporal structures, even though each author stresses this aspect to varying degrees. White analyzes the structure of opportunity in large organizations as chains of upward moves sequentially ordered in time. Zuckerman and Mullins analyze the connections between generations of scholars from different generations. Zuckerman employs connections between mentors and apprentices from different periods to explain the structure of an elite's formation and perpetuation; Mullins uses ties between professors and graduate students in explaining the formation of new theory groups in science, and particularly in sociology. Yet neither of these two authors suggests new methods for cross-temporal analysis. In the final chapter of this study, I will show how one can analyze the data of Zuckerman and Mullins from an alternative perspective. Not only will that demonstration show the advantages of the methods I use here, it will also provide additional evidence for the hypothesis underlying this study. In addition to White's aforementioned methodological contributions to cross-temporal research, which have yet to find a common application, Abbott's work is an important contribution to cross-temporal analysis.

Given the lack of diachronic methods, or their unimproved condition, even the work of some historical sociologists, who do employ network analysis methods, focuses on connections between social actors from the same period, or it treats social actors from different periods as if they were from the same period. As a result, this work differs little from studies of present-day social networks. Consequently, although historical sociologists study historical networks, and sociologists who are not interested in history concentrate on present-day networks, their questions, and therefore their methods, are synchronic in nature. In these studies, the social actors whose networks are analyzed are not separated from each other by time; instead, they are embedded in the same period. Nor do studies involving cross-temporal comparisons constitute an exception to this observation. They compare the results obtained from synchronic analysis of different time periods.

The Gap between Cross-Temporal and Cross-Sectional Research

Given the concentration of current network analysis methods on cross-sectional or synchronic structures, I need to retool myself, with the purpose of demonstrating how cross-temporal relations, side by side with synchronic relations, constrain action and produce authority. To this end, I have modified the available methods of social network analysis and combined them with methods from other disciplines, which I will briefly survey below.

Bibliometrics and Co-citation Research

Bibliometrics, information sciences, co-citation, and communication research, all newly emerging fields, use a wide range of methods to deal with scholarly communication. The methods used by these research families are possible sources of inspiration for the present study because their subject matter approaches that under investigation here: first, it is inherently cross-temporal;

second, it revolves around reported speech; and, third, it addresses social networks through time.

However, this avenue of research has to overcome a tendency to conflate the diachronic with the synchronic and the literary with the social. Likewise, the underlying traditional approach to language that characterizes these research fields—an approach that sees language as merely a means of communication—needs revision in light of recent developments, discussed earlier, in our understanding of language.

Borgman (1990), editor of a work that brought scholars together from a wide range of disciplines, defines these fields as follows: "We consider scholarly communication to be the study of how scholars in any field use and disseminate information through formal and informal channels and bibliometrics to be the application of mathematics and statistical methods to books and other media of communication" (Borgman 1990, 10). These fields "share essentially the same repertoire of methods: surveys, experiments, case studies, content analysis, and historical analysis" (Borgman 1990, 8).

I believe these fields would greatly benefit from interaction with the recent research on network analysis and reported speech, especially given the fact that they study three "variables": (1) *producers* of written communication, individual or aggregate authors; (2) *artifacts* of communication, that is, formal products, as when other documents are read, when ideas are translated into these producers' own terms, and when the producers talk with others; and (3) *concept* communication, which entails (a) studies that use the authors' own terms and (b) studies that focus on the purpose or motivation of a citation (Borgman 1990, 16). These variables bear upon reflexive speech and are studied extensively by linguists.

Research on Cohorts and Generations

Another field that is closely related in its methods and analytical concerns to the one considered here is cohort and generation research. This family of research includes a great diversity of methods and research questions. Common to all approaches, however, is an emphasis on the relevance of time in the explanation of social processes. Quantitative, qualitative, and network analysis methods are used to explore macro- and micro-level processes in relations between or within generations (Becker 1992).

There is no unanimity in the way cohorts and generations, two unifying concepts in this research tradition, are defined. For one researcher, a cohort is "the aggregate of individuals within some population definition who experience the same event within the same time interval" (Ryder 1965, 843–61). Another perceives a generation as "a grouping of a number of cohorts characterized by a specific historical setting and common characteristics on an individual level (biographical characteristics, value orientation and behavioral patterns) and a system level (size, generational culture and generational organizations)" (Becker 1992, 20). White offers an alternative definition. "A generation is a joint interpretive construction which insists upon and builds among tangible cohorts in defining a style recognized from outside as well as from inside itself" (White 1992, 31). White's observation is especially relevant to scholars of hadith, who display a high level of awareness about narrative style and about their positions in the diachronic network of hadith transmission.

Temporal Stratification, Periodization, and the Concept of Layers

I introduce an alternative yet similar methodological construction: the concept of layers, which was inspired by the way medieval historians originally categorized the cohorts. A layer, as operationalized here, is a cluster or block of structurally equivalent social actors in a diachronic social network who reflect similar behavioral patterns. This similarity manifests itself in the way social actors establish network connections.

The advantage of employing the concept of layers, as opposed to using cohorts or generations, comes from the way its boundaries are demarcated by network connections. The concept of generations or of cohorts is defined by reference to a multitude of cultural and social features, whereas the concept of layers is defined merely by reference to the position of a group in a cross-temporal network structure. Each layer acts as a building block of the network and derives its identity exclusively from its position in the network. Without reference to the network, and to the interrelations of the group within it, it is impossible to conceive of a layer. Another advantage afforded by using the concept of layers is that it enables a sophisticated and dynamic system of periodization based on cross-temporal network dynamics. Nevertheless, the parallels between the findings of this research and of the research on cohorts and generations research will become clear in the remainder of this work.

A layer (*tabaqa*; the plural is *tabaqat*, and this key term is commonly used in the intellectual history of Islamic civilization) is a particular type of academic community, organizationally analogous to an invisible college, differentiated by its affiliation to a generation of scholars in an academic discipline. There are layers of jurists, linguists, sufis, and the like. The network position of a scholar determines his layer; his tie to his eldest teacher, or to the one who belongs to the earliest layer, is used as a criterion. Members of a layer do not register as members of a formal community or association, in the modern sense. Group identity, belonging to a particular layer or scholarly generation, is generated through awareness of a shared generational position in the intellectual network.

The term *tabaqa* has come to be translated as "layer," "stratum," or "class." It is a useful construct that historians of medieval Islam used to group the figures they studied into categories. Explicit in the concept of stratum is the internal differentiation and stratification of scholars. This stratification is twofold: stratification by virtue of human capital, such as competence, knowledge, and academic production; and stratification by virtue of social capital, such as proximity to the original source, the Prophet. Yet these two types of stratification hardly exist separately.

The first type of stratification produced the scholarly hierarchy that we have already described, namely, differentiation of hadith scholars into the categories of *shaykh al-Islam, hafiz, hujjah, muhaddith, musnid,* and *talib.* The latter type of stratification is produced by social or network time, based on differentiation of scholars into layers. More concretely, members of the scholarly community are differentiated internally, by virtue of their earliest connections.

In the culture of hadith narrators, there is also a normative side to the high regard paid to earlier layers, a regard that can be traced to the teachings of the Prophet. Narrative has it that the Prophet Muhammad said, "The best of generations is my generation, then the one that follows, then the one that follows." Those who were closer to the time of the Prophet had a better chance of more easily obtaining access to his true teachings.

This study reflects both types of stratification, one based on competence, the other on time. The analysis concentrates on the internal stratification of the stratum of huffaz by virtue of time (that is, the layers of huffaz) and the inter-relations between the layers over time.

In a given period of time, only a limited number of strata exist. How can we determine how many strata exist in a given time? The answer depends on the way the boundaries of the layers are demarcated. In the time of the Prophet, there were only two layers: the Prophet (the first stratum), and his Companions (the second stratum). Yet it is possible to further divide the stratum of the Companions into the old, the middle-aged, and the young. The same applies to the Successors. By definition, a Successor is one who had a connection to a Companion. Again, if birth and death dates are used as criteria, it is possible to further divide the Successors into the more refined categories of old, middle-aged, and young.

Dhahabi divides the network of hadith transmitters into seventy layers in his grand work *History of Islam,* whereas he divides the same period into twenty-one layers in the *Biographical Dictionary of Huffaz.* Likewise, in the latter work, while he treats the Companions as one stratum, he divides the stratum of Successors into three categories: the old, the middle-aged, and the young. Similarly, the stratum of the Successors of Successors is also divided into three sublayers following the same logic: the old, the middle-aged, and the young.

To return to the question of how many layers exist together in a given time, it is clear, in light of the preceding explanations, that only two main strata, by definition, coexist in any given time. Yet it is possible to further divide each stratum into substrata by virtue of their locations in the network, which are indicated by the proxy of birth and death dates or simply age.

We can conclude that Dhahabi—and, following him, Suyuti—divided each main stratum into three substrata. Therefore, in our data, the adjacent six layers coexist in a given time, with the exception of the periods at the beginning and the end of the network. The boundaries, however, are not drawn so clearly.

Coexistence in a given time should not be confused with a stratum's network scope (that is, the maximum number of areas a layer can reach in the network). As we will see, below, empirical analysis of the data demonstrates that the network scope of a stratum expands toward four earlier and four subsequent layers, the total number being nine and including the layer under investigation. However, connections usually occur among five of the strata that coexist in a given time. In youth, when a scholar is a student, his layer is connected to three earlier layers. In contrast, when he ages and becomes a teacher, his layer is connected to the three subsequent layers from which the students are recruited.

For instance, the network scope of the layer 10 expands from layer 6 to layer 14. This does not mean that layers 6 to 14 coexisted in a given time. Layers 6–9 are the teachers of layer 10, and layers 11–14 are the students of layer 10. While new layers of students are being born, the layers of teachers are waning. That is why, for a student from layer 14, the earliest possible connection is to teachers from layer 10.

Yet we have to overlay on this map (the network operation of layer 10) the concurrent activities of the adjacent and coexisting strata, each of which has its own network scope of teachers and students. These network scopes overlap, but only incompletely, because each new stratum occupies a newly added time period. A new stratum cannot rise without the demise of an old one. The next stratum and the oldest stratum, or the ones with the shortest paths to the Prophet, fill the vacancy created by the stratum in demise. The vacancy created by this change, which entails an upward movement, is filled by subsequent generations, as in a chain of events.

The demise of a stratum brings about extended chains of narrative for students, because the scholars who replaced those who have gone do not have such short chains. Hence, even though there is a new stratum of teachers, which replaces the stratum that has gone, the opportunities for young layers become limited with respect to connections. This constraint determines their position in the temporal hierarchy within the network.

Paradoxically, from the perspective of the emerging strata, the demise of an earlier stratum brings constraints and offers opportunities. On the one hand, it makes possible the upward mobility of the next stratum and the rise of a new stratum to fill the vacancies in the temporal hierarchy of the system. Yet, on the other hand, the chance of establishing connections with an earlier layer, and thus rising in social status and honor, also declines with the demise of that stratum. Consequently, each stratum is inevitably anchored to its spot in the social structure by the web of its network connections.

The same principle prevails on the level of individual social actors as well.

Since students search for teachers with the shortest chains, the relative measure of the length of the chain of a mentor is inversely related to his authority. With the existence of a mentor with a shorter chain of narrative, a scholar with a longer chain has no chance of attracting promising students. A young scholar, therefore, has to wait for decades until his chain of authorities becomes the shortest before he can teach. This becomes possible with the death of his teacher and other mentors who are structurally equal to his teacher.

Even if he wants to recruit students, he will not be able to attract any. Nor would this be considered moral and appropriate in the culture of hadith narrators. In his book on the methodology of hadith narration, *al-Muqiza,* Dhahabi reiterates this principle and warns his students who are future teachers not to narrate hadith in the presence of another teacher with a shorter chain:

> Part of the moral code [*al-adab*] scholars have to abide by is to refrain from narrating hadith in the existence of someone else who is more qualified than him by virtue of his age and expertise. Likewise, he should not relate any narrative that someone else narrates through a shorter chain of authorities. Also, he should not confuse the beginners; in contrast, he should guide them to the most important knowledge. Religion is but sincerity [al-Dhahabi 1991a, 66].

This would be considered deceiving students and not acting in their best interest. An honest mentor must refer a student who mistakenly comes to study under him to one who has something better to offer, namely, narrative transmitted through a shorter chain. Failure to comply with these ethical codes is considered immoral by one's colleagues, for it eventually affects the future of the students. A good-hearted mentor is expected not to block avenues of opportunity for his students for his own benefit.

A scholar has to wait until his narrative chains become the shortest available for the students to turn to him; otherwise, students will not apply to him, nor is he supposed to teach them for the reasons explained above. He can become a mentor by filling the vacancy created by the death of the scholar with the shortest chain. This is a structural constraint that no one has control over.

Interlayer relations are thus bloody. New layers have to force themselves into existence by seizing social space from those who have passed away. Except in the event of their own deaths, they would never allow scholars from new layers to take their places. This is the structure of relations in a system that "evolves by its own logic, neither controlled by putative central authorities nor amenable to manipulation by its members" (White 1970, 317).

The concept of temporal stratification serves another methodological concern as well, namely, periodization of the lengthy history of a social network through time. The rise and demise of each layer demarcates the beginning and the end of a period. Network connections, rather than simple chronological time, define these periods. Another feature of this method of periodization is that it allows the overlaying of several periods in a given chronological time. The periods for adjacent layers overlap to varying degrees. More concretely, the periods of coexisting layers (six at a time, as explained above) intersect at a certain calendar time.

Each stratum corresponds to a time period. Hence there are twenty-six time periods in our network. These periods are not necessarily commensurate with each other in terms of calendar year, because their borders are determined by the network connections of their members to previous or subsequent strata. When the first connection is by a layer, its period begins. The establishment of such a connection may be an indication of the demise of a previous stratum because, as explained earlier, normally students would not seek a teacher from a later layer while an earlier one still persists. Likewise, the life of a stratum ends with the last connection to its members. Death dates can be used as a proxy in place of the last connection because a scholar in the Middle Ages usually did not retire from teaching until his life ended. Birth dates might also be used to determine the beginning of the lifetime of a layer. In this connection, it should be taken into account that there is a period in the early life of a student during which he is not academically active. Bulliet has demonstrated that there is an "age structure" in medieval Islamic education.

The periodization that utilizes "network time" has advantages over periodization based on calendar time. It helps better capture the cross-temporal structures that exist in a social network through time. For instance, without this method of periodization, I would not have been able to detect the pattern in the in-layer and out-layer connections that I use to explain authority formation. Besides, the two methods are not mutually exclusive. I alternate between calendar and network time according to my interest in a given analysis. The two methods, therefore, should complement each other rather than becoming mutually exclusive alternatives.

How Far Can Layers Extend Their Network Domains?

In a cross-sectional social network in which all the actors live in the same time period, stratification is not based on time, and consequently everyone is reachable by everyone else, without time constraints. In other words, in cross-sectional networks, stratification and differentiation are outcomes of features and processes other than time, such as wealth and status. In contrast, this is not true in a time-stratified network. In a time-stratified network, only the social actors whose lifetimes converge are reachable by each other. Nevertheless, a relationship between two actors becomes impossible if their lifetimes do not overlap, although they are part of the same network. This is a major point that any study of time-stratified networks must take into account. Otherwise, we might end up searching for direct connections between people who lived in different times.

This is as true for aggregate actors, such as groups, generations, or layers, as it is for individuals. Just as micro-level analysis must take into consideration the historical possibility of connections between individuals, macro-level analysis should take into consideration the historical possibility of connections between aggregate social actors. Consequently, prior to any analysis, we need to determine the network borders of maximum reachability for each layer in the hadith transmission network, which consists of twenty-six layers.

Examination of the data (see table 5.1) shows that the accessibility of layer 1, which is the generation of the Prophet, is limited to itself and to the subsequent layer, the layer of the Companions. As for the Companions, layer 2, their scope of accessibility includes the generation of the Prophet, their own layer, and three subsequent layers. Layer 3 can connect to layer 2, as well as four subsequent layers. For layer 4, the scope of accessibility consists of three earlier and four subsequent layers in addition to layer 4 itself. This becomes a pattern, beginning at layer 6, until layer 23: all layers can reach four earlier and four later layers. However, since our data end at layer 26, beginning with layer 23 we do not have information about connections to later layers.

We see that layers occupy a time period that partially converges with the time period concurrently occupied by several other earlier and later layers. In a way, these layers share the same period of time. However, convergence cannot be complete; it must be partial. Otherwise, the layers could not be treated as

TABLE 5.1

Maximum Reachability among Layers

(overlapping scope of layers)[a]

Layer no.	Up4	Up3	Up2	Up1	In	Down1	Down2	Down3	Down4
Scope of L1[b]					1	2			
Scope of L 2				1	2	3	4	5	6
Scope of L 3				2	3	4	5	6	7
Scope of L 4			2	3	4	5	6	7	8
Scope of L 5		2	3	4	5	6	7	8	9
Scope of L 6	2	3	4	5	6	7	8	9	10
Scope of L 7	3	4	5	6	7	8	9	10	11
Scope of L 8	4	5	6	7	8	9	10	11	12
Scope of L 9	5	6	7	8	9	10	11	12	13
Scope of L 10	6	7	8	9	10	11	12	13	14
Scope of L 11	7	8	9	10	11	12	13	14	15
Scope of L 12	8	9	10	11	12	13	14	15	16
Scope of L 13	9	10	11	12	13	14	15	16	17
Scope of L 14	10	11	12	13	14	15	16	17	18
Scope of L 15	11	12	13	14	15	16	17	18	19
Scope of L 16	12	13	14	15	16	17	18	19	20
Scope of L 17	13	14	15	16	17	18	19	20	21
Scope of L 18	14	15	16	17	18	19	20	21	22
Scope of L 19	15	16	17	18	19	20	21	22	23
Scope of L 20	16	17	18	19	20	21	22	23	24
Scope of L 21	17	18	19	20	21	22	23	24	25
Scope of L 22	18	19	20	21	22	23	24	25	26
Scope of L 23	19	20	21	22	23	24	25	26	
Scope of L 24	20	21	22	23	24	25	26		
Scope of L 25	21	22	23	24	25	26			
Scope of L 26	22	23	24	25	26				

[a]The number in a cell is the number of a layer within the scope of the layer identified in the first column.
[b]L stands for layer.

separate. Some layers arise while others end. A given date thus has a different meaning for each one individually, according to the point in the life journey. A birth date for one might be the death date for the others. Likewise, when one is young, the other might be old. A close look at the dates of rise and demise of layers on the scene of history will put the issue in its historical context. I have provided the dates for the times of rise and demise for each layer as well as the duration of the lifetime.

Social network analysis must take the role of time into consideration in a time-stratified network. Because of the difference between cross-sectional and time-stratified networks, MR (the total number of agents in the maximum reach) must replace N (the total number of social actors in the network) in the computation of the total possible connections within a network.[1]

Maximum-reach does not merely demonstrate the network borders of scholars from a layer but also serves a vital role in our obtaining relative scores of prominence in the network. In a cross-sectional network, everyone is reachable by everyone else and comparable to him or her with respect to network activity. However, in a time-stratified network, only those who are in the same network domain are comparable. Otherwise, we might end up comparing a Companion with a tenth-century scholar. More concretely, the relative local social prominence of scholars can be obtained only if their network activity is compared with that of their peers from the same layer.

A network through time, such as the hadith transmission network, is not a single network; rather, it is composed of successive networks, where each is gradually moved downward on the ladder of history yet knitted together with its predecessors and successors through social connections. Analysis of networks through time, especially at the macro level, is thus an internetwork analysis, with networks differentiated from each other by the chronological time slots in which destiny has placed them. In brief, from a macro-level perspective, as the foregoing exploration of maximum reach has shown, a time-stratified network is a network of networks.

The data concerning each layer are thus organized on the basis of the MR of the particular layer under consideration. Each layer is a network domain that gradually is disentangled from previous layers and expands toward future layers. With this explanation completed, we can now look at our data more closely.

The size of the network, represented by node variables, has an explicit relationship with the number of network connections, represented by link variables. These two units of analysis—node and link variables, that is to say, information about social actors and their relations—bear upon each other. The total number of connections changes from layer to layer because the size of the node, being the number of scholars in each layer, changes.

Over time, the size of the network remains variable and the volume of connections is fluid. There is a strong correlation between the size of a layer and the total number of its connections to neighboring layers. They increase and decrease together over time. This does not mean that the changing number of connections can be entirely explained away by the changing number of narra-

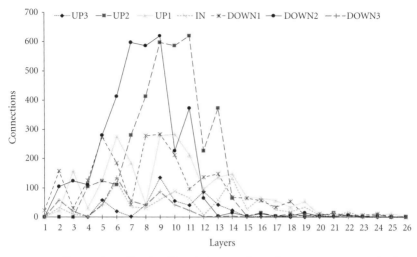

F I G . 5.1. Connections. For the abbreviations used, see chapter 4, pp. 118–20. A color version of this figure, and of figs. 5.2–5.3, may be viewed at www.sup.org/senturk.

tors. We will see in the following chapters that broader cultural, social, and political forces also may influence the level of networking activity.

For instance, layers 1 and 26 each consist of only one person, the Prophet and Suyuti, respectively. Yet layer 9, being the most populated layer, consists of 130 huffaz. For obvious reasons, layer 1 has 0 teachers, whereas layer 26 has 0 students; the former is the beginning, and the latter is the end of the network of huffaz. On average, however, each layer consists of 47 prominent scholars with 527 connections. Again on average, each scholar has around 5 teacher connections and 5 student connections, with an average total of 11 connections. The average number of students per scholar is highest for layers 1 and 2, followed by layers 5, 6, and 7.

The values can be broken down if the temporal locations of the social actors in the dyad are taken into account. Figure 5.1 breaks each connection down into nine categories: Up4 to Up1; In; and Down1 to Down4. These variables indicate the varying distance between the origins and the targets of the connections.

Figure 5.1 shows that most connections fall in the Up2 (n = 3564) and Down2 (n = 3564) categories (mean = 137.8), followed by Up1 and Down1 connections (mean = 89.04). They are followed by Up3 and Down3 (n = 519, mean = 19.96) and Up4 and Down4 (n = 18, mean = 0.69) connections.

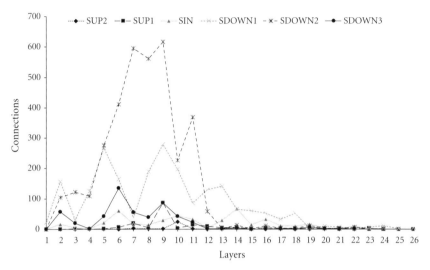

FIG. 5.2. Student Connections

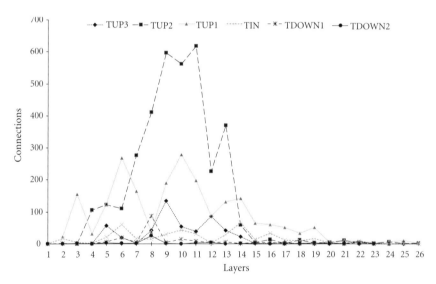

FIG. 5.3. Teacher Connections

Now, I will dissect the above measures even further, to student and teacher connections. Figure 5.2 illustrates the distribution of student connections, whereas figure 5.3 illustrates teacher connections.

An overview of student connections in figure 5.2 over 26 layers demonstrates that they concentrate on relations to subsequent layers, Down1 to Down4. The highest concentration of student ties is Sdown2 (n = 3515, mean = 135.19). It is followed by Sdown1 (n = 2134, mean = 82.08), and Sdown3 (n = 518, mean = 19.92). Sdown4 (n = 178, mean = 0.65) is smaller than "Sin," in-layer student connections (n = 440, mean 16.92) and Sup2 (n = 49, mean = 1.88). There is only one student connection to Up3 and Up4.

Similarly, figure 5.3 illustrates the fluctuations in the distribution of teacher connections over time, using variables based on the distance between the origin and the target of relations. An overview of the figure suggests that teacher connections are distributed over a large array, from Up4 (mean = 0. 69) to Down4 (mean = 0.04). Yet the highest concentration of teacher connections is Tup2 (mean = 135.19), followed by Tup1 (mean = 82.08). In-layer teacher connections are again low (mean = 16.92). However, from layer 23 to layer 26, there are no in-layer teacher connections.

Figure 5.3 also displays that Tup2 connections remain the highest from layers 6 to 13, at which point Tup1 connections gain prominence, from layer 14 to layer 20. It also shows the insignificance of in-layer and Tdown connections.

The above survey illustrates that the overall network scope for a given hadith scholar or a layer may cover nine layers in total. Yet there is a dynamic realignment of the network through the shifting focus on particular arrays, owing to the constraints imposed by the passage of time.

Authority Formation from Chains of Social Relations

Temporal constraints play a great role in the formation of authority by blocking or facilitating relations between actors from different generations. Social prominence, which is the dependent variable in this analysis, is typically defined as the total number of actual ties a social actor has to other prominent actors, divided by the sum of possible ties he could have. In our data, ties to nonprominent (non-hafiz) actors are not included; all ties in the data show a connection to another important hadith narrator who carried the title of hafiz.

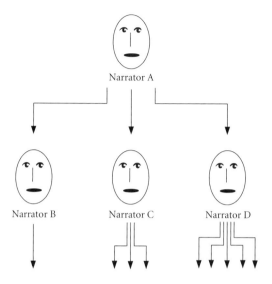

Which tie is more valuable for narrator A?
Which tie contributes most to the dissemination of narrative?

FIG. 5.4. The Role of Second-Step Ties

Therefore, one might be easily persuaded to conclude that there is no need to add weight to the ties to more powerful actors, as is usually done in prominence analysis. However, as previously mentioned, there is an internal differentiation among the prominent scholars; consequently, all ties do not have the same importance.

As figure 5.4 illustrates, not only first-step ties but also second-step ties count in the formation of authority. Suppose that scholar A has ties to three prominent scholars: B, C, and D. Scholar B has only one tie. Scholar C has three ties. And Scholar D has five ties. These ties could be either to teachers or to students; whether the ties are to teachers or students is not relevant to our present concerns. Among the three connections that scholar A has, which one is most important for him? Scholar A's connection to scholar D is more crucial to him than his connections to scholars B and C because scholar D is more central than the others. A connection to scholar D means access to more resources of information. The importance of a social network tie is proportional to the centrality of the person who is sought after.

Overall prominence can be further analyzed if prominence as a student and prominence as a teacher are both considered, to see if there is a relationship between the two. From this perspective, three types of prominence measures are created: overall prominence, teacher prominence, and student prominence. The total number of ties a scholar has may be seen as an indication of his overall prominence. From a closer perspective, the number of ties a scholar has to his students may be seen as an indication of his prominence as a teacher. The number of ties a student has to his teachers may also be seen as a sign for the level of his prominence. The relative volume of connections indicates the extent to which one is sought after by teachers, students, and colleagues, which helps us assess the relative degree of authority enjoyed by that scholar.

The relationship between these variables can be used to explore patterns in the network, to demonstrate whether there is any relationship between being a prominent student and being a prominent teacher. To put this issue more clearly, do prominent students become prominent teachers? Or is there a particular network configuration that is responsible for teacher prominence? For instance, how does the number of ties to three layers above affect the number of student ties from subsequent layers? To ask this question more broadly, how do network constraints on a novice student constrain his relations as a mature scholar? The example of hadith scholars attests to the fact that the impact is decisive. Not everyone was as lucky as Bukhari, who was an orphan but had a mother to travel abroad with him and facilitate his meeting with leading authorities and receiving hadith from them, or as lucky as Suyuti, whose father took him as a very young child to the circle of Ibn Hajar, the foremost scholar of hadith in his day. Both Bukhari and Suyuti, under the guidance of parents with foresight, made the right investment at an early age. They were prominent students who became prominent scholars.

Exploring the Micro Processes: A Constellation of Stars

The unit of analysis in this study has been connections between scholars: 1,226 scholars with 13,712 connections. Although it was possible to use these data on the macro level as aggregate values, on the micro level it is beyond the limits of the present study to examine the network of each scholar separately. Therefore, I need to create a subset of my data that will be feasible to handle

within the given limits of this study. This subset will consist of the three scholars from each layer with the highest number of connections. This selection
serves our purpose better than a random selection because the interest of this
study is to unearth the patterns in the network configuration of the most
prominent scholars.

Without such a subset, the analysis of the network on the micro level would
require a tremendous amount of research and computational work, which
might be a future project.[2] Each layer and even each scholar may require an independent study. In determining the "stars" to be included in our sample, the
total number of connections for each scholar is used as a criterion. From this
perspective, scholars can be ranked on the basis of total number of connections
or in a more refined manner, on the basis of teacher and student connections.
The three rankings for particular scholars do not always match each other. For
instance, Nafi' from layer 4 has the highest total number of connections in his
layer (n = 23); he is also first as a student (n = 14), yet as a teacher he is third (n
= 9). Similarly, Ibn Mandah from layer 14 is third with respect to total number
of connections (n = 29) and as a teacher (n = 18), yet he is first as a student (n
= 11).

In the subset I have thus selected, there are 76 scholars from twenty-six layers with 174 connections. Note that connections to scholars outside the subset
are not included here. Therefore, this number does not reflect all the connections a scholar has, but it reflects connections to the highly prominent scholars
within the subset. On average, each scholar has 6.69 connections. The majority
of these connections are not to the closest past and future generations but, on
the contrary, to the remotest previous and subsequent generations within the
accessible range, which I call the network zone of a scholar.

The network zone of each figure is demarcated by time, the most important
constraint for a hafiz. Because of the time constraint, a scholar's connections
cannot possibly expand beyond the adjacent four past and four future generations. Consequently, the total number of layers that constitute the network zone
of a scholar is nine. Yet they do not coexist in a given time. As earlier generations meet their demise, new generations emerge. When a scholar is born, four
earlier layers exist. As he ages, these earlier layers gradually decline one after another while new layers also gradually emerge one after another. Eventually, be-

fore his death, he may become the representative of the oldest layer in existence with four younger layers. As the layers decline and rise, network zones shift, and ties are constantly reconfigured.

Time plays an omnipotent or sweeping yet invisible role in determining who can have a tie with whom. Stratification based on time is so solid that it is impossible for social actors to evade it. No one has the power to encroach on the borders drawn by time; an invisible yet impenetrable wall separates the layers in a network through time and completely blocks the possibility for some to have connections with each other.

Simple Local Prominence

Determining the total number of direct ties a social actor has in a social network is the simplest method of determining his relative social prominence. Since direct ties in a time-stratified network may occur within a given scope, knowing their number provides us with a measure of what is termed here *local prominence.* Local prominence in time-stratified networks, which consist of intra- and interlayer connections, has different dynamics from those of cross-sectional networks, where generational phenomena are not even a concern. Therefore, following the logic used in the previous chapter on macro-level analysis, with micro-level analysis, too, MR (maximum number of possible connections for a social actor) will replace N (total number of connections in the network) in determining the maximum possible number of social actors with whom one can possibly establish connections. In reality, however, this maximum number is almost never reached.[3] Alternatively, from a more down-to-earth perspective, the number of connections for the locally most prominent scholar can be used as an indicator of the maximum number of connections that a scholar from this layer could have established.

The latter approach has advantages over the former because, practically speaking, it is impossible for a scholar from a given layer to establish connections with all the scholars from nine neighboring layers. Even if he could, hypothetically speaking, this would still be captured by the second approach. The maximum reach of the first and last layers, on the other hand, cannot expand to nine layers because the network is truncated in the beginning and at the end.

For instance, the first layer cannot go beyond the Prophet's generation, since it is the origin and formation of the network. Therefore, the maximum upward reach is limited to 1. .

Similar nuances can be observed for layers 2 and 3 because their upward expansion is also limited. The upward connections of layer 2 can extend only one step, to the layer 1. Analogously, the upward connections of layer 3 also can extend only one step, to layer 2. Likewise for the last layers: the downward maximum reach is limited solely because of the lack of data on their connections with future generations. Utilizing the number of connections established by the most prominent scholar, in the layer of the scholar under investigation, is a method of overcoming this problem and obtaining a relative measure of a scholar's social prominence.[4]

The local prominence (LP) measure is derived from the total number of connections, consisting of the student and teacher relations a scholar has had. Therefore, it is possible to dissect this total number into its components, which would then enable us to explore the interplay between the total number of student and teacher connections. Teacher prominence is derived from a scholar's total number of student connections divided by the maximum possible number of student connections he could have had. Student prominence, on the other hand, is based on the total number of teacher connections a scholar established divided by the maximum number of teacher connections he could have established.[5]

The three measures do not always match for particular cases. For instance, the general prominence score of Nafi' is 1.00, but his student prominence score is 0.42, while his prominence score as a teacher is again 1.00. The score of Ibn Mandah on general prominence is 0.69, his student prominence score is 0.53, and his teacher prominence score is 1.00.

Student prominence, teacher prominence, and the relationship between them can be used to explore more deeply some of the processes in the network. How is the total number of connections distributed between student and teacher connections over centuries? What is the impact of student connections on teacher connections, and vice versa? What role do teacher connections play in student connections? In other words, do prominent students always become prominent teachers?

The matrix of relations drives our attention to fluctuations over time in network patterns as well. For instance, there are no in-layer connections in layers 1, 2, 3, 8, 11, 12, 13, 19, and 20 or in layers 23 to 25. In contrast, there are in-layer connections in other layers, though in varying density. Similarly, in the majority of cases, scholars do not have teachers from later layers, yet it is possible to observe that a number of scholars have teacher connections to a layer one step earlier.

Adjusted Local Prominence: Interlayer Brokerage

Local prominence, as illustrated above, is derived simply from the number of connections. However, this approach may be quite misleading because, as we have observed, the concomitant social and cultural processes that must be reflected in the model influence social ties. In other words, what matters is not only the existence of a tie but also the network distance between those who are involved in a relationship. Consequently, alternative measures are proposed below, to demonstrate the effects of these processes on network ties. The outcome is adjusted measures of social prominence, based on the effects under investigation.

Networks through time reflect relations between and within generations and hide patterns of interlayer social relations. At first sight, the members of each generation might be expected to be thickly connected to each other simply because they are peers and thus easily accessible to each other. Yet empirically, the opposite is true: the prominent social actors in a layer are closer to prominent actors in other layers than they are to actors in their own. Peers from a given layer are never connected to one another as strongly as they are with scholars in adjacent layers.

Yet this observation needs further elaboration. Peers do in fact have a very strong relationship: that of rivalry. Their connection with each other can be characterized as unbending competition, which is a very intense form of social relationship. Thus what appears at first sight to be a network of entirely disconnected individuals is actually a network of individuals intricately connected via competition because, as Simmel (1995) has observed, competition can be taken as one of the strongest social ties. As social actors become more prominent, the competition among them becomes more taxing.

The apparent paradox of disconnection among peers is best illustrated by the enduring patterns in the interlayer relations within the hadith transmission network. The portion of in-layer connections in the composition of the total number of social connections remained the lowest, over a millennium, vis-à-vis the portion of connections with earlier and successive generations. The total number of in-layer connections never went beyond a very minute portion. In the subset, there are only 18 in-layer connections out of 174.[6] This example is sufficient to sustain the argument that the analysis of social prominence in networks through time must be adjusted in such a way as to take intergenerational structures into account.

Prominence from Proximity

Closeness to the center of the network plays an important role in determining the prominence of individuals in social networks. Each node in the network is connected to the center through a path, yet the length of the path between them varies from person to person. Some reach the center directly, and some reach the center via a number of nodes. A path in a social network is defined as an "alternating sequence of nodes and lines beginning and ending with nodes" (Wasserman and Faust 1994, 143). From this perspective, usually a figure is produced where nodes n_i and n_j are connected through a path, whose length varies according to how many nodes are needed to cover the distance in question.

As the distance grew between the Prophet and later generations, proximity to the Prophet gained even more importance. The chains relentlessly competed with each other in terms of closeness to the center, which meant greater reliability and authenticity for the narrative and greater authority for its holder.

The length of the path between a social actor and the central figure(s) in the network is an important indicator of the actor's prominence. The shorter the path, the greater his prominence. The higher the number of nodes in the path between two nodes, the more difficult is the access between them. Suppose that n_i is the most central social actor in the network and is connected to n_j and n_k, who are also actors within the same network. They may be connected to the central actor by one or more paths, among which the most valuable will be the shortest one, the one with the lowest number of nodes.

The value of a path can be conceived as equal to the cost of access to a given node in a social network. If the path is shorter, then the connection will be easier and less costly. Otherwise, each unit of increase in the length of the path will also increase the cost of access. This concern leads to the elimination of mediators because the only way to shorten a chain is to eliminate nodes, that is, the number of mediators. Yet there are constraints on the extent to which that can be done.

Moreover, connection to a central figure via a relatively shorter path would bring more prestige to a social actor by contrast with other actors who must painstakingly pursue longer paths to the center. The best illustration of this point is the status of the Companions of the Prophet, the center of the hadith network; they are connected to him through the shortest path, since there is a distance of only one link between them and the Prophet. Next to them in social status are the Successors, who have only two links between them and the Prophet. This is quite analogous to the status of the disciples of Jesus in Christianity.

Path Distance

Path distance has its correlates in time and space, since each node is anchored in a different time and space. However, actors from a given time period or geographical location do not necessarily reach the Prophet via paths of the same distance. The path distance varies between the Prophet and individual scholars from a given generation, with the result that the scholars with the shortest paths, or narrative chains, are put in a more prestigious position. Consequently, the number of a scholar's layer—the layer to which the scholar belongs—is not necessarily an accurate reflection of the scholar's distance from the Prophet. Nor does the time period in which a scholar lived reflect how many steps it takes for him to reach the Prophet. Mere geographical and temporal distance are simply not accurate indicators of network distance.[7]

Most student connections concentrate on earlier layers (Sdown1 and Sdown2). As an exception, however, Sdown3, Sin, and Sup1 connections can be found. There are only three Sup2 connections, and two of them are from the same layer (layer 21). There are no Sdown4 connections.

Teacher connections concentrate on antecedent layers. Tup2 and Tup1 connections get the highest share. They are followed by Tin and Tdown1 connections. There are only three Tdown2 connections, accounted for by two scholars, and 4 Tup3 connections, accounted for by four scholars. Again, the number of in-layer connections is very low compared to out-layer connections.

An important manifestation of the effect of path distance on academic prestige can be observed in the way students of hadith selected their teachers. Historical records indicate that, all other qualifications being equal, students of hadith always sought the teachers with shorter narrative chains. Consequently,
one could not become a prominent teacher of hadith unless one could compete
with one's colleagues with respect to path distance from the Prophet. Longevity,
over which scholars could exert no control, made such competition possible. To
draw more students, a scholar simply waited until he had outlived his cohorts
so that his own narrative chains become the shortest.

This preference for the shortest path emanated from a commonly accepted
concern on the part of transmitters to preserve the veracity of the original oral
text. The possibility of damage to the original text of the narrative, and thus to
its authenticity, during transmission between successive scholars increased with
a parallel increase in the length of the chain. The longer the path, the higher the
probability of damage to the original text, and consequently the lower the value
of the narrative.

Most important of all, longer paths mean increased scholarly dependence,
reflected in increased levels of reported speech. If n_i is connected to n_j through
n_a, n_b, and n_c, then n_i and n_j are dependent on n_a, n_b, and n_c. The interests of
n_i and n_j would best be served by elimination of the discourse mediators from
the path altogether, if at all possible. If complete elimination is not possible,
then the interests of n_i and n_j are best served by reduction of the number of discourse mediators on the path. Social actors in a temporal network must know
how to manage the temporal constraints they face.

The distribution of connections is to five ranges. In-layer connections constitute Range1; Up1 and Down1 connections constitute Range2; Up2 and
Down2 connections constitute Range3; Up3 and Down3 connections constitute
Range4; and Up4 and Down4 connections constitute Range5. Through comparison of how the ties are distributed to various ranges, it is possible to observe the contrast between, first, in-layer and out-layer connections and, second, Range2 and Range5 connections. To put this idea more clearly, the
connections to Range1 are not as high as one might normally expect among the
members of a prominent group. Likewise, the sudden drop in Range4 connections and the complete waning of Range5 connections show the constraints
posed by time in shaping the configuration of networks through time. Scholars

tried to expand the gaps they bridged, yet they could not overcome the limitations arising from the network borders that time had drawn. Therefore, shortening the path distance to the center of the network was desirable because of the advantages it had to offer, yet it was possible only to a limited extent because of temporal constraints.

Geodesic Distance between Teachers and the Prophet

It became clear from the above discussion that the work of the huffaz was characterized by a search for the shortest path to the Prophet. Scholars were not just after narratives; rather, they were after narratives through particular network channels that would gain them distinction in the community. Consequently, the value of a tie to a scholar, for them, depended on how close his chain of authorities was to the Prophet (see fig. 5.5). I will call this the geodesic value of a tie. An aspiring student of hadith sought ties with an extensive geodesic value. Geodesic value summarizes the logic behind the search of students for particular ties.

Geographical distance, however, despite its great vastness, was not an issue for the huffaz. Consequently, they did not attribute importance to the geographical distance bridged by a network connection. They were primarily concerned not with geographical distance but with social distance. They traveled long distances with the means of transportation available at that time. Political stability was required for the safety of roads.

The shortest path between scholars and the Prophet, which determines what is called here geodesic value, thus plays an important role in prominence. Attention needs to be paid, nevertheless, to the layer of the scholar as well. If the layer of the scholar is not taken into consideration, then scholars from different layers with the same path distance will end up being treated the same way. For instance, if n_i from layer 5 is connected to the Prophet via a path that includes three nodes, it will have the same value as n_j from layer 7, who is also connected to the Prophet through three nodes. Paradoxically, if a scholar belongs to a later layer but his chain is relatively shorter, this actually adds value to his chain because he has traversed a longer distance at less cost. To put it plainly, reaching the center with less effort from a greater distance will increase the importance of a path.

In this connection, geodesic distance is used here to indicate the shortest

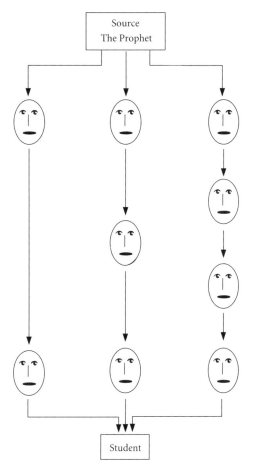

Which tie is more important for the student?
Which one invokes fewer levels of reported speech?

FIG. 5.5. The Role of Geodesic Value

path distance a social actor can travel to reach the most central figure(s) in the network. In our case, it is the shortest chain between a scholar and the Prophet. It should be noted that "geodesic distance" is generally smaller than the layer number because the extent of the network of scholars is not limited to the immediately adjacent generations. Conversely, it is desirable to go as much as possible beyond the immediate generations upward (teacher ties) and downward (student ties). Geodesic distance is 1 for the Companions because there is only one "arch" in the graph between them and the Prophet; it is 2 for the Successors (layers 2 to 4 in our dataset, which correspond to the old/early, middle-aged, and young/late Successors) because there are only two arches between them and the Prophet. For successive layers, it varies.

The most striking aspect is the difference between layer location and number of nodes to the center. This phenomenon demonstrates the difference between geodesic distance to the center and the number of the layers from the node under investigation to the center. For instance, scholars from layer 15 had to go through nine nodes to reach to the Prophet. Similarly, it took thirteen nodes for scholars from layer 25 to reach the Prophet. The scholar with the shortest path in a layer is given the score of 1, and the rest are ranked accordingly.

There are six cases for which geodesic distance value cannot be obtained for a scholar because these scholars did not have any of the top three scholars from the previous layers as their teachers. Nevertheless, they had other huffaz as their teachers. In the rest of the cases, the scholars all had at least one teacher from among the three with the highest scores.

It is important to pay attention to the role of increase in the social temporal gap that a tie helps to bridge. Therefore, the role of this temporal structure needs to be accounted for in assessing the dynamics of authority formation. Thus a weight value needs to be introduced into the equation, to reflect the effect of generational distance on the value of path distance. As explained above, in order to avoid treating an equal path distance from different generations in the same way, we need to take layer distance into consideration. The layer number is equal to the number of the generation a scholar belongs to. The total number of the layers equals the total number of generations in the data set (n = 26).[8] Proximity to the center bears upon social prominence.[9] The stars are, for the most part, connected to the center via the shortest possible chains among their cohorts.

Global Proximity from Local Distance

The previous section explored prominence from proximity to the center of the network. This section focuses on the processes that lead to proximity, which is the temporal distance between nodes. Shorter paths are produced by greater time distance between nodes of a path in a network through time. Closeness to the center, as previously mentioned, depends on shorter path distance, which in turn is contingent upon greater distances between nodes. Consequently, the greater the time distance between ego and alter, the more valuable the tie. Applied to the hadith transmission network, this formula says that the greater the layer distance between a scholar and his teachers and students, the more prominent the scholar becomes.

Direct access to prominent teachers from earlier generations increases the prominence of students. Similarly, to be sought after by younger generations increases the prominence of a teacher and shows his extended influence. In both cases, dependence on otherwise necessary ties is eliminated. The direct consequence of eliminating dependence on mediators, as elaborated earlier, is reflected in reduced levels of reported speech.

Geodesic Distance to Teachers and Students

Here, the term *geodesic distance* means generational distance in one's connections. More specifically, it is the number of layers between a scholar and his students and teachers. In other words, local prominence is adjusted by the distance between alter and ego. The value of a tie increases as the distance it helps to bridge increases.

Following this logic, the total number of ties to colleagues from the same layer is assigned the index value of 1. The number of ties to a one-unit distance is multiplied by 2. Ties to a two-unit distance are multiplied by 3. Ties to a three-step distance are multiplied by 4, and ties to a four-step distance are multiplied by 5. Upward and downward distances are treated the same way because both have a similar impact on prominence, owing to the reasons explained earlier.

On rare occasions, however, scholars from earlier generations have cited scholars from younger generations (Tdown1). Teacher connection from Down1 also must be given special treatment because distance of this type does not usually work in favor of the older scholar, since it demonstrates that he became a student of someone who was younger than himself. For this reason, Tdown1 connections are not weighted in the same way as are student connections to the same layer.[10] Our finding demonstrates that the greater the distance between oneself and one's alters (teachers and students), the greater one's social prominence; the smaller the distance between oneself and the people in one's network, the less one's social prominence.

Coupling Literary and Social Dynamics

The social phenomenon described above is an unintended outcome of an underlying linguistic phenomenon. More concretely, the reason why prominent scholars avoid in-layer connections is that they want to reduce the levels of reported speech. This hypothesis can be tested with historical, social, and sociolinguistic methods.

The Effect of Levels of Reported Speech

The temporal constraints on action are best exposed through analysis of the dynamics behind the levels of reported speech. Only a few scholars can speak with object language about scientific phenomena; this is an important privilege in the scholarly community. The rest have to cite and report. In reporting, the rule is to use the fewest possible levels of reflexive speech because prestige is inversely related to the levels of reported speech one uses in one's talk.

Only eyewitness narrators—whether they are scientists working in a well-endowed lab, anthropologists visiting a strange Australian tribe, or historians reporting an important event—enjoy the prestige of using object language when they tell their stories about the phenomena under investigation. Others can tell stories only by citing them. Moreover, citations from secondary or tertiary sources are ill received in the scholarly community. For instance, if a student cites the work of his professor from the paper of a fellow student, in which the text of their mutual professor's work is quoted, the citation will not go without criticism even if it is completely accurate. This rule about language use concerning reporting and narration unintentionally affects the network configuration of scholars; the outcome is either complete elimination or minimization of academic ties, in the form of citing and reporting, to fellow scholars from the same layer. A weight value based on social geodesics is assigned to each academic tie.

This particular system of language use concerning reported speech in present-day academia closely resembles the practice that existed among medieval Islamic scholars. Such was particularly true in the case of hadith scholars, whose sole preoccupation revolved around carefully selecting the shortest available chains of authority while narrating hadith.

In hadith culture, the shorter the narrative chain to the Prophet, the more prominent the scholar who used it. But why? This finding can be attributed to language use. Layers closer to the Prophet used fewer levels of reported speech because they could then report hadith with relatively reduced or shorter chains of authorities. Conversely, later layers had to use increasingly multilevel reported speech as links in the chains of authorities multiplied through the passage of time. More concretely, a Companion used object language and eyewitness narrative when he told stories of the Prophet because usually he had also participated in the event he was reporting.

Since, in narrative, only eyewitnesses can use object language, the Companions enjoyed this privilege in the case of hadith. The segment of Companions considered to be huffaz in the entire network is extremely small: only twenty-six narrators belonged to the layer of the Companions. Those who heard stories from eyewitness sources and conveyed them to others could not use object language; they had to use reported speech. They had to say, "I heard from such-and-such person that such-and-such event took place." The same rule applied to those who heard a story from this discourse mediator. But this time, these listeners had to use two-level reported speech, and they had to mention in their reports the name of the mediator who had heard from the eyewitness that such-and-such an event had taken place.

As the story was disseminated, each new node in the network added a new level to the levels of the reported speech. The number of ties in the social network increased simultaneously and at the same rate with the increase in the levels of reported speech. In brief, the question this observation brings to mind is, how does the use of language implicitly configure academic networks among prominent scholars?

Relying on reported language is a sign of dependence; it is an acknowledgment that one cannot have direct access to information. Worse is to use multiple levels of reported speech, an acknowledgment of distance from the central figures in the network, and thus from the original sources of information.

How Many Levels of Reported Speech Does a Tie Save?

Suppose that a scholar from layer 6 has two ties. One is to a teacher from layer 5, the other to a teacher from layer 3. Which tie is more valuable to him (see fig. 5.5)? The tie to the teacher from layer 3 is of course more valuable than the tie to the teacher from layer 5. The reason is that the connection to the teacher from layer 3 is an important asset in the hadith community because it reduces the levels of reported speech for the student by skipping three nodes between layers 3 and 6.

Similarly, suppose that there are two hadith scholars from layer 6, each with a total of four teacher ties. But one of them has all his ties to teachers from layer 5, and the other has one teacher tie from layer 5, one teacher tie from layer 4, and two teacher ties from layer 3. Which of these two scholars will be the more prominent? Although the total number of ties they have is the same, the latter will be more prominent because his ties are closer to the original source and allow him to speak with fewer levels of reported speech.

Likewise, suppose that a student from layer 7 cites one of these scholars from layer 6, and the other is cited by a student from layer 9. Which of these student connections will be the more important? From the perspective of interlayer brokerage, the latter tie will be more important because it will show that the cited scholar has a more extensive influence on the young. Furthermore, since his student will have a relatively shorter chain of authorities, his prominence will increase in proportion to the prominence of his young student (see fig. 5.6).

This leads us to conclude that the greater the network distance between one's own layer and the layer of one's teacher or student, the more valuable the teacher or student tie. Consequently, ties are weighted in a way that reflects the distance between the origin and the destination of a tie. The bigger the gap between the origin and the destination of a scholarly tie, the more important the tie.

In this study, the distance between origin and destination is indicated by the variables constructed for this purpose: all teacher and student ties are recorded in such a way that they include information about the distance of the tie. The numbers at the end of the teacher and student variables indicate the distance. For instance, Tup4 means a teacher tie from four layers earlier. Sdown3 means a student tie from three layers later.

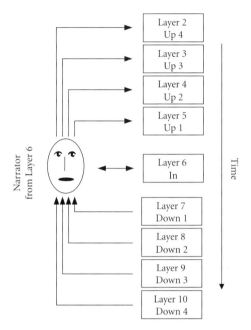

Which tie is more valuable for the narrator?
Which one invokes fewer levels of reported speech?

FIG. 5.6. The Role of Levels of Reported Speech

Each tie should be weighted by the distance it bridges. For instance, Tup4 connections may be multiplied by 4; similarly, Sdown4 ties also may be multiplied by 4. Tup3 ties may be multiplied by 3, and Sdown3 ties may also be multiplied by 3. For the same reason, ties within the same layer, or to only one upper and one lower layer, have no weight value. These ties include those designated as the variables Sin, Tin, Tup1, Tdown1, Sup1, and Sdown1.

Authority Formation from Diachronic Social and Literary Dynamics

Authority formation is a chaotic process that cannot be properly understood unless analytical tools from different fields are harnessed together in the analysis. This study combines social network and time series analyses because the social network analyzed here extends over a millennium and includes twenty-six layers of scholars. It also combines network analysis methods with sociolinguistic and socionarrative methods because social networks are constructed jointly by social and literary structures. Furthermore, the hadith transmission network analyzed here developed solely around a linguistic structure, hadith.

Methods for the analysis of time-stratified social networks are still in an embryonic state. This is true not only because time is an elusive phenomenon but also because it is almost impossible to collect social network data for more than a very limited number of generations. According to Wasserman and Faust (1994, 731),

> network analysis and network models have often been criticized for being static. Although much work has been done on longitudinal models, applications of this methodology are sorely lacking. Models are quite complicated, and often require continuous records of network changes, which are often hard to collect. . . . Good, easy-to-use methods for longitudinal network data would be an important addition to the literature.

From this perspective, hadith data provide us with an excellent site on which to develop methods for analyzing interlayer and time-stratified networks.

Figure 5.7 (compare with fig. 3.3), which Saussure drew years ago to explain the "internal duality of all sciences," facilitates illustration of the interaction between the synchronic and diachronic features of a structure. Saussure (1993, 103a) drew two axes and explained their meaning as follows: He called the first one *axis of simultaneity or contemporaneity* (AB). This axis concerns relations between coexisting things, relations from which the passage of time is entirely excluded. Saussure called the second one *axis of succession* (CD). This axis reflects the relations between successive things, things multiplied by time. Along

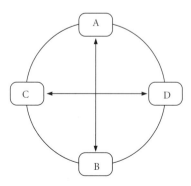

FIG. 5.7. Internal Duality of Sciences according to Saussure. Source: Saussure (1994, 80).

this axis one may consider only one thing at a time. But here we find all the things situated along the first axis, together with the changes they undergo. To put this more clearly, synchronic analysis is about relations between coexisting elements, while diachronic analysis is about relations between succeeding elements of a system.

The need to accommodate time in social network analysis has increasingly been emphasized; however, another potential area of expansion for network methodology has yet to be noticed by scholars in the field—namely, the interaction between social networks and social narratives. Current methods in sociology reflect the gap between literary and social structuralism. The methodological approach adopted in this study could pave the way toward the creation of methods that would be based on a new conceptual foundation, with an emphasis on interaction between literary and social structures.

CHAPTER SIX

Social and Literary Dynamics
of Authority Formation

The Macro-Level LRS Effect

Reporting speech from past generations is a must in the scholarly community, regardless of the discipline. Those who know how to do it successfully gain prominence. "The ideas I wish to describe are old ideas" said Richard P. Feynman, the prominent twentieth-century physicist and Nobel laureate, at the outset of a lecture on the philosophy of science (Feynman 1998, 3). This must have been disappointing and disturbing to the select members of his audience, who had come to hear the latest ideas about the philosophy of science from one of the leading physicists. Therefore, Feynman felt the need to defend himself: "Why repeat all this? Because there are new generations born every day. Because there are great ideas developed in the history of man, and these ideas do not last unless they are passed purposely and clearly from generation to generation" (Feynman 1998, 4). Feynman's frankness in this confession, far from diminishing his prestige, instead exposed a fundamental structure of scientific process—namely, that scholars gain prominence by reporting speech. In fact, scholars gain prominence by reporting speech from remote generations and relating it to current problems. Yet this is not an easy task; it takes an eminent scholar like Feynman to do it.

If Feynman's observation is true for philosophy and science, it is even more applicable to the humanities, art, and religion, even if it seems to contradict popular expectations about originality. The prominence of huffaz also came from their having successfully reported speech. Yet the mechanisms involved in this process are much more sophisticated than they might appear at first glance.

Having seen, in the preceding chapters, that the connections of prominent scholars of hadith are distributed in varying degrees over adjacent layers within a possible range, a situation that creates partly overlapping and continuously shifting network scopes over time, we can now explore whether there is a pattern in such distribution over time. The demonstration of a persistent and relatively stable pattern in the relations among layers would in turn prescribe some consideration of cause from within the broader intellectual context of the huffaz network.

Changing and Immutable Features over Time

Collins's recent work (1998) has demonstrated that patterns in the relations of intellectuals survive the test of time and do not simply fade away. Analysis of the connections between layers as aggregate social actors allows us, with the help of time series analysis, to test the claim that enduring patterns in social relations generate social structures through which social inequalities in academia are produced and reproduced over time.[1] In order for patterns in social relations to endure, they must be rooted in fundamental social processes, such as language use. Are there such patterns in the scholarly community that bear upon authority formation? If so, what are the processes through which inequalities are reproduced in each layer? Below, I will explore these questions on the macro level by analyzing the network of huffaz.

Why Does the Level of Networking Change over Time?

In the hadith transmission network, it can be inferred from a comparison between average numbers of connections for different layers that not all layers were equally active in establishing ties with other layers. As a result, the average number of connections per scholar in different layers fluctuates over time. Despite these fluctuations, some patterns are discernible over time.

If we examine figure 6.1, the first striking feature is that the average in-layer connections per scholar remained stable at a very low rate, despite fluctuations in the values for other variables relative to the volume of upward and downward variables over time. Even though some layers were not as active in networking, all layers were virtually static with respect to maintaining in-layer connections at a minimum level. The former is exemplary of change, while the

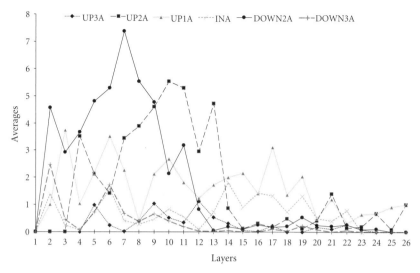

FIG. 6.1. Average Connections per Scholar. A color version of this figure, and of figs. 6.2–6.7, may be viewed at www.sup.org/senturk.

latter demonstrates continuity. Besides the stability of in-layer ties at a minimum level and the significant difference in the ratio between in-layer and out-layer connections, another striking observation is the fluctuation in the volume of out-layer ties over time, which begs for an explanation. The changing average number of connections for a scholar indicates the changing level of activity.

This observation brings to mind the following question: Why were scholars at certain times more actively involved in seeking higher numbers of teachers and students, as compared to their colleagues from other layers? The fluctuation in the average number of academic ties to prominent scholars over the course of history may be due to the political and cultural unrest that Islamic civilization underwent during certain periods in its history. A look at concurrent events during the lifetimes of layers may reveal the influence of these historical events on the network. Examples of such major historical changes and turbulence, with possible impacts on network patterns, include transfer of power between dynasties, Mongol attacks, and the Crusades. More important, changing internal dynamics of the network—such as evolving modes of narration, and particularly the shift from the relation of a single hadith to the relation of huge hadith collections—may also have been responsible for some of these changes.

There is a heightened level of activity until layer 14 (361–486 AH/971–1093 CE). Beginning with layer 15 (404–540 AH/1013–1145 CE), the level of activity increasingly vanishes along with the diminishing number of huffaz. The high level of activity in the first period, from the first to the fifth century of Hijrah, can be seen as peculiar to hadith transmission. In contrast, the level of activity in the second period, after the sixth century of Hijrah, can been seen as common to all the discourse networks.

What changes from the sixth century of Hijrah onward is not only the volume of activity but also the striking decrease in the maximal span of relations or the distance between the layer under consideration and the layer of scholars who are sought after as teachers and students. Until layer 14, we observe that the highest portion of ties from a layer is directed to scholars who are at a distance of two layers. However, beginning with layer 15, this distance between the target and the origin of the connections shrinks; instead of a two-layer span, a distance of one layer became dominant. We can thus conclude that both the level of networking activity and the maximal span of relations decreased at the same time, around the fifth century of Hijrah, which corresponds to the 11th century CE.

The transition from a predominant distance of two layers, upward and downward, to a distance of one layer is a significant and consequential one, which needs to be interpreted within the broader dynamics of Islamic history. It may be argued, from a Weberian perspective, that the routinization of activity, through standardization of the processes involved in finding reliable hadith, led to the decrease in the search for a maximal span in relations. The search for the shortest chain gradually lost its principal role and gave way to other criteria used in the evaluation of hadith. The primary focus increasingly shifted away from narration through the shortest chain and toward interpretation of content. The types of works in the hadith literature emerging after this time testify to this assertion. Moreover, the rivalry between the Qur'an, hadith, and reasoning (analogy) in Islamic law had been consolidated by that time because hadith had gained the status of being one of the main sources of Shariah, second only to the Qur'an, with primacy over analogical reasoning, even in the view of the People of Opinion (*ahl al-ra'y*). This period also corresponds to the time of consolidation reached among the four schools of law that earlier had competed for juridical evidence—in this case, the hadith—to solidify their positions against their rival schools. These changes can be cited as possible reasons why heightened level of interest in the shortest chains and maximized spans of relations gradually diminished until the transmission of hadith came to follow transmission patterns for other types of narrative. I will elaborate on this issue in the next chapter, in the context of discussing the relationship between hadith and associated disciplines.

Where Do Prominent Scholars Invest the Most?

Yet as the illustrations and tables in this chapter show, even after the search for the shortest chains was no longer the primary goal of scholars, their investment was still directed mainly at those other than their own contemporaries—directed, that is, at the preceding and emerging generations. Networking by prominent scholars is a self-reflexive process. It is commonly known that scholars do not randomly choose their students. Nor do students, especially those who aspire to become prominent scholars in the future, randomly choose their teachers. The teachers had to compete for students, even in the time of the Companions. The following dialogue took place between a prominent Companion, Abu al-Darda, who served as a hadith mentor to youth, and his wife, Umm al-Darda:

> Umm al-Darda': Abu al-Darda' would smile whenever he recounted a hadith, so I told him, "I am afraid that people say of you that you are a fool [ahmaq]." She said Abu al-Darda' replied, "I did not hear Allah's Messenger ever tell a hadith except he smiled as he was telling it."[2]

The dialogue expresses the concern of a wife, Umm al-Darda, about the career of her husband, who is so meticulous about his mission, and about the possibility that he may no longer attract students if he causes himself to be misjudged. The husband, Abu al-Darda, insists on taking the risk because he thinks this is what the Prophet did. History proved him right, since he became one of the most respected narrators of hadith. The students were not misled by their first impressions of Abu al-Darda, and they kept taking hadith from him.

There is a latent logic at work here, which determines who is more appealing to whom among teachers and students. The constraints involved make one-sided choices difficult if not impossible. A mutual decision of student and teacher is required unless there is a highly centralized educational system. This

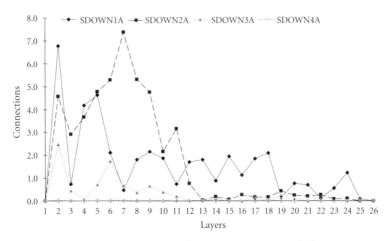

FIG. 6.2. Average Student Connections per Scholar

is especially true for the relationship between hadith students and teachers because hadith education always remained decentralized or, better, polycentric,
outside the control of governments and large institutions, such as those that we
are familiar with today. The values indicating average numbers of connections
through time expose the logic of strategic investment on the part of scholars,
since they display enduring patterns in the way the scholars invested their time
and energy.

Teachers and students persistently refrained from establishing academic ties
to their peers, a pattern that, we observe, remained stable until the end. Yet
when we look closely at out-layer ties, we see a striking change in the logic of
investment after layer 14. In figure 6.1, illustrating average connections per
scholar to particular distances, it is clearly observable that while scholars persistently invested in Up2 and Down2 connections until layer 14, they then began
investing in Up1 and Down1 connections, reducing the distance between themselves and their connections. This observation is also confirmed by the figures
illustrating average teacher and student connections over time.

As figure 6.2 shows, students invested for the most part in mentors from two
generations earlier (Up2) connections, until layer 14, after which they began investing mostly in mentors from a single generation earlier. This change may be
seen as an indication of decreasing interest on the part of students in the shortest chains.

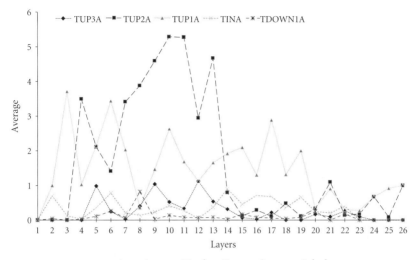

FIG. 6.3. Average Teacher Connections per Scholar

Teachers, as figure 6.3 illustrates, also invested in the youngest students who belonged to the layers two steps down from their own. This pattern continued until layer 14, where the intense search for the youngest possible students waned. Beginning with layer 15, teachers invested in students who were not as young as had been the case in preceding centuries.

Density in a Time-Stratified Network

Network density is equal to the proportion of actual as opposed to possible connections within a network. Measures of density are used to analyze how thickly layers are connected to each other. The concept of network density, as developed and applied to cross-sectional networks, is not suitable for the analysis of time-stratified networks. Proper modifications need to be made in order to make current density-analysis methods applicable to time-stratified networks. According to Scott (1992, 74), "The density of a graph is defined as the number of lines in a graph, expressed as a proportion of the maximum possible number of lines. This measure can vary from 0 to 1, the density of a complete graph being 1." This analysis is suitable for nondirectional graphs, which disregard the direction of ties by ignoring whether they are giving or receiving ties. For directional graphs, which take into account whether ties are giving or receiving, certain modifications are needed. In the case of the hadith transmission network, a direction graph consists of student (receiving) and teacher (giving) connections.

> In directed graphs the calculation of the density must be slightly different. The matrix for directed data is asymmetrical, as a directed line from A to B will not necessarily involve a reciprocal line directed from B to A. For this reason, the maximum number of lines which could be present in a directed graph is equal to the total number of pairs that it contains. This is simply calculated as $n(n-1)$.[3] The density formula for a directed graph, therefore, is $l/n(n-1)$ [Scott 1992, 74].

In a time-stratified network, this formula can be used only in the analysis of in-layer density. For the density of connections between layers, certain modifications need to be made. If we do not take into account what we call the *maximum reach (mr)* of a layer, most of these connections exceed the maximum reach. Yet if we take the indirect ties into consideration, we realize that all layers are indirectly connected to each other.

In cross-sectional networks, the highest possible level of density is measured by multiplying the number of cases by itself (N multiplied by N), but in the analysis of the highest possible density in diachronic networks, the total number of the maximum reachable cases *(mr)* must take the place of the total number of cases (N). However, in time-stratified networks, since not all layers reach each other, density is an outcome of n (total number of social actors in a layer) multiplied by $mr(-1)$ (total number of social actors within the reach of the layer in question, with the exception of self-reflexive ties).

$$D= c/n(mr-1)$$

where D stands for maximum possible density, c stands for number of connections present in the network, n stands for number of social actors in a layer, and *mr* stands for the number of social actors reachable by n (n = the layer in question + 4 previous layers + 4 future layers).

We can further analyze this global value of density by breaking it down into the different domains to which a layer is connected. From this perspective, we can analyze the density of connections within a layer as well as between layers. Multiplying the number of social actors in the origin layer by the number of social actors in the target layer (the product is equal to the highest possible number of connections) and dividing the product by the actual number of connections produces the relative measure of density of the network connections between two layers.

$$D_{ot} = c/n_o(n_t)$$

where D_{ot} stands for the density of connection between the origin and target layers, with o standing for origin layer and t for target layer, c stands for the number of connections present in the network, and n stands for the number of social actors in a layer.[4] This model gives us the density of connections between two temporally different social groups or clusters embedded in a broader network over time. The borders of each group, conveniently termed *origin* and *target*, are demarcated by the time period they occupy. These temporal borders must partially overlap for the relations to be possible.

The total possible number of connections between two layers, a number that is equal to the highest level of density, may actually occur only if everyone is connected to everyone else in the reachable domains. This is a hypothetical situation and is never the case in social life. There is always a huge discrepancy between what is possible and what is actual with respect to social density, for it is beyond the limit of social actors to exhaust all the resources they have at their disposal. The relations we actually have are insignificant in number compared to our possible relations. The constraints we knowingly or unknowingly face eliminate most possibilities, and we end up with a highly limited number of relations. Among these constraints, time features prominently.

There is only one exception to this rule: the Prophet. Only the Prophet exhausted all the possibilities. By definition, he was connected to all his Companions. But, regarding all the other layers, no one even came close to that point. In this regard, there is an asymmetry with the beginning and the end of the network. The last layer also has one figure, Suyuti, but with only three connections to hafiz teachers and no hafiz students.

How Thickly Are Layers Connected to Each Other?

A comparative analysis of actual measures of the density of connections for all layers across time demonstrates changes over time. Figures 6.4, 6.5, and 6.6 demonstrate both the contrast between what is possible and what is historical and the fluctuations in network density among layers through centuries. The figures reflect fluctuating values for different layers, yet one can notice that fluc-

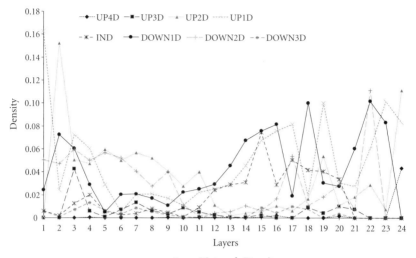

FIG. 6.4. Network Density

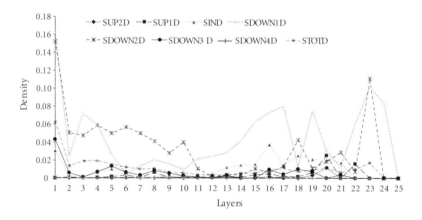

FIG. 6.5. Density of Student Connections

tuations in density are not as sharp as fluctuations in the average number of connections between layers, which we have just surveyed.

For further analysis, it is possible to break the aggregate density measures down into density of student and teacher connections. Dissection of the connections demonstrates that the density of student connections concentrates on future layers, while the density of teacher connections concentrates on connections to earlier layers.

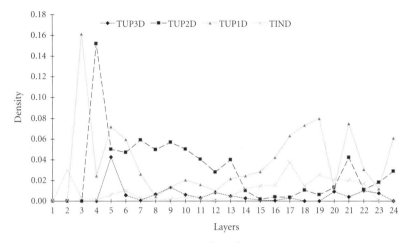

F I G . 6 . 6 . Density of Teacher Connections

This is displayed in figures 6.5 and 6.6, which allow us to observe the changes in the density of teacher and student connections between layers over twenty-six generations. Figure 6.5 illustrates the tension between Sdown1 and Sdown2 density. In the beginning, Sdown2 density is higher, until layer 11. Beginning with layer 11, Sdown1 density gains supremacy until layer 18, where it falls sharply, but it rises again in layers 19 and 20. In layers 18 and 20, density of connection to students at a distance of two layers (Sdown2) again gains prevalence.

Figure 6.6 shows competition between Tup2 and Tup1 density. In the beginning, density is concentrated in Tup2, until layer 14. Beginning at layer 14, density shifts to Tup1 connections. Density of in-layer teacher connections for 26 layers follows a low degree; the highest degree it reaches is at layer 17, where it becomes higher than the density of Tup2 connections.

In earlier generations, the maximal span characterizes the majority of connections. Consequently, layers are for the most part connected to the remotest possible generations. Connections between layers, however, do not remain equally thick throughout the centuries. Earlier layers are more thickly connected to each other. In contrast, later layers are progressively less thickly connected both to each other, particularly to remote layers: a sign of the vanishing network. The density of connections within a layer as always remains extremely low compared to the density of connections to preceding and future layers. This is a manifestation of interlayer brokerage (ILB).

Are Prominent Scholars Closer to Those Who Are Far from Them?

In the preceding discussion it is already noticeable that there is, approximately speaking, a symmetry between the volume of upward and downward connections of a layer. For instance, the measures for Up1 connections are close to the measures for Down1 connections, and the measures for Up2 connections are close to Down2 connections. In other words, there is symmetry in the volume of the giving (teacher) and receiving (student) ties. This symmetry is an important feature of the hadith transmission network, and it remains almost unchanged throughout its history. Also, the internal domain of a layer itself is not the center of activity. Most activity takes place outside, in the interaction between a layer and its distanced neighbors.

The symmetry between measures regarding connections to equal past and future distances allows us to put these measures together so as to see the volume of connections from a layer to its neighbors at equal distances. I thus created five scopes, indicated by capital S. Each scope encompasses temporal connections to equal distances, past and future:

$$Scope_X = Up_X + Down_X$$

In-layer connections constitute $Scope_{in}$ (Sin). Connections to Down1 and Up1 constitute $Scope_1$ (S1). Connections to Down2 and Up2 constitute $Scope_2$ (S2). Connections to Down3 and Up3 constitute $Scope_3$ (S3). Connections to Down4 and Up4 constitute $Scope_4$ (S4).[5]

We can observe and analyze, from this perspective, how close a layer is to its neighbors, both past and future, at various distances. As figures 6.1–6.7 have shown, a layer is not so closely knit within itself, but it is closely knit with those that are far from it generationally. The thickness of the connection between a layer and adjacent earlier and later layers is just as striking as the thinness of the fabric of the internal connections within a layer.

Figure 6.7 displays the differences between total numbers of connections to various network scopes. It is possible to observe the fluctuation in the actual values and the stability in the ratio. For instance, $Scope_2$ connections are always lower than $Scope_1$ connections. Here again we observe the manifestation of continuity and change.

Figure 6.7 shows that connections to $Scope_1$ (S1) and connections to $Scope_2$ (S2) compete with each other. $Scope_2$ (S2) connections are the highest from

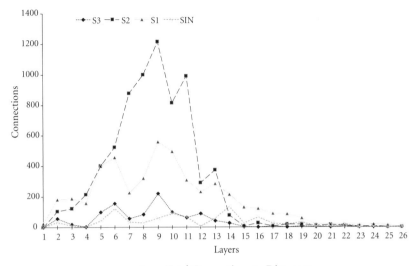

FIG. 6.7. Total Connections to Distances

layers 6 to 13, while Scope$_1$ (S1) connections are the highest in layers 2 and 3 and from layers 14 to 20. Internal connections within a layer (Sin), however, remain low at all times.

The average number of connections per scholar from a layer to the scholars from neighboring scopes also fluctuates, a finding that can be attributed to the historical conditions of the time as well as to network processes. However, the ratio between these values remains stable here as well.

A closer examination of the values for the variables under consideration captures the continuity better. The percentages for volume of connections to the same scopes remain stable over time. The ratio for Scope$_{in}$ values indicates that in-layer connections are the lowest. In contrast, the ratio for Scope$_2$ values is the highest.

Figure 6.7 also depicts the enduring tension between Scope$_1$ (S1) and Scope$_2$ (S2) connections. We can see that Scope$_2$ (S2) connections are highest from layers 3 to 13. From layer 14 until the end, with the exception of layer 22, Scope$_1$ (S1) connections prevail. Scope$_3$ (S3) connections, generally speaking, are higher than Scope$_{in}$ (Sin) connections. Figure 6.7 also lays out the tension between S1 and S2 density. S2 density is prevalent from layers 3 to 12, whereas S1 density is prevalent from layer 13 to the end, with the exception of layer 16. Scope$_{in}$ (Sin) density also fluctuates and sometimes reaches very high degrees. For instance, in layer 16, Sin density reaches its highest level.

TABLE 6.1

Time Series Used in the Analysis

(Period = 610–1505)

No.	Series name	Definition
	Series involving raw values or total number of connections	
1	Stotal	Total number of student connections from a layer
2	Ttotal	Total number of teacher connections from a layer
3	Total	Total number of connections (sum of teacher and student connections from a layer)
	Series involving average number of connections	
4	Saverage	Average number of student connections per scholar from a layer
5	Taverage	Average number of teacher connections per scholar from a layer
6	Staverage	Average number of connections per scholar from a layer (teacher and student ties together)
	Series involving in-layer connections	
7	Sin	Total number of in-layer student connections for a layer
8	Tin	Total number of in-layer teacher connections for a layer
9	In	Total number of in-layer connections, including both teacher and student connections
10	Stina	Average number of in-layer student connections of a layer
11	Tina	Average number of in-layer teacher connections of a layer
12	Sttina	Average number of in-layer connections, including both student and teacher connections
	Series involving percentage of connections to distances	
13	Su1d1per	Percentage of student connections per scholar to distance 1 (up1 and down1) of a layer
14	Su2d2per	Percentage of student connections per scholar to distance 2 (up2 and down2) of a layer
15	Sinper	Percentage of in-layer student connections per scholar of a layer
16	Tu1d1per	Percentage of teacher connections per scholar to distance 1 (up1 and down1) of a layer
17	Tu2d2per	Percentage of teacher connections per scholar to distance 2 (up2 and down2) of a layer
18	Tinper	Percentage of in-layer connections per scholar of a layer
19	Su2d3per	Percentage of student ties per scholar to distance 2 earlier (up) and distance 3 later (down)
20	Su2d4per	Percentage of student connections per scholar to distance 2 earlier (up) and distance 4 later
21	Tu3d2per	Percentage of teacher connections to distance 3 earlier (up) and distance 2 future (down)
22	Tu4d2per	Percentage of teacher connections per scholar to distance 4 earlier and distance 2 later

Time Series Analysis of Diachronic Networking Patterns

What we have intuitively observed by examining the preceding figures can be tested through time series analysis. We observed above that authority formation in the scholarly community depends on out-layer or, more precisely, upward and downward connections to past and future generations rather than in-layer connections. With the purpose of testing this claim by utilizing time series regression models, I employed the measures of in-layer connections as the dependent variable and the measures of out-layer connections as the independent variable.

The purpose here is to analyze the effect of in-layer connections on the number of student and teacher connections, which we take as a measure of social prominence. Measures of total number of connections, average number of connections per scholar, percentage of connections to other layers, and density of connections to other layers are used in the analysis. Table 6.1 lists the time series used in the analysis.[6] Brief definitions of the variables are also provided in the table. The 22 variables are aimed at reflecting the different aspects of network processes.

Time series concerning in-layer connections serve in the analysis as independent variables. They are variably constructed according to what type of measure is used in the analysis, whether total, average, percentage, or density. I have formed single-equation regression models to regress upward and downward connections on inward connections. As discussed earlier, the majority of upward connections are connections to teachers from earlier layers, whereas the majority of downward connections are connections to students from future layers. Yet there are upward student connections and downward teacher connections as well. These results enable us to see whether there is an effect of in-layer connections on upward and downward connections.

$$C = c + a \text{ incon} + \text{eteq.} \tag{1}$$

where C stands for connections of a layer and "incon" stands for in-layer connections.

Both the dependent and the independent variables are variably defined according to (1) type of the connections (student, teacher, or both), (2) direction of the connections (upward, downward, or inward), (3) destination of the con-

nections (up1, up2, up3, up4, in, down1, down2, down3, or down4), and (4) type
of measure (total, average, percentage, or density).

$$\text{Sxden} = c + a \text{ sinden} + \text{eteq.} \tag{2}$$

$$\text{Txden} = c + a \text{ tinden} + \text{eteq.} \tag{3}$$

$$\text{STxden} = c + a \text{ stinden} + \text{eteq.} \tag{4}$$

where S stands for student connections, T stands for teacher connections, ST
stands for both student and teacher connections, and x stands for one of these
network zones: up1, up2, up3, up4, down1, down2, down3, and down4. For instance, {Sdown1} stands for total number of student connections to a subsequent layer. Similarly, {Tup3den} stands for density of teacher connections to
three layers up. Consequently, the number of regressions I ran that derived
from these models, as we will see below, varied according to the number of
zones.[7]

Before these regression models were run, unit root tests were conducted to
see whether the series were stationary or not. If the series were stationary, they
could be used in the analysis. If not, they could not be used in a time series
analysis (Gujurati 1995; Dickey and Fuller 1979). The following models were
used to determine whether a time series had a root.

$$Y_t = c + aYt + \text{eteq.} \tag{5}$$

With insertion of a trend, eq. (5) became

$$Y_t = c + aY_{t-1} + bt + \text{eteq.} \tag{6}$$

where t stands for trend. If $a = 1$, there is a unit root. In time series econometric
analysis, the variables that have a unit root are known as a *nonstationary series*.
The results are obtained and evaluated as follows. If the computed τ (tau) value
is greater than the tabled τ value, then the variables are said to be stationary.[8]
Otherwise, they are accepted as nonstationary variables.[9]

The time series measures for density are stationary. Table 6.2 shows Dickey-
Fuller stationary test results. This means that these series can be used in regression analysis.

As shown in table 6.2, computed F values of five out of six regressions regarding student connections are less than the tabled F value of 4.30. Then we

TABLE 6.2

Dickey-Fuller Unit Root Tests for the Density Time Series

No.	Series	Eq. (4) without trend	Eq. (5) with trend
1	Sup2d	−3.96 (stationary)	−4.18 (stationary)
2	Sup1d	−4.83 (stationary)	−6.31 (stationary)
3	Sinden	−3.22[a] (nonstationary)	−3.13 (stationary)
4	Sdown1d	−29.7 (stationary)	−28.6 (stationary)
5	Sdown2d	−3.79 (stationary)	−4.57 (stationary)
6	Sdown3d	−4.81 (stationary)	−5.91 (stationary)
7	Sdown4d	−4.79 (stationary)	−4.66 (stationary)
8	Tup4d	−4.79 (stationary)	−4.93 (stationary)
9	Tup3d	−5.97 (stationary)	−6.28 (stationary)
10	Tup2d	−3.71 (stationary)	−4.92 (stationary)
11	Tup1d	−29.7 (stationary)	−28.6 (stationary)
12	Tind	−3.01[a] (nonstationary)	−3.24[a] (nonstationary)
13	Tdown1d	−4.79 (stationary)	−5.11 (stationary)
14	Tdown2d	−3.96 (stationary)	−3.89 (stationary)
15	Tdown3d	−4.79 (stationary)	−4.86 (stationary)
16	Tdown4d	−4.79 (stationary)	−4.67 (stationary)

[a] These series are stationary at the 0.10 level.

TABLE 6.3

Regression Results from Eqs. (2), (3), and (4) for the Density Time Series

No.	Regression equations	Coefficient	F statistics	Significance level
1	Sup2d = c + sinden + et	0.0679	F (1,22) 2.153	0.156
2	Sup1d = c + sinden + et	0.0875	F (1,22) 0.583	0.452
3	Sdown1d = c + sinden + et	−2.423	F (1,22) 0.375	0.546
4	Sdown2d = c + sinden + et	0.1663	F (1,22) 0.052	0.820
5	Sdown3d = c + sinden + et	0.4238	F (1,22) 7.79[a]	0.010
6	Sdown4d = c + sinden + et	0.0003	F (1,22) 0.121	0.730
7	Tup4d = c + tind + et	0.0128	F (1,22) 1.93	0.178
8	Tup3d = c + tind + et	−0.1174	F (1,22) 0.443	0.512
9	Tup2d = c + tind + et	−1.4367	F (1,22) 6.00[a]	0.022
10	Tup1d = c + tind + et	7.9165	F (1,22) 4.79	0.039
11	Tdown1d = c + tind + et	0.1934	F (1,22) 3.17	0.080
12	Tdown2d = c + tind + et	0.0604	F (1,22) 1.66	0.209
13	Tdown3d = c + tind + et	0.0004	F (1,22) 0.721	0.404
14	Tdown4d = c + tind + et	0.0004	F (1,22) 0.036	0.850

[a] Significant. Reject the null hypothesis.

accept the null hypothesis for student connections. Only one out of six regressions is significant. The series {sinden} has some explanatory power for {sdown3d}. All other results are supportive of our model, with respect to the insignificant impact of in-layer connections on scholarly prominence, since the coefficients of the regressions are insignificant.

Computed F values of regressions are less than the tabled F value of 4.30 at the 0.05 significance level, with only two exceptions. One therefore fails to reject the null hypothesis that {tind} has no explanatory power for independent variables. As for the two exceptional results, the variable {tup2d} can be explained by {tind}, and {sdown3d} can be explained by {sinden} at the 0.05 significance level. Yet the variable {tind} has a negative coefficient on {tup2d}, whereas it has a positive coefficient on {tup1d}. I can therefore conclude that the results shown in table 6.3 support the prediction of our model: that in-layer connections either have no role in authority formation or negatively influence it.

The LRS Effect on the Macro Level

The preceding analyses, based on a comparative exploration of synchronic and diachronic variables, indicates both intuitively and statistically that prominent scholars from a layer avoid connections with their fellows from the same layer, a pattern that persisted over a millennium. It is time to ponder the possible causes and ask why. Why do prominent scholars stay closer to those who are far from them than to their peers from the same layer? In other words, why are prominent scholars thickly connected to those who are distant from them but thinly connected to those who are close to them?

The answer lies not in the social domain alone. On the contrary, only by recognizing the interplay between social and linguistic patterns can we explain this phenomenon. The recent trend, as outlined at the beginning of this book, in social and literary theory to couple long-isolated discursive and social structures has already prepared the ground for the line of argument I develop here.

I argue that the generative mechanism of the particular network configuration that we have identified above, using network concepts along with time series analysis, is an unintended outcome of language use on the part of scholars. Ties to fellows from the same layer are avoided because they would increase the levels of reported speech (LRS), which would be an indication of increased level of dependence on discourse mediators. Increased LRS can be avoided only if connections are established to layers far from one's own. The logic of invest- ment in particular network ties is thus rooted in sociolinguistic mechanisms.

As a stratum within their community, the huffaz gained unparalleled au- thority, not because they were closely connected to each other but, paradoxi- cally, because they were not closely knit together. This paradox finds its expla- nation in metalinguistic processes. Time series analysis, armed with concepts of network and discourse analysis, helps us discover these patterns in the unstable network of huffaz with fluid relations.

The preceding analysis also indicates that cross-temporal structures, but not synchronic structures, are responsible for the formation of authority on the macro level. Giving priority to out-group connections enabled the stratum of huffaz to gain social prominence as a group and to shape the paradigm of their discipline. Diachronic relations, but not synchronic ones, are responsible for scholarly prominence.

Interlayer brokerage (ILB) characterizes the network of prominent scholars from all the layers analyzed. Playing the role of bridge between otherwise dis- connected generations helped the stratum of huffaz gain authority. They trans- ferred this authority to their students, whom they recruited from among the youngest layers. ILB is responsible for the production and reproduction of au- thority, and hence for social inequality, in the network of huffaz. This claim could have been nullified if there had been some layers of huffaz with extensive in-layer connections. Yet the preceding analysis documents that there is not even one such layer of huffaz. It also suggests that in-layer connections are not significantly related to total number of student and teacher connections.

These findings provide additional evidence about the explanatory power of weak ties (Granevetter 1973) and social capital in social networks (Coleman 1990; Burt 1995). The network of the stratum of huffaz, in all twenty-six layers, is characterized by extensive numbers of weak ties, which I take to be responsi- ble for the unparalleled authority of the huffaz in the entire community of ha- dith transmitters, despite the minute size of their stratum. Implicit in this line of argument is that what counts in the process of authority formation is not only what is commonly called *human capital*, such as knowledge and skills, but also, and most important, what is commonly known as *social capital*, such as a particular position in a social network.

In the network of huffaz, human capital is closely associated with social capital, yet use of the former is contingent upon the existence of the latter. In other words, in the process of authority formation, social actors are constrained not only by the content of what they have to say but also by their network positions. In the market of narrative, metaphorically speaking, a client critically reflects upon what the patron has to say and, more important, on the network configuration in which he is embedded. In the presence of a teller who is closer to the original source, listeners are not attracted to one who has a lengthy chain of narrative. Herein lies the long-ignored link between chains of narrative and chains of opportunity (White 1970).

The findings also confirm the perspective of linking social and discursive patterns via metalanguage. Silverstein, Harrison White, Shotter, and Habermas, as discussed in chapter 2, successfully used this method in displaying uninterrupted interaction between speech and action. Employing complex structures newly discovered in language use helps us in further exploring sophisticated patterns of interaction between discursive and social relations over time.

Most important, the circular relationship between literary and social structures is laid bare in the interrelations of the twenty-six layers. The preceding analysis exposes the fact that, on the one hand, reported speech and narrative produce and reproduce the social network but that, on the other hand, the survival of narrative is contingent upon the endurance of the social network and social relations. The rise and demise of the huffaz tell us that a dynamic social organization requires dynamic patterns in reported speech and social narrative. Well before the demise of the huffaz as a class, there was a decline in the heightened dynamism characterized by the search for a maximal span in scholarly relations. This significant structural change indicated that, from that point on, hadith transmission had lost one of the major features that distinguished it from the transmission of other narratives. As bulky hadith collections became standard reference books, the payoff from the shortest chain was no longer as crucial.

When hadith gained stability in content vis-à-vis fictional narrative, and status vis-à-vis the Qur'an and reasoning (*ra'y*) in Islamic theology and law, the dynamics of competition in the scholarly community shifted to the reorganization and interpretation of texts rather than to having the shortest chains and multiplied chains. With the authenticity and status of hadith now ensured, it was time to explore its uses and implications more fully, from varying and contesting perspectives. Parallel venues for scholarly competition were thus opened up before students of hadith. The dynamics involved in these attempts will be the theme of our discussion in the following chapter.

CHAPTER SEVEN

Narrative and Sociology of Intellectuals
From Ibn Khaldun to Collins

Narrative has an existential meaning for people in general, but in particular for those who are professionally involved in its creation, evolution, and transmission. This attachment manifests itself on the intellectual, emotional, and spiritual levels and leads certain specialists to dedicate their entire lives to narrative. Part of the task of these specialists is to think about the interpretation of the material they transmit, which opens another venue for competition through creativity, a source of potential contest and rivalry for control. Even if the words are the same, a narrative may mean different things to different people.

Consequently, when narrative is passed on to rising generations, it is transmitted not only as text but also with these conflicting interpretations. New generations inherit the narrative and its interpretations from preceding generations. Even if a community shares a particular narrative as a common intellectual legacy, intellectuals[1] employ myriad opposing perspectives to creatively interpret their heritage and link it to current problems. Therefore, prominent intellectuals lead multiple lives as members of multiple intellectual networks, which require them to master different modes of thought and discourse and to continuously oscillate between them.

Hadith also meant different things for classical Muslim intellectuals from divergent disciplines and backgrounds. They all accepted its authority but differed on its place relative to reason, the Qur'an, mysticism, and local customs. For instance, cosmopolitan philosophers emphasized the role of reason, while the sufis emphasized the place of mystical experience and illumination of the heart. Local preachers tried to find religious justification for social customs that were not always consistent with the authentic teachings of the Prophet Muhammad.

Social Conflict, Consolidation, and Narrative

In the middle of all these conflicting currents, scholars of hadith strove to establish a hierarchy among the sources of knowledge and to secure for hadith the superior status it deserved. Eventually, with the prevalence of the Sunni approach, they achieved that goal; toward the end of the fourth century of Hijra, the majority of Muslim thinkers and scholars came to agree that hadith comes after the Qur'an in the hierarchy, but before analogical reasoning. And the mystical experience must comply with the external meaning of the Qur'an and hadith. Yet this consensus was not easy to reach; long fights took place between different schools, beginning in the recent years of the reign of the third Caliph, Uthman. The unrest took the life of Uthman and continued until Umayyad rule dominated the emerging and expanding Islamic empire. Political stability needed to be established before hadith narrative could be recorded and safely transmitted to future generations from a variety of races. Yet in this period, the two well-respected grandsons of the Prophet Muhammad, Hasan and Husain, were denied Caliphate by the Umayyads. They were both martyred in the conflicts, in a very tragic manner, which left lasting memories in the minds of the Muslim public, particularly the Shiites, who advocated the continuation of leadership on the hereditary line of the Prophet's progeny. This claim looked unacceptable to Sunni scholars, who gave primacy to intellectual genealogy over progeny. For the Sunnis, authority lay in being intellectually and spiritually linked to the Prophet Muhammad through a reliable chain of mentors. The Shiite community assigned unchallenged authority to the interpretations of the great imams, scholars, and leaders from the lineage of the Prophet Muhammad. For Sunni scholars, lineage had no bearing on the acceptability of the interpretation that one offered concerning a narrative; all interpretations remained open to challenge by other authorities.

Eventually the Umayyad rule collapsed and the Abbasids from the progeny of the Prophet Muhammad took over. The Shiites gained power. At the same time, the Mutazilites, with an emphasis on rational interpretation of narrative, became influential in the Abbasid palace. Translations of Greek philosophy also continued in that period, which brought about the question of consolidation between traditional Islamic and Greek views. The community of philosophers saw these views as compatible, but the puritan hadith scholars refused imported ideas and saw them as a threat to the indigenous purity of narrative. The sufis looked at hadith as a source of spiritual invigoration and thus de-emphasized the letter of the narrative and of the law, which was unacceptable to rational scholars of law.

Conflict over the place of hadith in Islamic theology and law characterizes the earlier and most dynamic period in the history of the hadith transmission network. The main cleavage had been between those who gave primacy to reason and those who gave primacy to tradition. The conflict between the Mutazilites and the Sunnites during the Abbasid period illustrates this intellectual opposition, which turned into a major political conflict. Ibn Hanbal (164–241 AH/780–855 CE, Baghdad), the leading scholar of the People of Hadith—or, in Arabic, *Ahl al-Hadith*—was persecuted in his time by Abbasid rule as, despite political pressure, he refuted the Mutazila doctrines.

The highest point of tension between the Mutazilites and the People of Hadith is characterized at the same time by the highest level of activity among the scholars of hadith. Opposition fueled dynamism in the network. The layers of that period, layers 9–11, are characterized by the highest number of huffaz and the maximal span of relations between teachers and students. Even the canonical Six Books of Hadith arose in that period.

The People of Hadith opposed not only Mutazila but also rationalist philosophers like Ibn Sina and al-Farabi, who allegedly propagated the ideas imported from Greek culture; Ahl al-Ray, who represented rationalism in jurisprudence; and the sufis, who represented spiritual innovation. In his canonical book, the renowned Bukhari frequently attacks Abu Hanifa, the founder of the Hanafi school, for not giving hadith the eminent place it deserved and for inclining toward rational or speculative thinking. He also attacks Shiite doctrine if there is an occasion.

The People of Hadith strove not only to control the chains of narration, with the purpose of precluding forged narratives, but also to control the way narratives were to be interpreted. It would have defeated their purpose to let ahadith be interpreted in ways different from those of previous generations, like the Companions and the Successors. They firmly believed that the text is both utterance and meaning and can be considered authentic only if both are preserved. Even the last *shaykh al-Islam* in hadith, Ibn Taymiya, relentlessly fought against Greek philosophy, logic, Mutazila, speculative mysticism, and the Shiite school.

These persevering scholarly efforts eventually produced pervasive results. The impact of Greek philosophy was tamed by Islamic theology. Sufi interpretations were brought into line with Sunni doctrine by Muhaddith sufis. This happened not through exclusion but through a consolidation reached between opposing sides in favor of the People of Hadith. The new synthesis can be seen as a moderate traditionalism that acknowledged the role of both rational and spiritual interpretations. Not only the conflict between representatives of imported ideas and rationality but also the conflict within the community of hadith scholars was reduced to a lower level. Consequently, the Mutazilite school was excluded almost completely from the intellectual scene as the Mutazilites lost the government support they had used to forcefully impose their ideas on traditionalist scholars during the early Abbasid period. Greek philosophy and logic were domesticated in the hands of Ibn Sina, al-Farabi, and, eventually, Ghazzali. The four schools of law (Hanefi, Maliki, Shafii, and Hanbali) made peace among themselves and recognized each other as equally valid. The Six Canonical Books were no longer seen as alternatives to each other but as a set of authoritative sources, to be condensed by later scholars into a single collection.

The coalition of ideas between the forces of tradition and innovation contributed greatly to the integration of Muslim society in general and of the intellectual community in particular. As Collins argues, new ideas are created as combinations or coalitions of old ones (Collins 1998, 52).[2] An intellectual cannot detach himself from past generations, although he needs for his own intellectual growth and independent thinking a necessary amount of relative detachment from the existing society and culture.

The overwhelming prevalence of the Sunni concept of hierarchical knowledge against rival camps did not mean the end of internal tensions within the Sunni school. Interpretation of hadith from differing and even opposing perspectives continued. Huffaz who transmitted the same texts charged it with different meanings. Attesting to this claim is the partial overlap between the network of huffaz and the networks of (1) scholars who specialized in the "recitation" of the Qur'an, (2) jurists, (3) historians, (4) philosophers, and (5) sufis. None of the huffaz specialized in hadith alone; rather, they were accomplished scholars in several fields. For instance, they were all outstanding jurists; some of them were even more renowned as jurists than as huffaz of hadith.

Similarly, there were prominent philosophers, historians, sufis, and literary artists among them.

Diachronic (intergenerational) relations, which bring about the tension between inherited and discovered knowledge, must be thought of in connection with synchronic (interdisciplinary) relations, which are responsible for the tensions between disciplines. The overlap between the networks of huffaz and other intellectual fields testifies to the fact that the huffaz did not merely memorize and mechanically transmit narratives of the Prophet Muhammad. Instead, scholars in each generation used narrative and metanarrative as an aid in their search for the meaning of life and explored the implications of narrative and metanarrative in divergent fields of social practice, as intellectuals from other parts of the world did with their own narratives and metanarratives. So precious to them was the narrative of hadith that they thought it worth an entire lifetime. In hadith they found answers to their legal, philosophical, theological, historical, spiritual, and moral questions.

The great huffaz severely criticized mere memorization and transmission of knowledge without critical study of contents and chains of authority. The great narrator Malik, who was also the founder of the Maliki school, is reported by Sakhawi to have said, "The science [knowledge] cannot be taken from those who exclusively rely on audition and memorization [sama']." Subki, another prominent hafiz, said, "The one who focuses exclusively on audition of hadith is not called muhaddith." Furthermore, Mawardi is reported to have said, "It [the word scholar] should not be used for the reciters of the Qur'an nor for the community of hadith scholars, because knowledge resides in meaning, not in what is memorized for recitation" (al-Sakhawi 1986b, 20).

A hafiz relied on one or more interpretive frameworks during interpretation. These frameworks are usually called disciplines. Disciplines are intellectual domains, with continuously moving borders, that have relatively autonomous social networks concomitantly running across time, yet with varying degrees of overlap among them. Joint membership in several networks makes this overlap visible to us. Ibn Khaldun's Muqaddimah explores the development of overlapping networks of Muslim intellectuals up to his time. The joint memberships of social actors in multiple intellectual fields implies that these actors played the role of broker and mediator between sociocultural domains.

Collins observes that creativity is an outcome of opposition or synthesis. Opposition characterized the first and most dynamic period in the history of the hadith transmission network, and synthesis characterized the second period, after layer 14. Yet the triumph of the People of Hadith over their rivals left them with no considerable opposition and thus hindered and eventually diminished their level of activity and creativity. By the time of Suyuti, the last hafiz in our network, there was no major threat to hadith from philosophers; the Mutazilites had vanished; the Shiites were contained within a limited geographical area; and speculative mysticism and the People of Opinion had come to acknowledge the authoritative place of hadith in their disciplines. The majority of Sunni scholars came to an agreement both on hadith chains and on the methods to be employed in putting the narratives into use.

Multiplex Structure of the Narrative Text

The role of huffaz who were involved in several fields at once can never be underestimated in this process of consolidation and integration. They came to conclude, after long conflicts, that the text may have multiple meanings because it has a multiplex structure. A particular group of scholars specializes in each layer of the text, and their interpretations are valid with respect to their particular layers. Such an approach to text, and the consequent relative validity of otherwise conflicting interpretations, was a great achievement that prevented intellectual contests from turning into social and political conflicts.

Early in Islamic history, classical Muslim scholars disagreed about what a text is. The concept of the text, because of its bearing on the concept of the Qur'an, was understood as a political, philosophical, and theological question rather than a simple linguistic or literary issue. The discussion over the nature of the Qur'an greatly contributed to the development of the human sciences.

The Sunni thinkers came to conceive of the text as being constituted by structure (*nazm*) and content or meaning (*ma'na*). The Mutazilites argued that the text is nothing but the meaning it carries. This discussion was not inconsequential, because it had implications for the nature of the holy book of Islam, the Qur'an. The Mutazilites made the mistake of turning this intellectual issue into a political matter during the Abbasid Caliphate, a strategy that backfired

when it met with great resistance by the Sunni scholars. The resistance of Ibn
Hanbal, the great hafiz of hadith and the founder of the Hanbali school of law,
is legendary.

Eventually, the Mutazilites lost the backing of the Abbasid palace, which
came to adopt the Sunni view. It has been unanimously accepted ever since that
the text is multiplex, comprising both structure and content. These two layers
are further divided into more refined ones. Meaning is accepted as being both
external (*zahir*) and internal (*batin*). External meaning is the domain of the rational sciences, such as theology and jurisprudence, while internal meaning is
the domain of the mystical sciences (*Tasawwuf*). They coexist in parallel fashion but are not mutually exclusive alternatives. Therefore, a rationalist jurist
who specializes in external meaning may at the same time maintain an interest
in the internal meaning of the text without feeling that the two are incompati-
ble. He acknowledges that neither interpretation entirely exhausts the meaning
of the text.

The multiplex concept of text and meaning allowed the coexistence of what
otherwise would have been conflicting interpretive frameworks (and their advocates) within the borders of the Islamic cultural milieu. The concurrent use
of a plurality of interpretive approaches to the same narrative resulted in a consolidation of conventional conflicts. The success of the Sunni scholars lay in the
construction of such a multiplex pluralist paradigm, whereby old rivals were allowed to have a voice, space, and identity. Therefore, it is more precise to see
Sunni identity as an umbrella sheltering a range of identities, an umbrella under which a scholar can momentarily activate any of the range of identities
through which he moves. Specialization in a particular layer of text bestows an
identity. The borders among layers of texts, identities, discourses, and networks
are always fluid and ever in motion.

Ironically, this triumph over rival methods of interpretation and uses of hadith was detrimental to the class of huffaz. Without considerable opposition,
intellectual activity ceases to be dynamic and creative, as Collins also shows in
the case of Japanese intellectuals in the Muromachi era (Collins 1998, 339). The
great controversy that had aroused students of hadith in earlier generations—
between important and indigenous ideas, rationalism and traditionalism—
came to an end, leaving students with fewer motives for devoting themselves to

hadith chains and methods of interpretation.[3] We will return to this issue in greater detail at the end of this chapter.

If we fail to keep in mind the multiplex structure of the text, which served as a tool of consolidation between perspectives that had been conventionally opposed and mutually exclusive, we may find it difficult to understand the multiple involvements of huffaz. The multiplex approach is in striking contrast to the view that a text is static and can have only one meaning over time, and within a particular period. Instead, various interpretations can be attributed to a hadith, and these interpretations are accompanied by the acknowledgment that all are valid within their own contexts, provided that they comply with the commonly accepted rules of interpretation. For a better illustration of this issue, we need to revisit Ibn Khaldun, who devoted substantial space to hadith in his time-honored book *al-Muqaddima* (The Introduction).

Ibn Khaldun: Multiple Involvements of Intellectuals

Hadith has it that "the Truth" (*al-Haqq*) is one of the ninety-nine beautiful names of Allah, or God. This approach to truth is significant because it pre-empts the distinction between the sacred and profane domains in intellectual activity. From this perspective, the truth, regardless of the domain to which it belongs, is perceived by Muslim intellectuals as a manifestation of God (a sign, or *ayat*) in countless ways. Therefore, those who study the signs in nature should not be seen differently from those who study religion per se. Besides, an intellectual's familiarity with God increases as he explores His countless manifestations in the world. Hence, one can think, there developed the encyclopedic scholarship of the Middle Ages, with individual scholars' involvement in several disciplines and networks. Yet multiple involvements cannot be attributed only to the epistemology of the Middle Ages, because even the leading modern intellectuals in our highly specialized age are involved in multiple domains of intellectual activity, without confining themselves to one discipline.

Huffaz also followed this pattern. They did not feel content with establishing themselves in one field. Instead, they continuously expanded their areas of interest to other intellectual domains. The huffaz were prominent not only in the field of hadith but in several others as well. Some of them came to the field of hadith after they had established themselves in other fields, while others expanded their interests after they had specialized in the field of hadith.

All these intellectual networks begin with the Prophet Muhammad and recognize him as the highest authority in their fields. The Prophet Muhammad serves as the ideal type of Muslim intellectual.[4] "Scholars are heirs of the Prophets," says a commonly circulated hadith. Yet the legacy of the Prophet was so monumental that each specialized group could claim only a part of it. The reciters of the Qur'an (*qurra'*), scholars of hadith, jurists, sufis, and philosophers all recognize him as the supreme authority in their fields and as the origin of their networks.

What accounts for interdisciplinary interaction and the overlap of social networks among various disciplines is not only their common origin but also the organic connection between them on the conceptual level. Although they have different goals and use different epistemological premises and interpretive methods, the Islamic sciences are all interconnected. The great philosopher Abu al-Hasan al-'Amiri writes:

> The religious sciences consist of three branches. One of them relies on sensual perceptions, namely, the science of the hadith scholars. The second rests on the intellect, namely, the science of the religious philosophers. The third involves both sensual and intellectual perception, namely, the science of jurists. Linguistics is an instrument serving all three branches [al-'Amiri 1967].[5]

According to al-'Amiri, there are three major branches in the Islamic sciences, with different methods: hadith, philosophy and jurisprudence. Al-'Amiri strikingly stresses linguistics as the foundation of all sciences. Hadith is an empirical vocation because it is based primarily on sense perception and data collection, whereas philosophy is a rational vocation, since it is based solely on reasoning. Jurisprudence, on the other hand, incorporates both methods.

A medieval Muslim intellectual had to master these sciences without exception before becoming part of the *ulama* class. Ibn Khaldun summarizes as follows the basic education of a scholar in his time:

> He must study the Qur'an, both with reference to the manner in which it has been transmitted and related on the authority of the Prophet who brought it from God, and with reference to the differences in the readings of the Qur'an readers. This is the science of Qur'an reading.

Then, he must study the manner in which the Sunnah is related to its originator [Muhammad], and he must discuss the transmitters who have handed it down. He must know their circumstances and their probity, so that the information one receives from them may be trusted and so that one may be able to know the part of it, in accordance with the implications of which one must act. These are the sciences of tradition.

Then, the process of evolving the laws from their basic principles requires some normative guidance to provide us with the knowledge of how that process takes place. This is the [science of the] principles of jurisprudence.

After one knows the principles of jurisprudence, one can enjoy, as its result, the knowledge of the divine laws that govern the actions of all responsible Muslims. This is jurisprudence.

Furthermore, the duties [of the Muslim] may concern either the body or the heart. The [duties of the heart] are concerned with faith and the distinction between what is to be believed and what is not to be believed. This concerns the articles of faith which deal with the essence and attributes [of God], the events of the Resurrection, Paradise, punishment, and predestination, and entails discussion and defense of these subject with the help of intellectual arguments. This is speculative theology.

The discussion of the Qur'an and *hadith* must be preceded by the [study of the] philological sciences because it is based upon them. There are various kinds, such as lexicography, grammar, syntax, and style, and literature [Ibn Khaldun 1967, 2: 437–38].

Implicit in the account of Ibn Khaldun is that narrative influences both the external and the internal life of social actors. Ibn Khaldun as a sociologist stresses the connection between intellectual culture and daily life by pointing out that the purpose of all this knowledge is to "enjoy . . . the knowledge of the divine law that governs the actions of all responsible Muslims." Jurisprudence links narrative to social life (Reinhart 1995). Berman (1983) shows that religious narrative in the West also permeated daily life in medieval Western history through jurisprudence.

Ibn Khaldun's approach is not exclusively focused on the external dimension of social actions. This can partly be attributed to the fact that Islamic jurisprudence, unlike its counterparts in the West, is more comprehensive. Yet, at this point, both philosophy and sufism, or *Tasawwuf,* come into play as well. Ibn Khaldun himself made his living for a while as a jurist of the Maliki school and is still considered one of the great authorities on sufism.

More important than the role of jurisprudence is the role of linguistic and literary studies in linking narrative to the daily life of individuals. Linguistics and the humanities were part of standard education at the time of Ibn Khaldun, since they were considered prerequisites for the study of the Qur'an and hadith. Consequently, a hafiz could not do without a solid knowledge of jurisprudence, linguistics, and what is today called the humanities.

In his *Muqaddimah,* Ibn Khaldun devoted a long section to the analysis of the sciences and of intellectuals (see chapter VI of *The Muqaddimah,* which is more than one-third of the book). He analyzed each discipline separately and also exposed the interconnections between disciplines. Ibn Khaldun's account shows how narrative permeates life via the channels paved by linguistics, literary disciplines, and jurisprudence; hence the overlap between the network of intellectuals who specialized in those disciplines. Now we can have a closer look at the overlap between the network of huffaz and the networks of reciters of the Qur'an, jurists, philosophers, historians, and sufis.

The Overlap between Networks of Huffaz and Reciters of the Qur'an

The Qur'an has a special way of recitation known as *Tajwid* (Cragg 1973; Jomier 1983; A. Jones 1983; Norris 1983; Paret 1983; Zubaidi 1983). According to the Islamic faith, not only the Qur'an but also the way it was to be chanted were divinely revealed to the Prophet Muhammad. The only way to preserve this vocal art was through oral transmission, although later on it developed as a branch of the traditional Islamic sciences, and its rules were recorded in writing. Moreover, initially, the recitation of the Qur'an was not in one dialect, as it is today, but in the different dialects of the Arabic language that were in use during that time. Scholars recorded, first in memory and later in writing, the different dialects in which the Qur'an was recited in the time of the Prophet. The various ways the Qur'an was recited in these dialects, reported to be ten in number, were also transmitted orally to future generations. Those scholars who specialized in the vocal arts of the Qur'an are called the *qurra',* or reciters of the Qur'an. They are also organized into a social network of masters and disciples across generations, with a history recorded in a rich literature of biographical dictionaries.

The network of Qur'an transmission is similar to, yet predictably much larger than, the network of hadith transmission. It continues even today, with no disruption analogous to that observed in the case of hadith transmission. Recitation of the Qur'an by highly reputable readers is still a public event in Islamic countries, with radios broadcasting such readings twenty-four hours a day. The reciters transmit not only the text of the Qur'an but also the way it is properly recited according to the rules of *Tajwid,* which became crystallized later in Islamic history, after the time of the Prophet. We can say that it also followed patterns similar to those usually found in the traditional vocal arts of other cultures. Many vocal arts in the modern world today also have their roots in the remote past and owe their existence to oral transmission between mentors and apprentices over the centuries. Ibn Khaldun briefly elucidates, as follows, the way Qur'an recitation evolved into a discipline:

> The Qur'an is the word of God that was revealed to His Prophet and that is written down between the two covers of copies of the Qur'an [*mushaf*].
>
> Its transmission has been continuous in Islam. However, the men around Muhammad transmitted it on the authority of the Messenger of God in different ways. These differences affect certain of the words in it and the manner in which the letters are pronounced. They were handed down and became famous. Eventually, seven specific ways of reading the Qur'an became established. Transmission [of the Qur'an readings], with their particular pronunciation, also was continuous. They came to be ascribed to certain men from among a large number of persons who had become famous as their transmitters. . . .
>
> Qur'an readers continued to circulate and transmit those readings, until the sciences were fixed in writing and treated systematically. Those readings, then, were set down in writing, along with the other sciences, and became a special craft and science in itself. People in the East and in Spain handed them down generation after generation [Ibn Khaldun 1967, 2:439–40].

The organization of the biographical dictionaries of the reciters of the Qur'an is similar to the organization of the biographical dictionaries of huffaz. The great hafiz Dhahabi has a monumental dictionary of *qurra'*. Dhahabi himself was an imminent scholar of Qur'an recitation and was trained under the greatest masters of his time. As in his biographical dictionary on huffaz, which is the primary data source of the present work, Dhahabi also classified the temporal network of readers of the Qur'an in layers up to his own time.

The network of the reciters begins with the Prophet Muhammad.[6] Muslims believe that the Qur'an was divinely revealed to him not as a text but as a vocal recitation, whose rules constitute the subject matter of the discipline of *Tajwid*. It is believed that not only the text of the Qur'an but also the way it is recited is based on divine revelation. Recitation of the Qur'an according to the rules of *Tajwid* is still intact among Muslims. According to this discipline, the Prophet Muhammad learned the particular way the Qur'an was recited from the Archangel Gabriel and practiced it among his Companions.

As is to be expected, some of the Companions of the Prophet were more talented than others in the recitation of the Qur'an. They became the mentors for the next generation. Only a very few Companions were prominent both in the field of hadith and in the Qur'an. Among them are Ibn Mas'ud, Abu Musa al-Ash'ari, Zayd bin Thabit, 'Alqama bin Qays, and 'Uqba bin 'Amir. Although the number of Companions who specialized in the disciplines of hadith and the Qur'an alone was much higher, there are only six Companions who were prominent in both fields.

Given its subject matter, the science of recitation was based mainly on oral tradition, and training required interpersonal contact. These interactions were recorded by succeeding generations as new students were trained under great masters in each generation. In the generation of the Successors as well, some great huffaz were at the same time great *qurra'*. Among them are Abu Abdirrahman al-Sulami and Abu al-Aliya.

The following is a brief list of huffaz who were also considered among the eminent reciters in subsequent layers:

Layer 4: Sa'id bin Jubayr, Mujahid bin Jabr, al-A'raj

Layer 5: Qatadah bin Diama

Layer 6: Abu al-Zubayr, Ibn Abi Layla, Amr bin al-Harith bin Ya'qub al-Ansari, Shayban bin Abdirrahman, Hammad bin Zayd bin Dirham

Layer 7: Abu Bakr bin 'Ayyash, Isa bin Yunus, Abdah bin Sulayman

Layer8: Umar bin Harun, Husayn al-Ju'fi, 'Ubaydullah bin Musa, Yunus bin Muhammad, al-Muqri' Abu Abdurrahman, Abdullah bin Salih bin Muslim, Zakariyya bin Adiyy bin al-Salt bin Bistam, al-Hawdi, Abu al-Jamahir, Ismail bin Abi Uways

Layer 9: Hisham bin Ammar, al-Zahrani, Yunus bin Abd al-A'la

Layer 11: Musa bin Ishaq bin Musa, al-Husayn bin Fahm, Abu Ja'far Muhammd bin Jarir al-Tabari, al-Mutarriz, Ibn Abi Dawud

Layer 13: Ibn al-Anbari, Ibn al-Munadi, Ibn Muzahir, Ibn al-Haddad, al-Naqqash, al-Tabarani, al-Hajjaji, Ghundar, al-Daraqutni

Layer 14: al-Hakim, al-Qabisi, Atiyya bin Sa'id, al-Talamanki

Layer 15: al-Dani

Layer 16: Ibn Sukkarah, al-Narasi

Layer 17: Ibn Hubaysh

Layer 18: Ibn Khayr, Abu Umar bin 'Iyad, Ibn 'Ubaydillah, Ibn al-Husari, al-Tajibi

Layer 19: Ibn al-Qurtubi, al-Dubaythi

Layer 21: Ibn al-Taylasan, Ibn al-Zubayr

Layer 22: al-Dhahabi, al-Qutb al-Halibi, Ibn Abdilhadi

Layer 25: Ibn al-Jazari

The above list shows that there are only sixty-eight highly prominent reciters among the huffaz. In addition to sharing the title of *qurra*', they are also known as *muqri*' and *mujawwid*. Their number might go up if we were to include each hafiz who had an interest in the science of recitation, or *ilm al-qira'ah*. Not only the huffaz but also ordinary Muslims who read the Qur'an practiced the basic rules of *Tajwid*.

The limited overlap between the networks of scholars of hadith and reciters of the Qur'an is to be expected because the two constitute the sources of Islamic law and theology. A religious intellectual must hold the Qur'an as the supreme authority, even above hadith. Yet he will be dependent on hadith literature as the most important commentary on the Qur'an. Hadith puts the Qur'anic verses in context by providing detailed information about the social, cultural, and historical circumstances in which they were revealed to, and dictated by, the Prophet. Furthermore, in the production of Islamic law, the Qur'an and hadith complement each other. Below, I will explore this relationship further.

The Overlap between Networks of Huffaz and Jurists

A hafiz has to be at the same time a jurist. This is one of the most important prerequisites in order to be accepted as a hafiz. A scholar of hadith who is not also well versed in jurisprudence cannot go further in the hierarchy of scholarship. He may stay in the lower ranks of the intellectual hierarchy for the duration of his career. The following excerpt illustrates the culture of huffaz on this issue:

> Al-Fariqi said: "The term should not be used for those who know chains of hadith but not the legal rulings derived from them. For one cannot be counted among the scholars of the law with only the former amount of knowledge." His student [Sharaf

al-Din 'Abd Allah ibn Muhammad] Ibn Abi 'Asrun [al-Tamimi al-Shafi'i, 492/1099–585/1189] also followed him in his book *al-Intisar* [The Victory]. Ibn Hajar stopped short of this view and said: "This is overemphasis because the divisions [of hadith sciences] are fourfold, the highest of which being the abundance in audition [*sama'*] and the knowledge of chains and their defects." I say: Perhaps the first two refused to call such a person *muhaddith* only because, literally speaking, he is a *musnid*, that is, one who simply conveys chains of authorities [without critiquing them]. The rest, however, use the term *muhaddith* figuratively [al-Sakhawi 1986b, 19].

One of the most important uses of hadith in Islam is in deriving legal and moral rules (Coulson 1964; Reinhart 1995). In this regard, the authority of hadith is second in Islam only to the Qur'an. These rules are highly comprehensive and are not restricted to a particular sphere of life. Since hadith is the second source of Islamic law and theology, a high degree of overlap between the networks of hadith and jurisprudence, or *fiqh,* is expected. The Sunnah, the conduct of the Prophet, provides the best example for his followers to emulate in their transactions and other affairs:

> . . . at the beginning Islam had no sciences or crafts. That was due to the simple conditions [that prevailed] and the desert attitude. The religious laws, which are the commands and prohibitions of God, were in the breasts of the authorities. They knew their sources, the Qur'an and the Sunnah, from information they had received directly from the Lawgiver [Muhammad] himself and from the men around him. The people at that time were Arabs. They did not know anything about scientific instruction or the writing of books and systematic works. There was no incentive or need for that. This was the situation during the time of the men around Muhammad and the men of the second generation. The persons who were concerned with knowing and transmitting the [religious laws] were called "Qur'an readers," that is, people who were able to read the Qur'an and were not illiterate. Illiteracy was general at that time among the men around Muhammad, since they were [Arab] Bedouins. People who knew the Qur'an were at that time called "Qur'an readers" with reference to the fact [that they were literate]. They read the Qur'an and Sunnah, which were transmitted from God, [in order to know the religious laws] because the religious laws were known only from the [Qur'an], and from the traditions which are mostly explanations of and commentaries upon the [Qur'an]. Muhammad said: "I left among you two things. You will not go astray as long as you hold on to them: the Qur'an and my Sunnah" [Ibn Khaldun 1967, 3:312].

Each hafiz was at the same time part of the network of jurists because scholars of hadith were not considered hafiz unless they were fully aware of all the possible legal implications of the narratives they handled. Consequently, one requirement for becoming a hafiz was to comprehend the multiple divergent ways hadith could be used in Islamic law by different schools as a foundation for legal rulings. The great hafiz Dhahabi is reported to have listed as follows the steps a student of hadith had to take:

> Today, the student of hadith should first copy by hand *al-Jam' bayn al-Sahihayn* [Convergence of the Two Sound Books (Bukhari and Muslim)], *al-Ahkam* of 'Abd al-Haqq (this is *al-Ahkam al-shar'iyya* [The Legal Rulings] by Abu Muhammad 'Abd al-Haqq ibn Abd al-Rahman Ibn al-Kharrat al-Ishbili [1116–1185 CE]), and *al-Diya'*. He should master these books. Also, he should frequently study the works of al-Bayhaqi, for they are beneficial. He should also study no less than a concise book like *al-Ilmam* (Muhammad ibn 'Ali Ibn Daqiq al-'Iyd [1228–1302 CE], *al-Ilmam fi Ahadith al-Ahkam* [The acquaintance with the prophetic narrations which serve as basis for legal rulings]), and teach it [al-Sakhawi 1986b, 21].

Abu Shame is reported to have said the following on the same issue:

> Imam Abu Shama [595–665 AH] said: "Today the sciences of hadith are three. The most honorable one is the memorization of the texts, the knowledge of rare hadith, and its relation to jurisprudence. The second is memorizing the chains of transmission, knowing the narrators, and discerning the reliable chains from the problematic ones. This used to be paramount, but now it suffices for the student of the science to know what is compiled and written in this branch, and there is no benefit in redoing what is already done. The third is collecting, writing, hearing, and learning the various chains through which a hadith has been narrated, searching for the shortest chains and traveling for this purpose. But the one who focuses on this is diverted from the most important of the useful sciences [that is, the first], in addition to being distracted from the actions which are the primary purpose: Allah the Most High says: 'I have not created jinns and humans except to worship me' (51: 56). However, it is acceptable for those who have freed themselves from distractions to spend time in this third branch because it helps perpetuate the unbroken 'from' chains [*silsilah al-'an'anah al-muttasilah*] back to the most honorable of mankind, God's blessings and peace be on him. These chains are one of the peculiarities of this Community."
>
> He also said: "One should stay away from that which is commonly shared by the young and the old, the mediocre and the intelligent, the ignorant and the scholar" [al-Sakhawi 1986b, 22].

The views of Al-A'mash, a prominent Successor (61–148 AH/681–765 CE), on the relationship between law and hadith are summarized in the following excerpt:

Al-A'mash said: "The hadith that jurists circulate among themselves is better than that which hadith narrators circulate among themselves." Someone criticized Imam Ahmad bin Hanbal, may Allah have mercy upon him, for attending the circle of Imam Shafi'i and leaving the circle of Sufyan ibn 'Uyayna. Ahmad told him: "Keep quiet. If you miss a hadith with a shorter chain, you can find it with a longer chain and it will not harm you. But if you do not have the reasoning of this man [Shafi'i], I am afraid you will not be able to find it." His words ends here [al-Sakhawi 1986b, 23].

Ibn Hajar, the last *shaykh al-Islam* in hadith, who came later, also followed the same tradition, as made clear by the following account:

Ibn Hajar said: "There is some disagreement in some of the above doctrine. Abu Shama's view that 'it suffices for the student of the science to know what is compiled and written in this branch' was rejected by the Savant Abu Ja'far ibn al-Zubayr and others. The argument can be made against him in the following way: If the number of compilations that have been written in the first branch makes reliance upon them necessary, without need for pursuing its sources, then the same can be said about the first branch that Abu Shama says about the second [that is, that 'it suffices for the student of the science to know what is compiled and written in this branch'], for the books written on jurisprudence of hadith and on rare hadith cannot be numbered.

"Indeed, if someone were to claim that the works in the latter fields [jurisprudence and rare hadith] are more numerous than the works about personality criticism and the works that distinguish sound from unsound hadith, he would not be far from the truth. To be sure, this is the reality. If studying the first branch is important, then the study of the second branch becomes even more important, for it is the staircase that leads to the first. Therefore, whoever neglects the second science [according to Abu Shama's classification] is bound to unwittingly mix unsound with sound hadith, and the narrator who is considered trustworthy with the unreliable. That is enough blame for such a method.

"The truth is, both the first and the second science are important in the science of hadith. There is no doubt that whoever can master both will attain the highest station, even if he is remiss in the third, while he who neglects the first and second can have no part in being called a hadith master [hafiz]. As for he who masters the first but neglects the second, he remains far from the definition of hadith scholar [*muhaddith*], while he who masters the second and neglects the first may still be called a *muhaddith*, although there is a deficiency in him with regard to the first science" [al-Sakhawi 1986b, 23].

Jurists, on the other hand, rely on hadith material in the construction of laws (*ijtihad, fatwa, hukm,* and the like) and thus are required to have a solid foundation in hadith literature. Islamic law has four major sources: the Qur'an, Sunnah (exemplary behavior of the Prophet recorded in the hadith literature), analogy, and consensus among scholars.[7] Thus each school of law developed its own methodology for the criticism of chains of authorities and the texts of narratives. In fact, most of the debate among jurists revolves around the use of hadith.

The legal rule that a particular scholar from a particular school has stipulated competes for public acceptance with numerous others produced on the same issue by other scholars. It is commonly accepted in Islamic jurisprudence that one legal opinion (*ijtihad*) cannot invalidate another. In the process of selection, foundations of rulings in hadith play a highly crucial role. If a ruling is based on a weak hadith with an unclear meaning, it has little chance to gain public acceptance. In contrast, if an alternative ruling on the same issue is based on a solid hadith with a clear indication of meaning, it will gain easy acceptance.

Therefore, all major jurists have to be at the same time prominent scholars of hadith. The founders of the four major schools of law are also listed among the huffaz. Imam Ja'far al-Sadiq, the founder of the Jafari school, is also listed as a hafiz by Dhahabi. The founders of other schools of law that have not survived up to the present day, such as al-Tabarani, Dawud al-Zahiri, and the like, are also renowned huffaz. Although there has been almost unanimous recognition over the centuries of these great scholars as huffaz and jurists, they have not been completely immune to criticism.

As has been true in the case of other prominent intellectuals, their reputations and places in the hierarchy of intellectuals have also occasionally been contested. Jurists who came to the field of hadith later in their lives are usually criticized for being incompetent in the field of hadith. Likewise, huffaz who came to the field of hadith later in their lives are criticized for not being competent in jurisprudence. Frequently, polemics among opponents from different schools have also induced this sort of criticism. For instance, Abu Hanifa was sporadically criticized by his opponents for having insufficient knowledge of hadith, whereas Ibn Hanbal was criticized for not using his own reasoning and for relying completely on inherited knowledge. These two highly preeminent scholars drew criticism for standing on the margins of the methodological continuum in Islamic jurisprudence that extends from reliance on personal opinion (Abu Hanifa) to reliance on inherited material (Ibn Hanbal).

The initially conflicting relations among different schools of law along this spectrum evolved over time until a consolidation was reached among the four schools of the People of Tradition and Community, or *Ahl as-Sunnah wa al-Jama'ah*. These four schools, conforming to Collins's law of small numbers, still dominate the Muslim world. The consolidation can also be seen as one of the sources of decreasing interest in the shortest chains, which had served as stronger evidence against the rival camp.[8]

The Overlap between Networks of Huffaz and Philosophers

Another important use of hadith has been in Islamic philosophy and theology. A hafiz is required to know the theological and philosophical implications of the hadith he is dealing with. Huffaz in general are traditionalist philosophers who profess that ultimate truth resides in the Qur'an and in hadith, the two authoritative sources of scripture in Islam. This creed does not mean that they assign no role to reasoning. On the contrary, there is still much room for speculation and debate because delegating authority to scripture does not entirely solve philosophical problems. There emerges, then, the question of interpretation of the texts of the Qur'an and of hadith literature; hence the major division in Islamic theology between those who give priority to individual thinking in the interpretation of texts and those who refer to other texts. If scholars in the latter group cannot find interpretations in other texts narrated from the Prophet and his Companions, they refuse further speculation.

The following huffaz also appear in the network of highly prominent Muslim philosophers analyzed by Collins:[9] Hasan al-Basri, Abu Hanifa, Al-Awza'i, Ja'far al-Sadiq, Malik bin Anas, Muhammad al-Shaybani (a great jurist-philosopher, but not listed as a hafiz by al-Dhahabi), Abu Yusuf, al-Shafi'i, Ibn Hanbal, al-Bukhari, Muslim, al-Hakim al-Tirmidhi, and al-Tabari. I intentionally focus on these names, derived from a recent study by a modern sociologist, to demonstrate how pervasive the influence of the huffaz is outside their native sphere.

The founders of four major schools of law—Abu Hanifa, Shafi'i, Malik, and

Ahmad bin Hanbal—occupy prominent positions in the network of philosophers, apart from their prominence in the network of jurists and huffaz. Ja'far al-Sadiq, the founder of Ja'fari school, was one of the masters of Abu Hanifa. Abu Yusuf and Muhammad al-Shaybani were the two major students of Abu Hanifa in the Hanafi school of law. Bukhari and Muslim, the authors of the most commonly accepted canonical compilations of hadith, are also considered to be prominent philosophers.

The Overlap between Networks of Huffaz and Historians

Hadith can be seen as a history of the first century of Islamic society (Duri, Khalidi, Margoliouth, Nicholson). Yet historians and scholars of hadith take different approaches to history and time. Historians use linear time to organize their material in consecutive order. Scholars of hadith, however, use disjointed narrative and are not concerned with ordering their narratives in linear time. Consequently, the genres of historians and hadith scholars reflect clear differences, despite the fact that both groups handle the same material. Differences in style gave rise to two different discourse networks.

Although disjointed structure characterizes the narratives of hadith, some scholars of hadith also mastered the genre of history. These scholars were involved in the networks of both hadith and history. Among the huffaz who were also historians are Hanefi, Maliki, Shafi'i, and Hanbali.

The total number of hafiz-historians is sixty-three. Their first appearance in the network of huffaz coincides with the sixth layer. This may be attributed to the phase of specialization in the intellectual community of the time, because before that point, hadith and history were not so clearly differentiated as two separate disciplines. History was born from hadith and greatly benefited from its methods. "The study of the Prophet's biography was developed by historians from among the scholars of *hadith*, not by storytellers" (Duri 10). The genre of history emerged first through an interest in the battles of the Prophet. This gave rise to a discipline called *maghazi* (J. M. B. Jones 1983; Kister 1983). "The founder of *maghazi* studies appears to have been the famous jurisconsult and *hadith* scholar 'Urwa ibn al-Zubayr (d. 94/712),[10] since he was the first to compose a book on the *maghazi*" (Duri 1983, 25; see also Monroe 1983). The following excerpt from Duri summarizes how the genre of hadith gave rise to the genre of history:

The study of *maghazi*, or military expeditions of the Prophet, began in Medina in conjunction with the study of *hadith*. The scholars of *hadith* continued to show interest in the *maghazi*, but some of them, in studying the life of the Prophet, began to do so in a manner which moved beyond the limitations of the juridical aspects of the subject. The pioneers of *maghazi* studies were scholars of *hadith*, as is confirmed by the way in which the learned regarded the *maghazi* authors. This also explains the importance of *isnad*, the chain of authorities transmitting a report, in assessing the value of the *maghazi*; this meant that the value of a *hadith* or other account depended upon the reputation of *hadith* scholars or transmitters who figured in the chain of authorities. This point of view very early on gave rise to a critical attitude towards *ruwat*, the sources who transmitted the information. It introduced the element of investigation and inquiry into gathering of the various accounts, and laid a firm foundation for historical studies. On the other hand, narratives and popular tales about *maghazi* were also passed along by word of mouth. Storytellers, the *qussas,* went to great lengths in relating these accounts and turned them into a kind of folklore, but although some of this did in later times find its way into certain biographies of the Prophet, the attitude towards transmitted accounts, and the methods employed in their criticism, essentially continued to follow the methodology of the scholars of *hadith* [Duri 1983, 23–24].

The historians who specialized in the history of Christians and Jews had been called *akhbariyyun,* which means those who transmit *khabar,* news, from the scriptures of the Children of Israel. Note that *khabar* is differentiated from hadith. These historians derived extensive information from Torah and the Bible regarding narratives about historical events, particularly the history of previous prophets. There is not a unanimous approach among Muslim historians toward whether Biblical accounts can be used as a reliable source in historical research. *Akhbari* historians adopt a favorable view of using the Bible and other Jewish and Christian historical sources, but strict scholars refute them as unreliable.

There is yet another genre pertinent to history: story, or *qissa.* Historians and scholars of hadith criticized the *qissa* genre for deviating from empirical narrative and involving fiction to produce attractive stories (Berkey 1995). There is only one scholar among the huffaz who is also known as *qass,* a storyteller: Abu Idris al-Khawlani, who served as justice and preacher of Damascus.

The Overlap between Networks of Huffaz and Sufis

Another use of hadith is in sufism because hadith literature reflects the way the Prophet Muhammad emphasized moderation in satisfying carnal desires and controlling mundane passions.[11] Sufism has myriad forms. Common to all is the goal of reaching the truth (*al-haqq*)—the objective of intellectuals, not via reason or sense perception but via the experience of the heart.[12] The following excerpt should be read in connection with the above excerpt from al-ʿAmiri, who classified traditional Islamic sciences according to the methods they employed. He argued that the science of hadith employs methods that depend primarily on sense perception, that philosophy and theology employ methods that rely principally on intellect, and that jurisprudence combines both methods. Ibn Khaldun adds to this list a new method, namely, experience of *dhikr*, a method that, according to him, supersedes all others:

> Mystical exertion, retirement, and *dhikr* exercises were followed by the removal of the veil [*kashf*] of sensual perception. The sufi beholds divine worlds which a person subject to the senses cannot perceive at all. The spirit belongs to those worlds. The reason for the removal of [the veil] is the following. When the spirit turns from external sense perception to inner [perception], the senses weaken and the spirit grows strong. It gains predominance and a new growth. The *dhikr* exercise helps to bring that about. It is like food to make the sprit grow. The sprit continues to grow and to increase. It had been knowledge. Now, it becomes vision. The veil of sensual perception is removed, and the soul realizes its essential existence. This is identical with perception. [The spirit] now is ready for the holy gifts, for the sciences of the divine presence and for the outpourings of the Deity. Its essence realizes its own true character and draws close to the highest sphere, the sphere of the angels. The removal of [the veil] often happens to people who exert themselves [in mystical exercise]. They perceive the reality of existence as no one else [does] [Ibn Khaldun 1967, 3:81].

Sufis constituted a separate discourse network. Not only the methods but also the language they used set them apart from the rest of the community of intellectuals of their time. Ibn Khaldun draws our attention to the way sufis created their own genre:

> Furthermore, the Sufis have their peculiar form of behavior and a [peculiar] linguistic terminology which they use in instruction. Linguistic data apply only to commonly accepted ideas. When there occur ideas not commonly accepted, technical

terms facilitating the understanding of those ideas are coined to express them [Ibn Khaldun 1967, 3:79].

Hadith scholars in general and sufis in particular saw the preoccupation with hadith as a way to get closer to God, but not a means to gain fame or social status. The great huffaz emphasized piety and criticized those who did not live up to the contents of the narratives of the Qur'an and hadith. Sakhawi writes:

> How well did the hadith master Abu 'Abdullah al-Dhahabi [d. 748 H] speak in what I read by his own handwriting about the above—even if he exaggerated, he is nevertheless excused: "Most of the hadith scholars have no understanding, no diligence in the knowledge of hadith, and no piety toward it. Worse, the sound and the forged look alike to them. The narrators do not correct their manners according to the ethics of hadith, and never wake up from the stupor of audition. At one and the same time, a scholar hears a book and his ego entertains the prospect of teaching it—in fifty years, perhaps? Woe unto you! How long is your hope, how evil are your works! Verily, Sufyan al-Thawri is excused for saying, according to the narration of Ahmad ibn Yusuf al-Taghlabi, 'Khalid ibn Khidash narrated to us that Hammad ibn Zayd narrated to us that Sufyan al-Thawri said: "If hadith was a good it would have vanished just as goodness has vanished."'
>
> By Allah, he has spoken the truth. What good is there in hadith where the sound is mixed with the unreliable, while you do nothing to sift one from the other, or to research its narrators, and you do not practice it or fear God concerning it? Today, in our time, the quest for knowledge and hadith audition no longer mean, for the *muhaddith*, the obligation of living up to it, which is the goal of hadith. The basis of hadith audition has become the prestige of narrating it. This, by God, is not for the sake of God! I am only addressing you, O hadith narrator—not those who do not listen, think, keep the five daily prayers, shun corruption and intoxicants, and strive for perfection in speaking the truth. O listener! Do not become a criminal like me [says the corrupt man], for we feel the worst afflictions [al-Sakhawi 1986b, 21–22].

The sufis are also known in Arabic to be *zahid* (ascetic), *faqir* (poor), and *rabbani* (divine). They studied the internal aspects of the Prophet's life and practiced exceptional piety. The following huffaz were at the same time highly prominent sufis: Abu Hazim Salamah, Habib bin al-Shahid, Jarir bin Abdilhamid, Abdullah bin al-Mubarak bin Wadih, al-Ma'afi bin 'Imran, Muhammad bin Fudayl bin Ghazwan, Ibn Abi 'Asim, Ibn Abi Hatim, Ibn al-A'rabi, Abu Ya'la, Abu Umar al-Zahid, Umar bin Sahl bin Ismail, Muhammad bin Dawud bin Sulayman, Ibn Shahin, Khalaf bin al-Qasim bin Sahl, Abu Abdirrahman al-Sula-mi, al-Naqqash, al-Malini, Atiyya bin Sa'id, Abu Nu'aym, Abu Dharr al-Harawi, al-Falaki, al-Kattani, Shaykh al-Islam al-Harawi, Abu al-Qasim al-Shirazi, Ibn al-Qaysarani, al-Shirazi, and al-Abyurdi.

Interdomain Brokerage and Prominence

Figure 7.1 shows that intellectuals with multiple involvements were not so numerous even among the most prominent scholars of hadith. Furthermore, disciplinary borders were fluid and far from fixed. For instance, in the early history of Islam, the traditional sciences were not completely differentiated from each other, and titles that came into existence later did not apply in any exact way; rather, they are projections from the present day onto the past, onto scholars who lived before the crystallization of disciplinary boundaries. The total number of scholars with multiple involvements is 178, excluding the number of hafiz-jurists because, as I argued earlier, the huffaz were all jurists as well. The

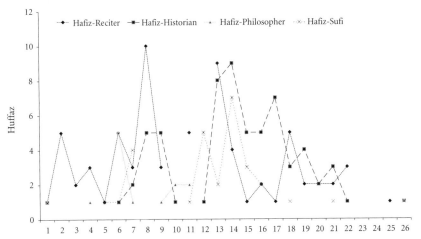

F I G . 7.1. Polyhistors over Time. In the earlier layers, titles are not applicable except as projections of more recent concepts onto earlier periods. The titles of disciplines and scholars came into existence later as the scholarly networks and disciplines gradually differentiated after the demise of the Prophet. Since a hafiz is required to be a jurist as well, this figure excludes the jurist-huffaz because complete overlap is assumed. Although the data are from Dhahabi's and Suyuti's biographical dictionaries of the huffaz, the names of the philosopher-huffaz are derived from Collins (1998). A color version of this figure may be viewed at www.sup.org/senturk.

number of polyhistors among the huffaz constitutes only 14.53 percent of all huffaz.

Among the total of 178 huffaz with multiple involvements, 70 connections were to the network of the reciters of the Qur'an (*qurra*) (39.3 percent), 64 connections were to the network of historians (35.96 percent), 14 connections were to the network of philosophers (7.87 percent), and 16 connections were to the network of sufis (16.35 percent).[13]

The above analysis documents that there was not a single hafiz who specialized in only one field. The best evidence comes from the fact that the huffaz were at the same jurisconsults, with varying degrees of reputation. But why? Why did these intellectuals not remain content to have mastered one intellectual domain? Why did they have the propensity to continuously expand their interests? Why, instead of feeling happy to have gained prominence in one field, did they readily accept the risk and fatigue of putting themselves under the burden of yet other disciplines?

This phenomenon, in brief, can be called *interdomain brokerage* because each discipline or field of academic study constitutes a relatively autonomous sociocultural domain with a distinctive mode of discourse or genre. I suggest that the propensity among highly prominent intellectuals to have multiple involvements and assume the role of interdomain broker can be attributed to the effect of levels of reported speech.

Multiple involvements reduce dependence on indigenous authorities in a discourse network other than one's own. Social actors try to reduce the constraints on their social activity and increase their independence as much as they can. This is true for corporate and individual actors, whether in markets or intellectual fields. A scholar has to cite an authority from another field if he is not an expert in that field as well. Yet if he specializes in that field also, he can speak as an authority in it without depending on, and reporting from, another authority. For instance, a sociologist who wants to speak about economic institutions has to cite authorities in the field of economics unless he also becomes an authority on economics. By also involving himself in economics, our sociologist eliminates the existing constraints on him as a mere sociologist and can now speak about economics without having to cite or refer to expert economists.

Furthermore, a scholar with multiple involvements serves as a discourse broker between the domains he is involved in, which increases his prominence in his native field. Our sociologist-economist may gain prominence among his sociologist colleagues because he will have advantages that others do not. He can be instrumental in the academic exchange and cross-fertilization of ideas and methods between two disciplines. This is a tradition some sociologists actually have followed, though with varying degrees of success, from the time of Marx and Weber to the time of Parsons and Coleman as well as many others.

In addition, the influence of a scholar with multiple involvements is no longer limited to his native field. Each additional field in which a prominent scholar gets involved means increased influence on his part. He will allow himself to be influenced by the perspectives of the new fields he becomes involved in, yet at the same time his influence will also expand to the new fields. For instance, the influence of Marx and Weber is felt both in and outside sociology because of these two figures' almost limitless interests, which defied all existing disciplinary borders.

A discourse mediator who is involved in multiple social and cultural domains carries the burden of mastering all the genres that characterize the fields he has a foot in. Furthermore, he has to be mindful of the invisible borders between discourse networks and able to switch promptly between them. Going back to the example of our sociologist-economist, he cannot expect a sociology journal to publish a paper he has written in the genre of economics just because he is a prominent sociologist. Likewise, if he sends a sociology paper to an economics journal, his paper will certainly be rejected, regardless of its excellence. A broker between different discourse networks can be successful only when he is fully aware of these constraints and masters the various genres of discourse.

Teachers with multiple interests may draw more students than their colleagues who are prominent only in one field, because they will attract students from all disciplines they are involved in. Students not just in sociology but also in economics will seek out our economist-sociologist. The more a teacher is sought after by students, the more prominent he is.

Ibn Khaldun: Why Are the Majority of Muslim Intellectuals Non-Arabs?

Ibn Khaldun observed in the fifteenth century that most of the Muslim intellectuals were non-Arabs, although Islam first emerged in Arabia, the Prophet

Muhammad was an Arab, and the language of the Qur'an and hadith is Arabic:

> It is a remarkable fact that, with few exceptions, most Muslim scholars both in the religious and in the intellectual sciences have been non-Arabs. When a scholar is of Arab origin, he is non-Arab in language and upbringing and has non-Arab teachers. This is so in spite of the fact that Islam is an Arabic religion, and its founder was an Arab [Ibn Khaldun 1967, 3:311].

I demonstrated earlier that the hadith transmission network had several shifting centers over time. Medina served as a center only in the early period, and later it lost this privilege to the cities that emerged on the edges of Islamic world (Bulliet 1994). As the intellectual center shifted away from the religious center (central Arabia, where Mecca and Medina are found) and toward the periphery, the number of prominent Arab scholars decreased while the number of prominent non-Arab scholars increased. The network of intellectuals had multiple shifting centers over the centuries, from Spain to India.[14]

Ibn Khaldun attributed this paradoxical development to the dialectic between sedentary and nomadic cultures. Civilization rests with sedentary culture, whereas nomadic culture is remote from civilization. According to Ibn Khaldun (1967, 3:315), "Scholarship was restricted to cities with an abundant sedentary culture." He also writes:

> We have mentioned that the crafts are cultivated by sedentary people, and that, of all the peoples of Arabia, [Bedouins] are least familiar with the crafts. Thus the sciences came to belong to sedentary culture, and the Arabs were not familiar with them or with their cultivation. Now, the [only] sedentary people at that time were the non-Arabs and, what amounts to the same thing, the clients and sedentary people who followed the non-Arabs at that time in all matters of sedentary culture, including the crafts and professions. They were most versed in those things, because sedentary culture had been firmly rooted among them from the time of the Persian Empire [Ibn Khaldun 1967, 3:312].

Arabs, who originally provided the raw material and initiated the process of creating new disciplines, had to relearn them from non-Arabs:

> The Arabs who came into contact with that flourishing sedentary culture and exchanged their Bedouin attitude for it were diverted from occupying themselves with scholarship and study by their leading position in the Abbasid dynasty and the tasks that confronted them in government. They were the men of dynasty, at once its protectors and the executors of its policy [Ibn Khaldun 1967, 3:313–14].

Ibn Khaldun shows how sweeping the contribution of non-Arab intellectuals was to the Islamic sciences. Even linguistic studies about Arabic were born in the hands of non-Arab scholars. Arabs thus owe the grammar of their language to non-Arabs, an interesting phenomenon with which I shall deal shortly in more detail. Not only linguistics and literary studies but also the study of hadith, the Qur'an, Islamic jurisprudence, and philosophy emerged through the contributions of non-Arab scholars who learned Arabic as a second language:

> Thus the founders of grammar were Sibawayh and, after him, al-Farisi and az-Zajjaj. All of them were of non-Arab [Persian] descent. They were brought up in the Arabic language and acquired their knowledge of it through their upbringing and through contact with Arabs. They invented the rules of [grammar] and made [grammar] into a discipline [in its own right] for later [generations to use].
>
> Most of the *hadith* scholars who preserved the traditions for the Muslims also were non-Arabs [Persians], or Persian in language and upbringing, because the discipline was widely cultivated in Iraq and the regions beyond. [Furthermore,] all the scholars who worked in the science of the principles of jurisprudence were non-Arabs [Persians], as is well known. The same applies to speculative theologians and to most Qur'an commentators. Only non-Arabs [Persians] engaged in the task of preserving knowledge and writing systematic scholarly works. Thus the truth of the following statement by the Prophet becomes apparent: "If scholarship hung suspended at the highest parts of heaven, the Persians would [reach it and] take it" [Ibn Khaldun 1967, 3:313].

Although Ibn Khaldun attributes this striking phenomenon to the dialectic between sedentary and nomadic cultures, I believe a related phenomenon must also be taken into consideration—namely, the pilgrimage to Mecca and the caravan trade, which must also have played a crucial role in the development and dispersion of the traditional Islamic sciences. The cities along the pilgrimage and trade routes, such as Cairo, Baghdad, Nishapur, and Bukhara, were also cultural centers of the time, which attracted students from around the known world. Trade contributed to the wealth of these cities. Most important, trade caravans also served as channels of communication between the various centers of learning, creating a huge pool of culture where ideas could circulate and interact with each other.

Cosmopolitan Intellectuals and the
Need for a Lingua Franca

The question raised by Ibn Khaldun about the ethnic composition of the huffaz leads us to yet another striking discursive aspect of the network of huffaz. If the majority of intellectuals were non-Arabs, and Persians in particular, then why did they continue to use Arabic? I suggest that the answer has to do with the need for a cosmopolitan group to have a lingua franca that would help them construct and maintain social relations for an extended period of time. In this regard, Arabic, for Muslim intellectuals, is comparable to Latin for Christian intellectuals of the Middle Ages and English for intellectuals in modern times.

This phenomenon is important if considered in connection with Collins' concept of "interaction rituals" in the intellectual community. Interaction rituals in a cosmopolitan community are facilitated by the existence of a lingua franca. Without one, it would not be easy for an international community to maintain its existence and coherence for an extended period of time. This is an additional reason why a single language prevailed in the network of the huffaz, despite their different mother tongues. Arabic occupied a privileged position and thus was more suitable to reign as the lingua franca than other major languages of the Muslim peoples, such as Persian, Berber, and Turkish.

Non-Arab intellectuals paid a price for maintaining Arabic as their lingua franca (Bohas, Guillaume, and Kouloghli 1990). Ibn Khaldun observes that the speed of their intellectual progress was hindered at the beginning of their educational careers because they had to spend an extended period of time mastering Arabic. A section in *The Muqaddimah* carries the following title: "A person whose first language is not Arabic finds it harder than the [native] speaker of Arabic to acquire sciences" (Ibn Khaldun 1967, 3:315). Even though it took a toll on non-Arab intellectuals, they maintained Arabic as their lingua franca, regardless of the small number of Arabs in their ranks, because it provided common ground and an expedient means of communication.

From Huffaz to New York Intellectuals

Modern intellectual communities, with their unconfined borders, face the same problems the huffaz faced in the construction and maintenance of a cosmopolitan intellectual community. Today, English plays a crucial role as a means of communication throughout the world. Intellectuals from other nations have to spend time to learn and master it if they want to belong to the international intellectual community.

For instance, the cosmopolitan community of New York intellectuals communicates in English, which is their lingua franca regardless of their native languages. The best example of this is the way German-speaking Jewish intellectuals who fled from Nazi Germany quickly adapted to the English-speaking New York community. Likewise, a great number of the books published by New York publishers are not by native speakers of English. Similarly, from Albert Einstein to Edward Said and Umberto Eco, countless foreign professors visit and teach at the academic institutions of New York City, primarily Columbia University. Furthermore, a considerable number of foreign students have also been trained at the academic institutions of New York. The libraries are full of books in foreign languages. What is more, even the newspaper kiosks on the street corners display newspapers and periodicals in numerous foreign languages. On the basis of these observations, one can say that, without English, it would be difficult for New York intellectuals to maintain communication and cohesive social relations among themselves.

In addition to the need for a lingua franca, it is possible to draw other parallels between the community of modern intellectuals and that of the huffaz. In the modern world, too, intellectuals are involved in multiple fields. Take New York intellectuals as an example. They belong to universities and are involved in academia. They also contribute to audiovisual and written media as experts or as columnists. One can be a historian as well as a novelist. Intellectuals may also belong to artistic circles of musicians and actors. Some may choose a political vocation as well, and some may be involved in trade and business.

Intellectuals, whether modern, medieval, or ancient, lead multiple lives. First, an intellectual has the world of his native language and the world of the lingua franca he has adopted. This intellectual capital is multiplied by the world of his home discourse network and by the other vocations to which he concurrently commits himself. He stands where all these different spheres overlap and plays the role of broker between them. He enjoys the privilege of speaking in each domain without having to report the speech of others. On the contrary, he is the one whose speech others report.

The contrast between the huffaz and New York intellectuals confirms the thesis of Collins, who argues that the hierarchical structure of the intellectual community has remained unchanged for the last two millennia. Ages ago, Ibn Khaldun made the same point. Both Collins and Ibn Khaldun, before coming to this conclusion, studied intellectual networks in their temporal contexts, paid extensive attention to the linguistic or discursive aspects of the networks of intellectuals, and highlighted the role of a tiny group as the leading element.

What intellectuals transmit to rising generations of students are languages, styles, and distinctive interpretations. Students are initiated into multiple discourse networks through polyhistor masters who transmit not merely narrative but also its opposing interpretations and ways of consolidating them in one's mind by building coalitions among them. A coalition of ideas, as Collins calls it, is a feature of an intellectual network and a source of creativity.

If such a coalition is carried too far in favor of one side, however, it may eliminate the opposition that is the fuel of intellectual dynamism and creativity. A clash of ideas and discourses on the intellectual level is needed by all parties involved in the conflict; otherwise, the overwhelming triumph of the strongest is ironically similar, in its ultimate effect, to one's unwitting preparation of one's own end. The triumph of the People of Hadith over rival paradigms testifies to this idea. As the interpretive approach of the Sunnite paradigm overwhelmingly prevailed in all the disciplines, through the efforts of polyhistor huffaz in the majority of the Muslim world around the eleventh century CE, the dynamism in the hadith community notably decreased because of the lack of opposition. Yet this outcome was never intended or foreseen by the huffaz.

Similarly, Collins (1998) has commented on the breach that resulted from extreme social fluidity at the clergy-layman boundary in Japan during the Muromachi period, around the fifteenth century CE, when religious schools became open to lay students as well as to monks. Collins emphasizes that although this is the path to the rise of the secular university, a pattern he has observed in Europe and India, in fifteenth-century Japan these developments did not produce that outcome. On the contrary, no philosophical creativity was produced. Instead, students persisted in memorizing the classics, which were used as textbooks. Collins attributes this "failure" to the lack of competitive networks with rival centers. The domination of a single center, without opposing schools of thought, stalled creativity and innovation (Collins 1998, 339). This is reminiscent of the energizing role of the polycentric structure of the hadith transmission network and the fluid movement of ideas within it, brought about through the bridging channels provided by polyhistors in the earlier history of Islamic civilization. Nevertheless, conceptual synthesis, social integration, and political consolidation eventually reached a level that became counterproductive as the basis of creative tension and dialectic in the intellectual community was eroded.

CHAPTER EIGHT

On the Shoulders of Giants
Chain of Memory and the Micro-Level LRS Effect

The links in the chain of collective memory are the personal relations between mentors and pupils on the individual, or micro, level. They help the intellectual community extend itself across generations. They usually represent relationships between grandfathers and grandsons, but not between fathers and sons, and infrequently between peers from the same generation. Books and other means of communication, regardless of how sophisticated they are, cannot take the place of personal association. Hadith scholars also greatly emphasized personal affiliation as the best way of acquiring and transmitting knowledge. They nevertheless acknowledged the validity of other methods as well. This view originated in the first generation, who considered that meeting the Prophet Muhammad was the sole criterion for determining who was a Companion, the greatest honor in the Islamic community. Later generations turned this into an enduring tradition: the mentor one personally met from the earliest generation determined one's layer. Consequently, that mentor also determined one's social identity, authority, and status within the intellectual community. Yet this feature is not peculiar to the huffaz of hadith alone.

Sociologists who study the structure of intellectual communities[1] commonly observe that where there is no climbing on the shoulders of giants from previous generations, intellectual horizons are closed to aspiring students in ancient as well as modern times. The ancient Latin aphorism states, "Pigmei Gegantum humeris impositi plusqam ipsi Gigantes vident" ("Pygmies on the shoulders of giants see farther than the giants do").[2] In early modern times, Isaac Newton reiterated this aphorism. Later, it drew the attention of Robert Merton, who explored its roots and sociological significance.[3] Collins's most recent work (1998), on networks of philosophers, also emphasizes the diachronic relations among intellectuals in the major civilizations of the world. His findings are basically in conformity with those of earlier scholars in the sociology of science and of intellectuals, such as Ibn Khaldun, Merton, Zuckerman, and Mullins.

Between Ancient Wisdom and Modern Query

Ultimate truths, or "decontextualized ideas," are what intellectuals search for, Collins argues. Yet Collins also claims that success in intellectual query depends on the opportunity structure in which one is placed. The opportunity one's social network offers shapes one's success as an intellectual:

> . . . the basic form of intellectual communities has remained much the same for over two thousand years. Key intellectuals cluster in groups in the 1900s CE much as in the 400s BCE. The personal contacts between eminent teachers and later-to-be-eminent students make up the same kinds of chains across generations. And this is true even though communications technology has become increasingly available, and the number of intellectuals has increased enormously, from on the order of hundreds in Confucius' China to the million scientists and scholars publishing today. Intellectual life hinges on face-to-face situations because interaction rituals can take place only on this level [Collins 1998, 25–26].

As the following analysis will show, the huffaz also conform to the same patterns. First, a hafiz is always the student of another hafiz from an earlier generation, from whom he inherits knowledge. Second, meeting in person is required for a transmission to gain greater credibility. Collins stresses in great detail the role of what he calls "interaction rituals" in the intellectual community (Collins 1998, 20–53). Interaction rituals, as we have already seen (chapter 7), are extremely important in the hadith transmission network as well. The etiquette of hadith transmission is repeatedly emphasized in the community. The mentor is advised to put on nice clothing and perfumes, brush his teeth, sit at a higher elevation, and speak slowly and clearly. Custom also requires the scholar, like any other Muslim, to greet the soul of the Prophet Muhammad by saying, "Peace and greetings be on the Messenger of God" each time the Prophet's name is mentioned. It is well known that Malik (93–179 H/711–795 CE), one of the greatest masters from layer 6, who lived in Medina, showed great respect for the words of the Prophet and set an example for later generations. He narrated hadith only after putting on his best clothes and sitting at a higher elevation. When he was asked why he dressed so well, he said, "Because all the scholars I received this knowledge from dressed well."

There should be at least one interaction ritual between a disciple and a mentor of hadith for the connection to be accepted as valid by the critics. Hadith scholars in the early period debated whether written correspondence was acceptable as a valid teacher-student relationship. For instance, Bukhari, the author of the most authoritative compilation, adamantly insisted on an actual meeting (*liqa*) between a mentor and a student, to ensure the credibility and validity of the tie. Otherwise, for him, the relationship bore no fruit academically: the knowledge acquired in the absence of personal contact cannot be used and cited in scholarly works or reported by students, nor can a scholarly opinion in law and theology be built upon it. Muslim, the author of the second most authoritative hadith compilation, severely criticized Bukhari on this issue and claimed that a personal meeting was not always necessary to the credibility of a narration. I have already demonstrated, in the preceding discussions, the self-reflexive approach with respect to these rituals and the ensuing codification of interaction rituals.

In the tradition of the hadith scholars, personal relations, through direct meetings or correspondence, represent the only route for the reliable and valid exchange of knowledge. Books are conceived as auxiliary tools to help in the process of transmission, but not as alternatives or substitutes for personal mentor-pupil interaction. The one whose mentor is books alone is not considered a scholar in the community and is not granted permission to transmit hadith, nor is he licensed to issue religious verdicts or opinions. Books do not transmit the emotional energy with which mentors charge their students, nor can they serve as role models in practicing what is learned. However, after obtaining a certificate from a master, one can utilize books. One is then well prepared to avoid the pitfalls in the literature.

The language must also be learned initially through personal interactions with previous generations. Then one can go to the books. Yet rarely can a language be reliably learned from books alone. Collins repeatedly draws our attention to the importance of speech in the construction and reconstruction of intellectual networks. He writes:

The crucial focus of an intellectual group is the consciousness of the group's continuity itself as an activity of discourse, rather than the particular contents of their discussion. . . . The ritual focus is not so much on the level of particular statements and beliefs (although groups can vary a good deal in conformity on this level), but on the activity itself. The focus is on a peculiar kind of speech-act: the carrying out of a situation-transcending dialogue, linking past and future texts. A deep-seated consciousness of this common activity is what links intellectuals together as a ritual community [Collins 1998, 28].

The process of hadith transmission from teacher to student provides an excellent example of Collins's arguments concerning the rituals in an intellectual community, in particular the role of language use in reproducing intellectual identity and regenerating the network. Furthermore, in the hadith transmission ritual, we clearly observe the role of reflexive language, in particular reported speech, in linking past and future generations. Without reflexive speech, it would be impossible to establish and maintain connections with intellectuals from past generations. Besides, what is related during these rituals is not just texts but, as Collins calls it, the "emotional energy" that is also transmitted to the new generations.

The relationship between prominent masters and disciples is quite ambiguous. It is not a relationship of complete submission. Nor is it a relationship of complete rebellion. It is characterized by both. In hadith culture, the emphasis on respect and loyalty to one's masters is paramount; yet it is also repeatedly said that relying merely on inherited knowledge keeps one from attaining high levels of scholarship. An aspiring scholar is expected to develop a critical mind while building upon his intellectual heritage. Those who fail to develop these intellectual qualities cannot enter the network of prominent scholars, since they are not considered huffaz.

Furthermore, there was competition not only among students from the same generation but also between students and their masters. The well-known Muslim competed with Bukhari while Ibn Hajar competed with his master Dhahabi and believed that he surpassed him. In like manner, Suyuti competed with his master Ibn Hajar and believed that he also exceeded him. Muhammad al-Shaybani and Abu Yusuf, the two prominent students of Abu Hanifa, the founder of the Hanafi school, disagreed with their great mentor on many issues. Students of the other great masters in the Islamic intellectual tradition also disagreed with them. Abundant historical examples demonstrate vertical opposition to great mentors by great students. Disagreement with mentors, and intellectual opposition to them (*ikhtilaf*), are general features characterizing the relationship between great mentors and great disciples. Among the most remarkable issues involving controversy are the interpretation of hadith and its implications for theological and legal questions.

Ironically, vertical relations with great masters may both block and promote creativity. One has to have a great mentor but, at the same time, manage to creatively develop a new approach of one's own. Striving toward the goal of originality and creativity brings forth a unique dichotomy, whereby one faces the following question: How can innovations and discoveries emerge if aspiring scholars and intellectuals have to be closely linked to past generations? Isaac Newton revolutionized his discipline, and his intriguing answer to a question about his own success—that in order to see farther than the giants, one has to stand on their shoulders—reveals the unfounded assumption on which that question was based (Merton 1993). Close ties to prominent intellectuals from antecedent generations do not hinder the process of innovation; on the contrary, they accelerate it. New generations build upon the work of previous generations instead of reinventing the wheel. Creativity and innovation, as Feynman (1998) also argues, are to a great extent outcomes of a critical dialogue with the past and are therefore ultimately contingent upon a deep familiarity with it.

Giants, however, are few in any generation. Collins argues that a survey of the lengthy history of the major cultures of the world demonstrates that the "law of small numbers" applies to intellectual networks everywhere, regardless of the time frame. The patterns that the present study has unearthed in the hadith transmission network also conform to the law of small numbers. The stratum of huffaz also remained tiny in size yet monumental in influence.

The same rule applies even more strikingly to the network of prophets of the ancient world, the divinely inspired intellectuals of their time. One man is believed to stand at the origin of the three major religions of today's world: the prophet Abraham. He can be seen as the ideal type of the seminal intellectual. The prophets of Judaism, Christianity, and Islam are all believed to be his descendants. The religions expressed in the Torah, the Bible, and the Qur'an originated with him. Jews, Christians, and Muslims, who constitute around half the world's population, revere him. In the tiny network of prophets, Moses, Jesus, and Muhammed, who have gained unparalleled authority in the long history of religions, honored Abraham as their grandfather. These prophets are all believed to be connected to each other, not only through intellectual and spiritual lineage but also through family lineage. The prophet Abraham, narrative has it, had two wives, Sarah and Hagar. The former was the mother of Isaac, from whose lineage Moses and Jesus descended, while the latter was the mother of Ishmael, from whose lineage Muhammad descended. Four figures, then, have shaped the religious culture of a significant part of humanity over thousands of years.

The prophets may be seen as the ancestors of the intellectuals. Yet they were not professional scholars, as we understand that term today, because theirs was a different vocation. For them, authenticity was the primary concern, not originality. For instance, the Prophet Muhammad did not claim to have offered entirely new rules and ideas.[4] Instead, he declared that he had come to restore the eternal wisdom of the prophets, from Adam to Abraham, reaffirming the divine revelation of the Torah and the Bible. Linked to the intellectual and familial lineage originating with Abraham, the Prophet Muhammad reclaimed the spiritual legacy of Abraham, the first architect of the ancient temple, the Kaaba in Mecca. Instead of building a new temple of his own, he symbolically expressed this act of reclamation by requiring his followers to turn five times a day to the Kaaba while praying. The act of turning toward Mecca in prayer followed on the custom of praying in the direction of Jerusalem, as Jews and Christians had long done, yet the Prophet Muhammad went back even further in time by turning to Mecca, an act that linked him to an earlier source, the tradition of the prophet Abraham.

For the most part, each new generation derives its authority for claims to truth from the connection to a grandfather who lived in an unknown and remote past. If Suyuti is connected through an intellectual genealogy to the Prophet Muhammad, and if the Prophet is connected to Abraham through a familial and intellectual genealogy, then there is a connection between Suyuti and the prophet Abraham. This is true not only for Suyuti but also for his Jewish and Christian counterparts. And the case of Abraham, father of prophets and of three major world religions, is not the only one in the world. His counterparts can be found in the eastern part of the world as well, in such examples as Buddha, Confucius, and Lao-Tzu.

At any rate, this unparalleled authority is bestowed upon the prophet Abraham even though he did not leave anything in writing, and even though it was a long time before his reported speech, transmitted orally, was recorded in sacred scripture. The same is true for Socrates. Like Abraham, Socrates has lived on through the writings of his students, in particular Plato. However, this is not the common pattern in an intellectual community. In general, the authority of intellectuals is embodied in the texts inherited from them and in the works that cite them. Accordingly, the authority of the prophets becomes manifest even today in the discourse networks of sacred scripture (Coward 1988; Cragg 1973; Smith 1993; Graham 1987). Likewise, the authority of Plato and Aristotle is also embodied in texts that are still passionately read and discussed in the modern world.

In the ancient world, however, ultimate truth was transmitted through generations, and the role of the intellectual was to receive, understand, practice, and build upon it. Collins shows that this pattern is observable in all the major cultures of the world, from Japan to Europe, and from ancient to modern times. In each major civilization, major thinkers are students of great thinkers from past generations, who in turn have built their thinking on the ideas of their own masters. In this regard, quite strikingly, there is no difference between the network structure of the scholars of hadith in Islamic civilization and that of philosophers from China, India, and Europe.

Contrary to popular perception, what we consider even today to be "the truth" is for the most part inherited, in varying degrees, depending on the discipline, notwithstanding the high value ascribed to self-discovered truth. When we examine the network of intellectuals in the modern era, we observe that they are also thickly connected to the network of prominent intellectuals from preceding generations (Zuckerman, Mullins, Collins). In light of this finding, we can deduce that in the modern intellectual landscape, the rise of a prominent intellectual with no connection to antecedent generations of intellectuals remains impossible.

There might be an aura of superiority in each new generation toward former generations, owing to a feeling of coming closer to the truth with the help of recent discoveries. This is true especially within the claims of the discourse of modernity because it is characterized by common faith in a linear "progress" toward an ideal society, by contrast with ancient cultures, which believed in a continuous "decay" or "fall" from a golden age that existed in the remote past.

Yet, despite their feeling of superiority, contemporary intellectuals cannot get away from supporting their claims with evidence derived from the ancient masters. Works of ancient masters are therefore still an important part of the curriculum in modern academia, and they are still more cited than the works of most modern thinkers.

At this point, the following question arises: Why do we still rely, both conceptually and socially, on intellectuals from previous generations, even though we believe that we have far superseded them in knowledge? The explanation offered by sociological studies is that aspiring students must be connected to the network of prominent intellectuals if they desire to be prominent intellectuals themselves. Likewise, aspiring authors must link their works and ideas to those of earlier masters if they wish to add more authority to their own claims. In brief, even modern intellectuals cannot dispense with previous generations, even if they perceive themselves as more advanced. This poses a paradox. I will further illustrate it below, in the context of the hadith transmission network, focusing both on internal relations and on external relations with rulers, and then offer an explanation from the perspective I have thus far outlined.

Mutations in the Chains of Collective Memory

Dissemination of hadith began in Mecca in 610 CE, the year the Prophet Muhammad announced his mission, though not so publicly, as the Messenger of God to humanity.[5] At the age of forty he received the first revelation on the mountain of Hira near Mecca, where he used to go frequently for retreat in a small and isolated cave. As the common tradition holds, the Archangel Gabriel conveyed to him the following divine command:

> Read: In the name of thy Lord Who createth, Createth man from a clot. Read: And thy Lord is the Most Bounteous, Who teacheth by the pen, Teacheth man that which he knew not [Qur'an, 96:1–5].

Shaken by the event, Muhammad rushed home and asked his wife, Khadija, to cover him with a blanket. He was also concerned about the possibility of a delusion or a spell. Khadija had been the wife of Muhammad for fifteen years and had never seen him in this condition. She was a woman of vast experience, with great love, loyalty, and compassion for her husband. She told her husband that God would never forsake him, because he cared for the needy and fed the hungry. She was a businesswoman dealing in international trade. She owned trade caravans to transport goods between Yemen and Syria. She hired Muhammad, who had been making his living as a businessman working for others, to oversee her caravan, which gave her the opportunity to directly witness his outstanding character and personality. The nickname of Muhammad in Mecca was "al-Amin," the Trustworthy, since he proved himself to be a businessman of persistent integrity. Khadija, who was then a widow of forty, proposed marriage to him. He was twenty-five years old at that time, fifteen years younger than she was. They got married and happily remained so for almost twenty-five years, until Khadija died.

While Muhammad was resting, wrapped in a blanket, as narrative has it, another revelation came, commanding him to act: "O thou enveloped in thy cloak, arise and warn! Thy Lord magnify, Thy raiment purify, pollution shun! And show not favour, seeking wordly gain! For the sake of thy Lord, be patient! For when the trumpet shall sound, surely that day will be a day of anguish, not of ease, for disbelievers" (Qur'an, 74:1–12).

Muhammad was worried that no one would believe him. Khadija responded by saying she would believe him because she had never known him to lie. She thus gained the honor of being the first Muslim to believe in the Prophet Muhammad. They decided to keep Muhammad's mission secret for a while between themselves and intimate friends. Abu Bakr, a businessman and a close friend, was the second to embrace Islam. The third convert was a young boy, Ali, the nephew of Muhammad. The fourth was an African slave, Bilal, who tried in vain to hide his conversion from his polytheist master. Upon discovering Bilal's conversion to the new monotheist religion, his master tortured him ruthlessly, until Abu Bakr purchased him and set him free. The small core of believers, comprising members from diverse segments of Mecca society, grew steadily but secretively for several years, until the new religion was publicly declared. In this period, the sayings of the Prophet Muhammad were disseminated secretly within the small network of the faithful.

Following the public proclamation of Islam, a new phase commenced for the believers, requiring great endurance of oppression at the hands of Meccan polytheists, which continued until the flight from Mecca to Medina, the Hijra, in 622. Yet the oppression failed in its attempts to silence the new monotheist religion, which continued to spread and gained new converts. Eventually the leaders of the Meccan tribes, motivated by tribal zeal, came together to discuss the problem and agreed, as a solution, on ending Muhammad's life. Since they wanted to forestall the possibility of revenge by his tribe, the Sons of Hashim, a person from each Meccan tribe was chosen to take part in the murder of the Prophet. They thought his tribe would not possibly dare to oppose such a powerful alliance comprising all the tribes.

Having somehow learned of the secret plot against his life, the Prophet Muhammad, accompanied by his closest friend, Abu Bakr, fled Mecca at midnight, heading south in order to mislead his enemies. The two hid themselves in a cave on the Mountain of Thawr for a few days before heading to Medina, a city north of Mecca, where the message of Islam found fertile ground.

With the flight from Mecca to Medina, the Hijrah, a new period began in the history of Islam. Muslims established a state under the charismatic leadership of the Prophet. This meant amending the purely spiritual teaching of the Mecca period with legal rules, to regulate social relations in the new community. The growth of Islam had begun in the commercial society of Mecca, whose entire income came from trade, since the land around Mecca was barren, impossible to cultivate. After its formative period in a society of traders, Islam continued its development in the society of farmers in Medina. In fact, with the arrival of the Meccans, Medina became both an agricultural and a commercial city. Those who came from Mecca were called the Immigrants, "Muhajirun," while the native residents of Medina were called the Helpers, "Ansar," because of the help they gave the newcomers. Islam had to respond to the regulatory needs of both agricultural and commercial relations of production. Therefore, Islamic law stipulated rules concerning trade, finance, farming, and land. This initial experience must have prepared Islam for its later role in various rural and urban settings characterized by different economic relations, and it can be considered a significant factor that contributed to its swift spread over a wide geographical area.

Brought together by a common religious identity and by brotherly love for the sake of God, a cosmopolitan community emerged in Medina around the Prophet Muhammad. For instance, Suhaib al-Rumi came from Rome or Byzantium; Salman al-Farisi came from Persia; Bilal al-Habashi came from Abyssinia; and Abu Hurayra came from Yemen. Furthermore, they all came from a wide spectrum of religions that included polytheism, Christianity, Judaism, and

Zoroastrianism. The rise of the new religion thus attracted pious people from remote lands and religions to Medina, where they found a deeper meaning in life, clearer spiritual guidance, and a more caring community. In the early years following the Hijra, the Prophet Muhammad encouraged the converts to move to Medina to learn more about Islam and contribute to the strength of the new community. The cosmopolitan nature of the first Islamic society may be seen as yet another major factor contributing to the sweeping dissemination of hadith across divergent cultures of the time.

The Prophet Muhammad sent mentors to the tribes who accepted Islam, thereby institutionalizing the spread of hadith. Yet a mentor was not required to rely exclusively on hadith. On the contrary the, Prophet Muhammad encouraged them to use their reason in matters not dealt with by his teachings. A conversation between the Prophet and Muadh, the mentor he was about to send to Yemen, is instructive in this regard. The Prophet posed the following question to Muadh: "According to what will you judge?" Muadh replied, "According to the Book of God." The Prophet asked again, "And if you find nothing therein?" Muadh responded, "According to the Tradition of the Messenger of God." The Prophet asked again, "And if you find nothing therein either?" Muadh answered: "Then I will exert myself [use my opinion, exercise *ijtihad*] to form my own judgment." Such incidents taught the Companions how to maintain a hierarchy between the Qur'an, hadith, or Sunnah, and reason. They also helped later jurists to develop an elaborate methodology for Islamic jurisprudence. But, more important, the space accorded to rationality along with revelation must have helped Islam adjust to local settings more easily, another significant factor that may have contributed to the swift dissemination of the Prophet Muhammad's teachings.

These teachings emerged and were spread under great duress and pressure, which is the case for all great religions and ideologies that challenge the status quo. Both the Qur'an and hadith were taught during times of great threat, fear, perseverance, sorrow, and conflict. At that time, the Arabian Peninsula housed a great variety of religions and religious adherents, including polytheist idol worshipers, followers of the ancient religion of Abraham, Christians, and Jews. Frequent clashes took place between the newly emerging religion and the pre-existing ones, which strove in vain to arrest the progress and spread of Islam. The message of the Prophet had been a completely peaceful one at the outset, opposing war even in the form of self-defense. For fourteen years the Muslim community was not allowed to defend itself against attacks, until two years after Hijrah. Muslims were then finally allowed to make defensive war against the frequent attacks by the alliance of polytheist tribes from Mecca who kept attacking Medina in an attempt to completely destroy Islam in its new home. Eventually, when the polytheist Arabs broke a peace accord, the Islamic army put Mecca under siege until it surrendered without a war. The Prophet forgave all his former enemies, who had expelled him from his hometown, and peacefully entered the Kaaba, the temple toward which pious Muslims turn five times a day in prayer. He banished all the idols inside and around the Kaaba, thereby firmly establishing faith in one God, the legacy of the prophet Abraham.

The Prophet Muhammad employed informal methods to instruct his followers and disseminate his teachings, without constraining himself with restrictions of time and place. Education was constant and everywhere. Apart from congressional prayers on Fridays, the Prophet rarely gave public lectures. Instead, he educated his Companions as life went on at the dinner table, at wedding parties, on the battlefield, in sports races, on the farms, in the marketplace, and in other quotidian settings. Simply put, hadith may be described for the most part as the table talk of the Prophet Muhammad. The Companions who were present at an occasion shared what they had learned and observed with those who had been unable to attend. Figure 8.1 illustrates the exchange patterns among the most prominent Companions, who are considered huffaz.

The demise of the Prophet in 632 initiated an entirely new phase in the spread of his narratives. His Companions were determined to carry his message with great enthusiasm to the farthest lands they could reach, from North Africa to Yemen, from Anatolia to India. A culture of travel beyond Arabia already existed among them. The Companions from Mecca were particularly familiar with remote lands, since they traveled with trade caravans to distant places. Yet this time they were bound to take the new faith with them. In these lands they met new disciples who learned the new religion from them. Their preexisting experience with the cultures and geography of non-Arab peoples and lands must have helped them in their efforts to win converts to the new faith.

Not all the Companions were equally involved in the education of the new generations. The greatest teacher among them was Aisha, the wife of the Prophet Muhammad after Khadija's death, who had the highest number of students from the generation of Companions and Successors. Respected as the Mother of the Believers, she served as a great authority to men and women alike

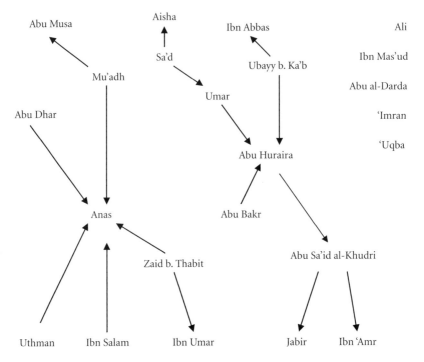

FIG. 8.1. Exchange of Hadith among the Prominent Companions

on matters pertinent to all religious, moral, legal, and political issues. On many occasions she had to defend the rights of women by not letting pre-Islamic Arab culture gut the rather egalitarian teachings of the Prophet Muhammad. Figure 8.2 shows that Aisha drew a great number of students. Among them were Nafiʾ, Shaʾbi, Saʾid bin al-Musayyab, and Shaqiq.

Abu Hurayra, the second most crucial of the Companions in the dissemination of hadith, had embraced Islam only a few years prior to the demise of the Prophet Muhammad. He eagerly attached himself to the Prophet to observe his behavior more closely and memorize his speeches. He also acquired knowledge of hadith from other Companions who had accepted Islam before he did. Umar was among his mentors, as can be seen in figure 8.2. On the path of knowledge, he gave up work and relied on charity. At times he had to endure hunger for days. He belonged to the Fellows of the Antechamber, "Ashab al-Suffa," which comprised the eager Companions who spent most of their time in the Mosque of the Prophet, listening to his sermons and teaching newcomers. The Prophet Muhammad selected from among them the mentors he sent to converted Arab

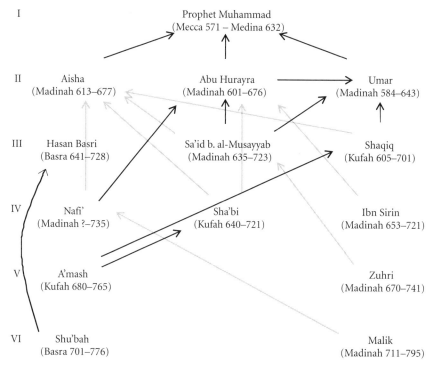

FIG. 8.2. The Companions and the Successors, Layers 1–4. Roman numerals represent layer numbers in the HADITHNET dataset.

tribes. As figure 8.2 shows, a number of great figures from the following generation, such as Nafi', Sa'id al-Musayyab, Sha'bi, and Ibn Sirin, studied under Abu Hurayra.

Yet Umar, the third Companion with the most significant role in the dissemination of hadith, could not afford to commit himself entirely to learning because of his family responsibilities. With the purpose of compensating for what he had missed, he established a partnership with another Companion. The partners alternately took off from work to spend the day with the Prophet, and in the evening each in turn shared his experiences with the other upon his return from work. Later, Umar was to become the second Caliph after Abu Bakr. He served in that capacity more than a decade. During his rule, he greatly contributed to the development of Islamic law. Umar taught Abu Hurayra, Sa'id bin al-Musayyab, and Shaqiq, among many others. He strove to establish the principle of justice in law, which gained him the title "Umar al-'Adil," Umar the Just.

Yet justice was hard to maintain in this new cosmopolitan society. The first civil war in Islamic history erupted toward the end of Uthman's reign. The Caliph Uthman fell victim to civil war, which continued during Ali's reign. Yet scholarship continued even during times of social and political turmoil. Eventually, internal conflicts brought an end to the rule of the Four Rightly Guided Caliphs (Abu Bakr, Umar, Uthman, and Ali) as the Umayyad period commenced.

With the transfer of power to the Umayyads, the new capital, Damascus, became a center of learning and attracted many great scholars from the generations of the Companions and the Successors. Kufah and Basra also emerged as new centers of learning, attesting to the polycentric structure of Islamic learning at that time. Nonetheless, Medina remained one of the important centers of hadith scholarship.

The Companions were not professional scholars as we usually perceive them today. They were primarily merchants, farmers, rulers, and warriors. Scholarship only gradually came to be differentiated from these roles. Their education was not ordered by school schedules. They learned and taught as life went on in the marketplace, at home, on the battlefield, and at the mosque. They did not separate action from knowledge or faith from practice. Scholars did not expect payment from the government or from their students for their services; they had to make their own livings. For them, teaching what they knew was spiritual fulfillment, an obligation, and a way to please God. Even though it was a greater burden on the scholars to generate income for their families while maintaining their scholarly work, it ensured greater autonomy for them. This tradition continued later; the majority of the pious scholars tactfully stayed at a distance from the rulers of their time and thus avoided co-optation by the state.

The first Umayyad Caliph, Muawiya (661–680 CE) reunited the community after the civil war that ended the rule of the Rightly Guided Caliphs. With a strong central authority, he reestablished social and political stability, which was needed for intellectual growth to continue. The Umayyads reigned not by overwhelming consensus but by force. Yet they maintained stability and expansion of the empire. Under their rule, Islam spread to North Africa, Spain, Transoxania, and Sind.

Hadith scholarship continued to grow steadily during the Umayyad period, without interruption. Without the legendary political skills and genius of Muawiya, the newly emerging cosmopolitan society would have shattered into pieces. If the civil war had continued for a longer period of time, the chains of narration could have suffered interruption. However, Muawiya was blamed for the transformation of a meritocratic system of Caliphate to the rule of his own dynasty, since he transferred power to his son, Yazid, before his death.

This was unacceptable to some segments of the society and triggered another civil war, lasting from 680 to 692. The Umayyads did not refrain from shedding blood to maintain their power. The victims included even the grandson of the Prophet Muhammad, Husayn, who was martyred in Karbala (Iraq). His martyrdom permanently divided the entire Muslim community, "more than any dispute over law or theology or any antipathy between tribes, races and linguistic groups" (Lapidus 1988, 59). The Shiite scholars of hadith thus formed a separate network of hadith transmission and developed distinctive concepts and methods for hadith criticism, since they refused to narrate hadith from the opponents of their political views concerning the Caliphate of Ali and his progeny. They also accorded great importance to the sayings of their religious leaders, imams, and treated them as hadith. Yet the Sunni scholars treated all scholarly views equally, irrespective of their proponents. A governing principle was established in Sunni thought that "a scholarly opinion (*ijtihad*) cannot invalidate another."

During the Umayyad period, new intellectual centers emerged. As shown in figure 8.2, the number of scholars from Basra and Kufah in the generation of the Successors attests to that. Basra housed such great Successors as Hasan al-Basri (21–110 H), while Kufah housed Shaqiq (17 BH–83 H) and Sha'bi (19–103 H). Sa'id bin al-Musayyab (14–105 H), Nafi' (d. 117 H), and Ibn Sirin (33–110) resided in Medina. These scholars taught in their homes and mosques while also producing written compilations.

Among the most prominent scholars from the generation of the Successors, Malik enjoys the longest-lasting impact because he authored one of the early canonical works of hadith literature, *al-Muwatta'*, which is still commonly used and cited. The Maliki school of Islamic law originated with him. He gave primacy to the customs of Medina as a major source of Islamic law, since, as he argued, these customs had developed under the guidance of the Prophet Muhammad and his Companions. Despite requests by the Umayyad Caliphs, he refused to allow his book, *al-Muwatta'*, to become the official law of the state. Nor did he agree to teach the princes in the palace of the Caliph; instead, he asked them to come to his home if they desired to learn from him.

Unlike Malik, Zuhri, who had lived a generation earlier, preferred to collaborate with the Umayyad palace. He used the sources at his disposal to collect more hadith. His efforts proved very effective, for he became the fountainhead of many narrations. In the palace, he also served in the education of the princes and in advising the Caliph on religious matters.

The Umayyad Caliph Umar ibn 'Abd al-'Aziz—or, briefly, Umar II—was also a great scholar of hadith. Even though he is not among our three most prominent scholars, he was known as a hafiz. His rule lasted for only three years (717–720) before his death. Yet his efforts for a virtuous state became as legendary as those of Umar I, who was seen as the symbol of justice. Unlike his Umayyad predecessors, who perceived their state as an Arab empire, Umar II returned to the meritocratic approach of the Rightly Guided Caliphs. He saw that domination of one ethnic caste over other peoples was anachronistic after the advent of universal Islamic unity:

> The antagonisms of Arabs and non-Arabs would have to be dissolved in a universal Muslim unity. As Umar saw it, the problem was not just to placate the converts while retaining Arab supremacy. Rather, he held that the empire could no longer be an Arab empire but had to be the imperium of all Muslims. He thus stood for the conversion of all of the peoples of western Asia to Islam, and their acceptance as equals of the Arabs [Lapidus 1988, 63].

Yet his successors did not maintain the vision of this "philosopher king" and their failure to do so eventually led to the collapse of the Umayyad dynasty, in 750 CE, and then to the rise of the revolutionary Abbasids, with a more inclusive and egalitarian ideology. "Under the Abbasids the empire no longer belonged to the Arabs, though they had conquered its territories, but to all those peoples who would share in Islam and in the emerging networks of political, social, economic, and cultural loyalties which defined a new cosmopolitan Middle Eastern Society" (Lapidus 1988, 70–71). The Abbasids established coalitions and incorporated Persians, Nestorian Christians, Jews, and Shiites into their administration.

In a sense, the Abbasid revolution demonstrated the power of the periphery

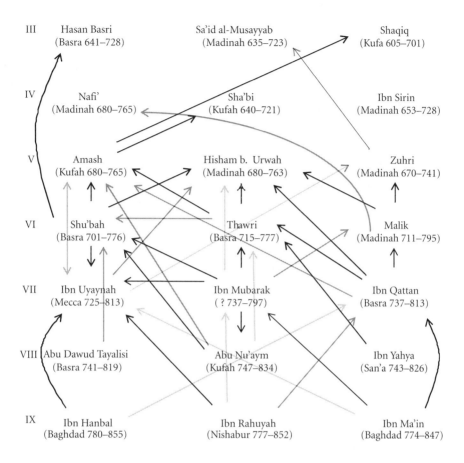

III   Hasan Basri   Sa'id al-Musayyab   Shaqiq
       (Basra 641–728)   (Madinah 635–723)   (Kufa 605–701)

IV   Nafi'   Sha'bi   Ibn Sirin
       (Madinah 680–765)   (Kufah 640–721)   (Madinah 653–728)

V   Amash   Hisham b. Urwah   Zuhri
       (Kufah 680–765)   (Madinah 680–763)   (Madinah 670–741)

VI   Shu'bah   Thawri   Malik
       (Basra 701–776)   (Basra 715–777)   (Madinah 711–795)

VII   Ibn Uyaynah   Ibn Mubarak   Ibn Qattan
       (Mecca 725–813)   (? 737–797)   (Basra 737–813)

VIII   Abu Dawud Tayalisi   Abu Nu'aym   Ibn Yahya
       (Basra 741–819)   (Kufah 747–834)   (San'a 743–826)

IX   Ibn Hanbal   Ibn Rahuyah   Ibn Ma'in
       (Baghdad 780–855)   (Nishabur 777–852)   (Baghdad 774–847)

FIG. 8.3. The Successors of Successors, Layers 5–7. Roman numerals represent layer numbers in the HADITHNET dataset.

over the center: it emerged in Khurasan, especially around the city of Marw, and toppled the rule in Damascus. However, the Shiite opposition, based in Kufah, a city closer to the center, remained ineffective in its revolutionary impulse against the Abbasids. Intellectual life was not so different. The power of the periphery steadily increased as non-Arab scholars gradually took over intellectual life, including the religious sciences and hadith scholarship.

During Abbasid rule, as figure 8.3 illustrates, each generation maintained the tradition of the previous generations by extending the chain of memory further in time.

Baghdad, which was founded by the new Abbasid regime, emerged as the new center of intellectual life and played an everlasting role in the intellectual history of Islam; "it crystallized the culture which became Islamic civilization" (Lapidus 1988, 70). Baghdad remained the largest city in the world outside China until the rise of Istanbul in the sixteenth century.

By establishing Baghdad, the Abbasids aimed to distinguish themselves from the ancien régime. They called it City of Peace (Medinat al-Salam). It could be reached from the main roads between Iraq, Iran, and Syria and was accessible by land and by sea. It was a convenient station for travelers, for religious, academic, and commercial purposes, between the eastern and western parts of the empire. For instance, hadith scholars from Iran, Azerbaijan, and south and central Asia, on their way to and from Mecca, stopped in Baghdad and exchanged narratives with the local scholars.

The relationship between the Abbasids and the intellectuals remained ambiguous. Their efforts to co-opt such scholars as Abu Hanifa and Malik failed. Yet they succeeded in the co-optation of the Mutazilites. Abu Hanifa and Malik did not commit the detrimental mistake that Mutazila did. The Mutazilites paid the price in the long run: they disappeared. But the schools of Abu Hanifa and Malik survive today. Ibn Hanbal was the leading figure against the Mutazilites and was persecuted for that. The period of the persecution of scholars, who disagreed with the Mutazilites on the question of whether the Qur'an was created or uncreated, prepared the end of both the Mutazilites and the Abbasids. The Abbasids lost legitimacy in the eyes of intellectuals and the general public and came to be suspected of heresy and oppression. The scholarly community distanced itself ever further from their rule and became more conscious of its autonomy with respect to the state. "Henceforth Islam would evolve in full autonomy . . . under the aegis of the religious teachers" (Lapidus 1988, 125).

Consequently, hadith and Islamic law developed in the urban centers at the hands of the relatively autonomous *ulama* class, without direct control by or contributions from the state. The Abbasids established an academy, Bayt al-Hikmah, to promote the natural sciences, astronomy, and the translation of Greek philosophy into Arabic. Yet there was not a parallel organization for the religious sciences; that was left to the private efforts of scholars, who refused co-optation by the state and strove to maintain their autonomy. The scholars maintained critical discourse without active political involvement or rebellion.

"The urban 'ulama' affirmed religious equality, political accountability, and personal values based upon the Quranic revelation and the Arabic identity of the town populations" (Lapidus 1988, 123).

Maintaining intellectual autonomy was further facilitated as the central authority of the Abbasids began disintegrating when the regional powers gained prominence after the ninth century (c. 833–945 CE). The weak Abbasid state allowed intellectual discourse to develop freely while at the same time ensuring the political stability needed for intellectual growth. None of the founders of the Sunni schools, who were all huffaz, had close ties with the state. Indeed, they had striven to evade the Caliphs. Abu Hanifa chose to die under torture at a prison in old age rather than accept co-optation by the Caliph.

The same observations are true for the authors of six canonical hadith compilations: Bukhari, Muslim, Nasa'i, Ibn Majah, Abu Dawud, and Tirmidhi. The latter, Tirmidhi, does not appear in figure 8.4, because our data do not indicate that he was among the three most prominent scholars of his generation. These scholars also avoided control by the ruling elite and preferred to maintain their autonomy, even if it involved enduring financial burdens and oppression. Bukhari, for instance, endured hunger during his travels. Yet he declined invitations from the rulers. Toward the end of his life, as the pressure mounted to an unbearable degree, he chose to live out his remaining days in an isolated village near Bukhara, where he had been born.

As we examine the geographical origins of the authors of the Six Books, we observe not only the polycentric structure of the network of hadith transmission but also the power of the periphery over the center. Bukhari came from Bukhara; Muslim from Nishabur; Nasa'i from Nasa'; Ibn Majah from Qazwin; and Tirmidhi from Tirmidh. With the exception of Bukhari, who came from central Asia, these great scholars were from Persia. This phenomenon may be seen as a confirmation of the genuinely international character of hadith scholarship, with Arabic as its lingua franca.

Figure 8.4 demonstrates a higher rate of activity among scholars in this period. Both the number of scholars in each layer and the number of ties among them were higher. Furthermore, scholars displayed a greater desire to maintain the maximal generational span between mentors and students. However, a comparison between figures 8.4 and 8.5 would make it clear that the subsequent generations were characterized by a smaller number of huffaz, by fewer ties

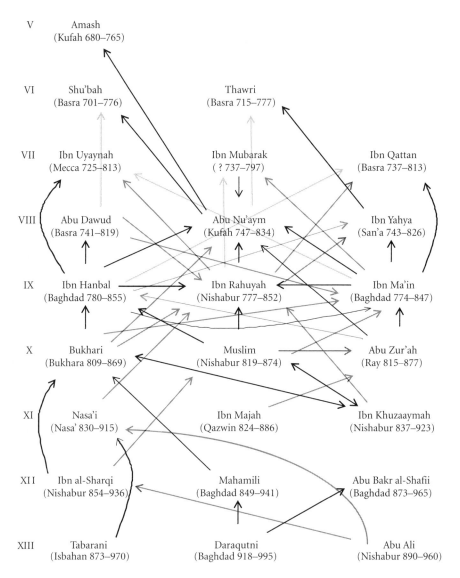

FIG. 8.4. Rise of the Canons (the Six Books), Layers 8–12. Roman numerals represent layer numbers in the HADITHNET dataset.

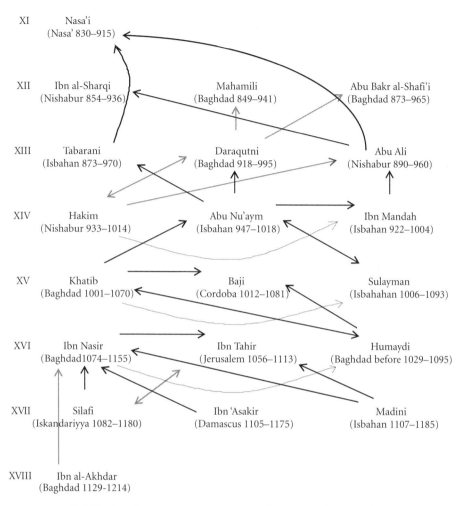

FIG. 8.5. Stabilization, Layers 13–16. Roman numerals represent layer numbers in the HADITHNET dataset.

among the huffaz, and by decreasing interest in the maximal generational span of ties.

We can also observe further expansion of the hadith transmission network toward eastern and western Muslim lands, from Cordoba (Qurtuba), the homeland of Baji, to Isbahan, which produced the great Tabarani, Abu Nu'aym, and Ibn Mandah, as well as to Nishabur, which was the homeland of Abu Ali, Hakim, and Suleyman. We also see the increasing importance of Jerusalem,

Quds, home of Ibn Tahir. Baghdad was still an important center where such great scholars as Daraqutni, Khatib, Ibn Nasir, and Humaydi resided. These scholars worked on refining the earlier works, reorganizing them and writing commentaries on them so as to make them more easily accessible to students and to the general public.

Their efforts greatly contributed to the further rationalization and stabilization of hadith transmission. Transmission of the six collections became a standard part of training in that period, which brought great efficiency to hadith education. A student could acquire knowledge of hadith in a relatively shorter period of time by studying these books, by contrast with the earlier period, during which a student was required to collect hadith in a piecemeal manner. Instead of collecting and transmitting individual narratives, it was more efficient for teachers and students alike to learn and transmit the Six Books as a set.

Since collecting hadith was no longer such a greatly time-consuming task, students of hadith shifted their primary focus onto interpretive activity. They produced great commentaries on the canonical compilations of hadith by exploring the theological, legal, and moral implications of hadith. In these commentaries, they usually compared previous interpretations before presenting their own.

With the collapse of Abbasid power, independent successor states emerged, beginning in the tenth century (945–1220), prior to the Mongol invasions in the thirteenth century (c. 1220–1260 CE). The Abbasid caliph, however, maintained his symbolic role for a longer period of time. The dynasties that emerged in this period included Fatimid rule (969–1171), Mamluk rule (1251–1517) around Egypt, and Saljuq rule in Anatolia and Syria (1081–1307).

In this phase, we observe greater self-reflexivity on the part of scholars with respect to their activity and their network. Mizzi and Dhahabi produced the most comprehensive works on the history of their discipline and its network. They also criticized their colleagues for not living up to the highest standards their vocation required.

The trends we observed above from layers 13 to 16 became even more visible in this period, which corresponds to layers 17–26 (see fig. 8.6). The institutionalization of hadith education increasingly broadened as the hadith colleges (*dar al-hadith*) spread all over the Muslim world, from the Balkans to India. The

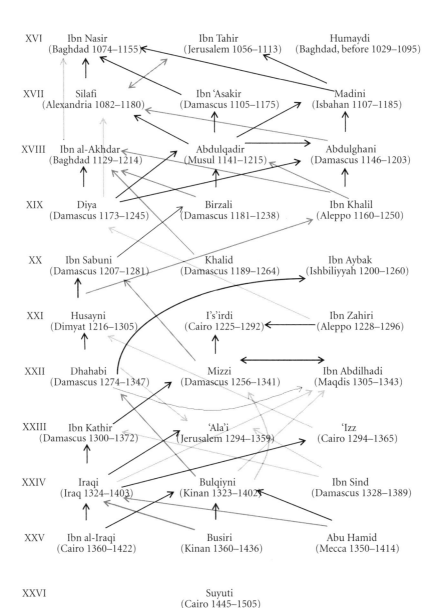

XVI   Ibn Nasir   Ibn Tahir   Humaydi
      (Baghdad 1074–1155)   (Jerusalem 1056–1113)   (Baghdad, before 1029–1095)

XVII   Silafi   Ibn 'Asakir   Madini
      (Alexandria 1082–1180)   (Damascus 1105–1175)   (Isbahan 1107–1185)

XVIII   Ibn al-Akhdar   Abdulqadir   Abdulghani
      (Baghdad 1129–1214)   (Musul 1141–1215)   (Damascus 1146–1203)

XIX   Diya   Birzali   Ibn Khalil
      (Damascus 1173–1245)   (Damascus 1181–1238)   (Aleppo 1160–1250)

XX   Ibn Sabuni   Khalid   Ibn Aybak
      (Damascus 1207–1281)   (Damascus 1189–1264)   (Ishbiliyyah 1200–1260)

XXI   Husayni   I's'irdi   Ibn Zahiri
      (Dimyat 1216–1305)   (Cairo 1225–1292)   (Aleppo 1228–1296)

XXII   Dhahabi   Mizzi   Ibn Abdilhadi
      (Damascus 1274–1347)   (Damascus 1256–1341)   (Maqdis 1305–1343)

XXIII   Ibn Kathir   'Ala'i   'Izz
      (Damascus 1300–1372)   (Jerusalem 1294–1359)   (Cairo 1294–1365)

XXIV   Iraqi   Bulqiyni   Ibn Sind
      (Iraq 1324–1403)   (Kinan 1323–1402)   (Damascus 1328–1389)

XXV   Ibn al-Iraqi   Busiri   Abu Hamid
      (Cairo 1360–1422)   (Kinan 1360–1436)   (Mecca 1350–1414)

XXVI   Suyuti
                    (Cairo 1445–1505)

FIG. 8.6. Decline, Layers 17–26. Roman numerals represent layer numbers in the HADITHNET dataset.

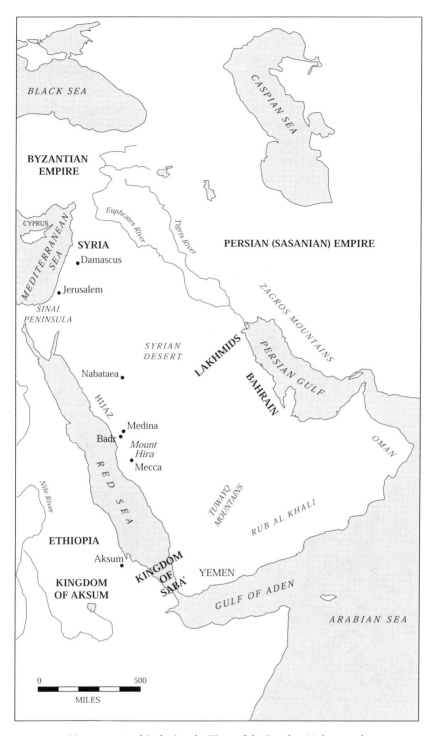

M a p 8.1. Arabia during the Time of the Prophet Muhammad

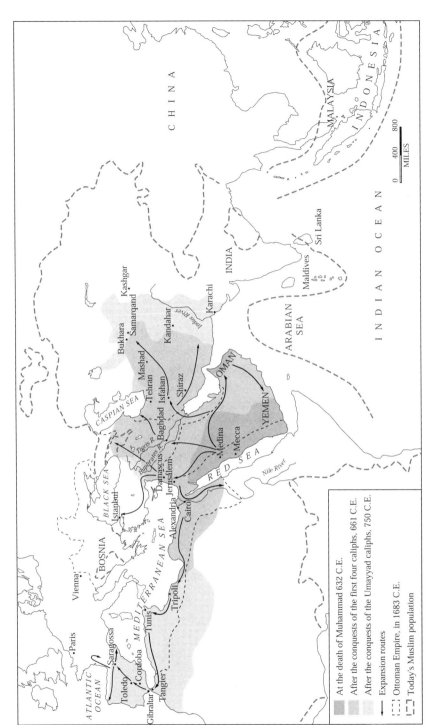

Map 8.2. The Spread of Islam

At the death of Muhammad 632 C.E.

After the conquests of the first four caliphs, 661 C.E.

After the conquests of the Umayyad caliphs, 750 C.E.

Expansion routes

Ottoman Empire, in 1683 C.E.

Today's Muslim population

teaching in these colleges revolved around the Six Books. Students studied their chains and texts. Hadith transmission finally became routinized as it reached greater efficiency through successive stages of rationalization, from the narration of single narratives to the narration of the set comprising the Six Books.

These achievements did not leave much to be done; as Ibn Khaldun mentions, later scholars concluded that these prior achievements left little more to do than maintain the tradition. This is what the Ottoman colleges of hadith did in Istanbul, the Balkans, and Anatolia. The Ottoman Empire emerged during the late thirteenth century in western Anatolia, but its eastward expansion came much later, after the sixteenth century (see maps 8.1 and 8.2). The Mamluks reigned in Egypt prior to the Ottoman expansion. Such well-known huffaz as 'Izz ibn Abd al-Salam and Suyuti lived under Mamluks. These later scholars also maintained the tradition of their pious predecessors by evading the rulers and criticizing them when they deviated from Islamic law. In particular, 'Izz became legendary for his civil disobedience of the Mamluk regime. When the Ottomans conquered Egypt, they could not find the great huffaz, for they had just disappeared. In any event, the focus of the Ottoman rulers and scholars had not been on hadith but on Islamic law, to establish and maintain order in the vast cosmopolitan empire.

A Legendary Case: Ibn Hajar between Knowledge and Love

After this swift survey, we may now focus on a particular example to shed more light on the world of hadith scholars. In this way, we may be able to compensate somewhat for insufficient detail in a journey of centuries taken in a few pages. Indeed, each generation and each scholar deserves to be studied independently, yet that is beyond the intent and reach of the present book. I will use the biography of Ibn Hajar (773–852 AH), written by his renowned student, the historian Sakhawi, in two huge volumes.[6]

Ibn Hajar is one of the most esteemed scholars of hadith in the history of Islam. A closer look at his life will shed more light on the upbringing and career trajectory of hadith scholars. Hadith education in medieval Islam can be understood as analogous to humanities education in our time. In addition to religious content, it housed a rich source of knowledge about Islamic history. Consequently, hadith was an integral part of the education and literature of Muslim societies. Furthermore, for the majority of students, such as Ibn Hajar, to study hadith meant to follow a calling, a vocation for spiritual and intellectual fulfillment.

Ibn Hajar first studied in Cairo, under the most prominent scholars. Subsequently, as all serious students of hadith did at that time, Ibn Hajar also prepared himself to make academic journeys abroad, termed *rihla*, to collect hadith with shorter chains and to study under the oldest and most prominent masters of hadith. He was reported to be an excellent rider.[7] This, he considered, was part of being a good student because it saved time. His student al-Sakhawi (831–902 AH) reported that he said, "A good student must be speedy in reading, writing, eating, and walking" (al-Sakhawi 1986b, 18).

As a young student, Ibn Hajar made his first trip to Aleppo, a Syrian city on the trade routes, well known as an intellectual and commercial center. There he met some of the oldest masters of hadith. The respected hadith teachers of Aleppo offered Ibn Hajar narratives with fewer nodes in the chains of authority and more parallel chains for the narratives he had already learned from his mentors back in Cairo. They also shared with him their interpretations of the narratives.

His was a competition with fellow students for shorter chains as well as for more parallel chains of authority along with a better understanding of their content. The shortest chains of narrative—which meant the fewest levels of reported speech—could be collected only if one traveled abroad to study with the oldest authorities. Ibn Hajar's future prestige as a scholar depended on his opportunity to study under the most renowned authorities of his time. His friends back home had exactly the same narratives, yet from younger teachers, and thus with longer chains of authority and more levels of reported speech.

When he first arrived in Aleppo, he did not know that not only knowledge but also love was awaiting him. There he met Layla, a girl who stole the heart of this bright young student of hadith. This development could have put his scholarly aspirations on trial and jeopardized all the plans he had made before leaving home. His unexpected love for Layla might have preoccupied Ibn Hajar and distracted him from his studies. Fortunately, however, as a student of religion, Ibn Hajar did not have to suppress and hide his love, unlike his contemporary, the young Christian scholar in Umberto Eco's historical novel *The Name of the Rose*. In Islam, asceticism is forbidden, and a religious scholar is no different from a layman with respect to love and marriage. Moreover, love and marriage are even praised as customs of the prophets. Therefore, Ibn Hajar and Layla decided to get married while he continued his studies and his quest for more valuable narratives from respected authorities.

Ibn Hajar, following the custom of the time, either copied the books of the reputable scholars of Aleppo or hired a scribe to copy them for him. Yet owning a copy of a hadith book had little value beyond one's personal use. In order to get the copy sanctioned for prospective use in instruction and citation, one had to study the book under the authority either of the person who had written it or of one of his licensed students if the author was not alive. Studying a book entailed reading and discussing the book thoroughly with a teacher, from cover to cover, unless the teacher decided otherwise, in consideration of the student's previous knowledge and level of understanding. Depending on the circumstances, either the teacher or the student performed the reading. In the terminology of hadith instruction, the former is called "reading" (al-qira'ah) while the latter is termed "auditing" (al-sima').[8] This exercise was also an excellent way of proofreading the manuscript. Permission to use a book, or a segment of it, even if it was a single hadith, was registered in a written document called al-ijazah. Without this permission, a scholar's use of another's work was not considered ethical (Makdisi 1981, 1991).

After each book was read, either by Ibn Hajar to a master or by the master to Ibn Hajar, the master signed in the back of Ibn Hajar's copy, thereby authorizing him to relay the narratives to his students, perhaps forty or fifty years later, if he was lucky enough to live that long. Future students would have been interested in Ibn Hajar as a teacher only when he had outlived his peers, since only then would his chains have become the shortest ones. Thus Ibn Hajar, while writing and memorizing narratives, was also hoping to relay them one day to younger generations, a prospect that depended on his outliving his fellow students, and over which he had no control.

At that point, Ibn Hajar had to make a choice between staying with Layla or following the prerequisites of a successful career. Since Ibn Hajar strictly adhered to the aforementioned principles of success, which had become crystallized over centuries in the community of hadith scholars, it did not take long for him to finish collecting the hadith of Aleppo from the oldest masters of the city. Layla was also under pressure because she also faced a dilemma: she had to choose between following Ibn Hajar to an unknown future in the remote lands her beloved would travel to or staying with her family in Aleppo. One of these choices entailed extensive travel back and forth to such centers of hadith education as Arabia, Yemen, central Asia, Iran, India, and Spain.

Layla and Ibn Hajar jointly decided to sacrifice their love. Ibn Hajar made the difficult decision to leave his beloved behind, just as his contemporary, the young Christian scholar in Eco's novel, had done. But in the case of Ibn Hajar, it was a voluntary sacrifice of love for the sake of knowledge. This was an extremely painful decision for both Ibn Hajar and Layla. Ibn Hajar always remembered Layla and voiced his mourning for their love in his poems:

> I departed, and left my beloved in her house,
> Against my will. I never inclined to any other,
> But only to engage in the study of hadith,
> All my days, and at night, to long for Layla.
> [...]
> Rise, and listen to some tavern song! For Layla is in the dead of night,
> Sleeping in my embrace, but only in my dream,
> And my streaming tears lead a dance with her shadow.
> Do you suppose those who see me know this, and what befell me?

Ibn Hajar did the right thing, some may think in retrospect, by giving supremacy to his inner drive for more knowledge over his passion, because he later became one of the greatest scholars of all time in Islamic culture. His authority still goes unchallenged in the field of hadith. His colleagues, students, and future generations came to address him with the title *shaykh al-islam*. This title means, in the culture of hadith scholars, the highest authority in Islamic knowledge, and it is bestowed upon exceptionally outstanding scholars, whose number does not exceed forty in all of Islamic history (al-Sakhawi 1986b, 14–17).[9] There was a traditionally accepted stratification among scholars of hadith, *shaykh al-Islam* being the highest, followed by *hafiz*. Ibn Hajar successfully gained recognition in the community and quickly climbed the ladder of the scholarly hierarchy until he reached the highest level.

Ibn Hajar traveled all his life between centers of hadith. He went to Yemen a few times, where he met one of the greatest linguists of Arabic, Fayruzabadi. He traveled to Damascus, Jerusalem, Mecca, and Medina. In Mecca, his wish when he drank from the holy well of Zamzam, near the Kaaba, the symbolic House of

God, was to reach the level of Dhahabi, the highest authority of that time. It is still believed that these wishes are accepted by God. Sakhawi wrote:

> Some of his students asked him, "Who has more knowledge in memory, you or al-Dhahabi?" He kept silent. This was an expression of humility from him, may God be pleased with him. He told us that he drank the waters of Zamzam when he made a pilgrimage to Mecca in the year 800 or 805—the doubt is from me—to reach the level of the hafiz al-Dhahabi. He also said, "When I made another pilgrimage, around twenty years later, I found myself desiring more than this level, and I wished for a level that is higher than that. I hope that God will help me to reach that level." I say that God granted him this wish, and everyone without exception bore witness to that [al-Sakhawi 1986b, 106].

One of Ibn Hajar's youngest students was al-Suyuti. He was even more rigorous than his teacher. He even took pains to travel to India and Morocco in addition to the places where his teacher had traveled. Since childhood, his purpose had been to reach and surpass the level of his teacher, Ibn Hajar, the highest authority in the world. In his autobiography, Suyuti writes:

> Thanks to God, I traveled to the cities of Syria, central Arabia [Mecca and Medina], Yemen, India, and the West [what is known today as Morocco]. When I made my pilgrimage, I drank the water of Zamzam for several wishes. Among them were that I should reach the level of al-Bulqini in *fiqh* and the level of Ibn Hajar in Hadith. I was given the authority to issue legal rulings (*fatwa*) in the beginning of 71 [871 AH, which means at the age of twenty-two, since he was born in 849 AH] and in the beginning of 72 [872 AH] I conducted my first dictation of hadith [*imla al-hadith*] [Suyuti 1984, 8].

It is evident from his account that al-Suyuti was in competition with his great master and proud of reaching such a high level at an earlier age than his famous teacher had done. These accounts illustrate the competition even between teachers and students as well as the role of traveling.

Alas, Ibn Hajar was the last of his kind in the history of hadith. In the generations that followed, no one could reach his level. Not only the stratum of the *shaykh al-Islam*, with the death of his student al-Suyuti (1505 CE), but even the stratum of hafiz became beyond the reach of the following generations. According to the majority of historians, Suyuti's death marked the end of the tradition of the huffaz, the eminent hadith narrators who committed hundreds of thousands of hadith to memory and embodied them in their lives (Fadel 1995).

After the deaths of the great hadith scholars, such as Ibn Hajar and Suyuti, the academic scene was left to relatively minor figures from the stratum of the *muhaddith*. The nine-century-long network of huffaz, from the time of the Prophet Muhammad to the sixteenth century, expanding all over the Islamic world from the gardens of Spain to the steppes of central Asia, came to an end. Suyuti, a well-known polymath, wrote in his biographical dictionary about the death of Ibn Hajar, whom he had met at a very young age: "The gate was closed after him, and this vocation ended with him" (Suyuti 1984, 553). Later generations fatalistically accepted this as an irreversible process, and scholasticism was bound to prevail.

However, some hadith scholars challenged this view of their history. They claimed that there was much to be done in each age, and the huffaz from each century carried on the work in a distinct manner. al-Kattani represents this view in his book *Fahras al-Faharis*, where he provides a long list of scholars from subsequent centuries, from Suyuti until his own time. He tries to demonstrate the continuity in the chain of memory through the efforts of scholars whom he considers huffaz. Yet, even if we agree with al-Kattani, it cannot be denied that none of these later authorities had the impact of their predecessors. Visionary scholars of hadith kept remembering "things past," yet at the same time they realized how deeply times had changed.

The LRS Effect on the Micro Level

The foregoing analysis has demonstrated that a scholar avoided connections to his fellows from the same layer, although it was expedient for him to obtain narratives from his friends. This is a paradoxical issue. Having identified the network patterns of prominent scholars, we now need an explanation for the pattern of authority formation—an explanation of why such a network configuration emerged and persisted for centuries.

The answer, and I reiterate my earlier argument, lies on another plane, namely, that of metalanguage. These scholars, like everyone else, were trying to reduce the levels of reported speech by obtaining narratives from the individuals who, in their times, were closest to the original source. Had they taken narratives from their peers, their chains of narrative, and thus their levels of reported speech, would have extended to an undesirable degree. The attempt to reduce the levels of reported speech prompted them to seek out teachers who had fewer nodes in their narrative chains.

Yet, in the process, their social network gained a particular shape, though this development took place out of sight. In other words, metalanguage implicitly configured and reconfigured the network of scholars. Those who were more successful in reducing their levels of reported speech as students became prominent teachers later in life because their network positions attracted aspiring students.

Therefore, the role of metalanguage needs to be taken into account in exploring how students selected their teachers, why they had to wait until a certain age before they could teach, and why students were attracted to them. Without incorporating linguistic processes in our analysis, we cannot find an explanation for the particular network configuration that characterized the social relations of prominent hadith scholars.

CHAPTER NINE

Conclusion

Speech and Action Conjoined on the Diachronic Axis

I have so far highlighted the problems triggered by the gap between discursive and social structures, on the one hand, and synchronic and diachronic structures, on the other. I also showed the advantages afforded by bridging these gaps on the conceptual and methodological levels. Structuralism cannot deliver what it promises without bridging these gaps, which divorce speech and time from social action and thus ignore the temporal and discursive constraints that social action faces. Social action is certainly bound to fail, however, if it does not take temporal and discursive constraints into consideration.

The image of structure suggested by Ferdinand de Saussure, whose work has served as the fountainhead of structuralism since the beginning of the last century, can be summarized by the interaction of two axes: micro and macro, on the one hand, and diachronic and synchronic, on the other. Almost a century has passed since Saussure, yet his project has only been partially realized, despite the popularity it has enjoyed in intellectual and academic circles. This is because, notwithstanding the extensive attention paid to the link between macro and micro levels in social theory, the time axis that Saussure used to differentiate between diachronic and synchronic relations has yet to be fully explored.

Saussure's approach was also very sensitive to the uninterrupted synergy between discursive and social structures. He even considered putting linguistics under the newly emerging field of sociology. But later developments in social and human sciences have not taken this strong relationship into account. The results have been images of narrative without social organization, and images of the social actor without speech.

In the first phase of social theory in the modern era, the founding fathers of sociology took language as an epiphenomenon and did not incorporate it into the images of social actor, relation, and structure that they variously constructed. The only exception was Marx, who gave language a peripheral place in his social theory. In the next phase, however, humanists and social scientists alike discovered the importance of language. Also in this phase, however, language remained subordinate to the social, which was considered to be the real world. But the third phase, which we are in now, increasingly gives equal importance to language and action in the construction of social relations and structures. The third phase became possible with the rise of a constitutive approach to language, as opposed to the traditional referential approach that was common to the humanities and the social sciences. Adopting a constitutive approach to language implies a sweeping rapprochement of our concepts and methods in the social and human sciences.

From this perspective, bringing language back in, or the "linguistification" of social theory, as Habermas puts it (1984–87, 2:2), can occur through the coupling of long-isolated discursive and social structures by way of a reciprocal or circular model. An increasing number of scholars from various disciplines have adopted such an approach. Besides Habermas, striking examples include Harrison White, Tilly, Shotter, Silverstein, and Lucy. Notwithstanding the claims of their predecessors, these scholars have responded to language by paying it due respect.

Moreover, there have been other advances in the study of discursive patterns as our understanding of talk has evolved. Language is no longer seen as operating only on one plane. Instead, as Silverstein maps it out, there are several planes overlaid upon each other, namely, language and metalanguage, pragmatics and metapragmatics. Plainly put, there is talk, and there is talk about talk. The former is termed *object language,* while the latter is referred to as *metalanguage,* or *reflexive speech.* Studies on reflexive language demonstrate how language constantly acts upon and reacts to itself, and this bears directly upon social action and relations. Patterns in the use of reported speech provide an excellent example of this point. In line with Silverstein, Harrison White also offers a dynamic and a multilayered image of language use and shows how we continuously and reflexively revise our stories and accounts in everyday social relations.

In the remainder of my concluding remarks, I will do three things. First, for the argument developed here, I will display evidence from modern scholarship as well as from major civilizations of the world, using the work of Mullins, Zuckerman, and Collins. Second, I will elucidate how cross-temporal analysis might bear upon synchronic network analysis. And, third, I will discuss the possibility of applying to other social networks the interpretive perspective developed here. The last two sections will demonstrate how my perspective contributes to ongoing broader debates in sociology.

Revisiting Mullins, Zuckerman, and Collins

My argument about the role of diachronic relations in the formation of authority is also substantiated empirically by the data that Mullins, Zuckerman, and Collins have collected concerning prominent scholars and intellectuals. Mullins collected data on the network of prominent social scientists (see Mullins 1973, 42, esp. fig. 3.1),[1] whereas Zuckerman gathered data on the network of Nobel Prize winners (see Zuckerman 1977, esp. figs. 4-1, 4-2, and 4-3).[2] Collins collected data about the most prominent philosophers in the major civilizations of the world, from Japan to India to the Islamic world and Europe.[3] These data also show extensive out-layer/cohort connections parallel to the patterns displayed by the hadith transmission network. Likewise, all three authors, deriving data from different fields and different time frames, stress that in order to become a prominent scholar one has to become the student of a prominent scholar.

However, all three authors merely stress the existence of a connection, without giving due attention to the generational difference between the parties and to the gap in the ratio of in-layer and out-layer ties. True, prominent scholars were the students of other prominent scholars—which is only a partial explanation of the phenomenon, but I should add that they were not from the same generation. This observation shows the role of diachronic connections in generating and regenerating authority in ancient and modern scholarly communities across the world.

Earlier, I discussed how Saussure's image of structure gave long overdue recognition to the temporal dimension of social action. However, one important dimension is still missing from this image of structure—namely, the spatial dimension. In addition to synchronic (Saussure 1966, 101–39) and diachronic (Saussure 1966, 140–90) structures, Saussure stressed the importance of structures emanating from geography (Saussure 1966, 191–211). However, subsequent structuralist query in the social sciences, with the exception of geography, has not pursued this idea seriously and has yet to develop methods of displaying the interaction of time and space in the operation of social systems. The field of geographical information systems is a new and fast-developing one that combines social scientific and geographical data and methods with the most recent computer technology.[4]

This limitation is also reflected in my work here. At times, I also had to put the spatial dimension aside in order to concentrate more fully on the temporal dimension. Bulliet's work presents an excellent example of how to trace developments on both axes, although within a very limited scope. The space variable remains fixed in Bulliet's work, since he analyzed the network of hadith scholars in only one city, Nishapur (Bulliet 1972). In my data, however, which represent a polycentric network structure, I have briefly described how centers shifted across time.[5]

The present research, while making no claims to be exhaustive, further analyzed how social ties are anchored not only in time but also in social and geographical space. Narrative travels and is disseminated in time and space through networks, following certain patterns and thereby giving rise to social structures. In the present work, I have concentrated on some of the structures emerging from time, leaving further discovery of spatial patterns for future research. For instance, mapping out the network on the vast geography of Islam over centuries would demonstrate the international routes of narrative from Spain to central Asia, routes that would probably overlap with the trade routes of those ages, in particular the silk and spice routes (Abu-Lughod 1989; Eickelman and Piscatori 1990). In this connection, the role of pilgrimage to Mecca, and to the cities that served as stations on the way, must also have played an important role (Gellens 1990, 50–65). These issues, which I could touch upon only tangentially in this research, can be fully explored in a future study.

The focus of this work, limited to the most prominent scholars, the huffaz,[6] needs to be widened in the future to include the less prominent scholars, the *muhaddithun*, and those who were stigmatized as liars. For instance, the grand dictionary of Dhahabi (*History of Islam*) and his specialized dictionary on the fictive narrators or storytellers (*Register of the Weak and the Abandoned*) provide information about different strata of narrators over an extended period of history. This would help us determine the social conditions that played an important role in forgery, and in the conflict between fictive and historical modes of narrative. It could also facilitate comparisons between the network structures of prominent and less prominent scholars.

Furthermore, the network of hadith scholars, which I have reconstructed here, needs to be confounded with actual chains of authorities, *isnad,* and texts of narrative, *matn.* My initial exploration showed that, in Bukhari's *Sahih,* among 1,528 transmitters (Kalabazi[7]) featuring 7,563 *isnad* trees (Bukhari), there are 430 huffaz, 28 percent of the total population. Yet we still do not know how big a role they played in the transmission of hadith, a role whose extent and impact could be determined through analysis of the frequency with which their names occur in the actual *isnad* trees. Analysis of the network can further be linked to content analysis of the texts, to see whether there are recurring patterns.

The conflict between the Shiite and the Sunni branches of Islam is reflected in the network of narrators of hadith as well as in their respective metanarratives. In this study, the data are derived from Sunni sources. Yet it seems that the authors of biographical dictionaries, including Dhahabi and Suyuti, paid only limited attention to school-based differences between scholars, for they also included many well-known Shiite scholars. The division between the Sunni and Shiite schools in Islam emerged toward the end of the first century and gradually crystallized. Prior to this division, there had been only one network, but after the conflict took root in society, the network of scholars also began differentiating according to the two different schools of thought (Kohlberg 1983). However, prominent hadith scholars, such as Bukhari, took hadith from scholars who did not belong to the same school of thought as their own. Thus, despite the difference in schools, we find many scholars who are today considered Shiite—such as Ja'far al-Sadiq, the founder of the Jafari school—included by Dhahabi as huffaz in his biographical dictionary.

Is the Idea of Synchronic Structure an Illusion?

Is the idea of synchronic structure an illusion? Yes, says Saussure. Yet, paradoxically, he argues that it is a profitable and necessary illusion. Social actors are unaware of temporal order, although they are embedded in it. The scholar who wants to understand the perspective of social actors must also adopt it and bracket his awareness of time. Saussure writes (1966, 81):

> The first thing that strikes us when we study the facts of language is that their succession in time does not exist insofar as the speaker is concerned. He is confronted with a state. That is why the linguist who whishes to understand a state must discard all knowledge of everything that produced it and ignore diachrony. He can enter the mind of speakers only by completely suppressing the past. The intervention of history can falsify his judgment.

Temporal structure is about succession in time of sounds, letters, words, sentences, actions, actors, relations, and events, from the most minuscule microscopic level to the most gigantic macroscopic level. Succession is also called an event.[8] Each level has its own notion of time. What is diachronic at one level can be treated as a synchronic fact at another level. What is diachronic for phonetics and morphology, succession of sounds, is synchronic for syntax. What is synchronic for syntax, succession of words, is synchronic for narratology.

Saussure mistakenly identifies diachronic laws with evolution because he applies the diachronic perspective only to the macro level and confuses succession in time with succession in space (or, more precisely, on paper, as in writing).[9] He uses the following statements as examples of synchronic laws (Saussure 1966, 91–95; emphasis added):

> 2. Stress never falls on a syllable *preceding* the antepenultimate syllable of a word.
> 3. All words *end* either in a vowel or in -s, -n, -r; but no other consonant.

As the italicized words ("preceding" in law 2, and "end" in law 3) show, these laws are also about time. The coexistence of words on paper when we read them may leave us with the misperception that they coexist.[10] In contrast, as the event of speech makes clear, sounds succeed each other in an orderly manner. Similarly, if we are operating on the macro level, the succession of elements on that level will appear synchronic to us. These laws are synchronic only if we are looking at them from the level of "language" but not that of "speech."

Study of discursive and social structures that ignores temporal constraints is called *synchronic analysis*, as first suggested by Saussure (1966). This perspective has been highly prominent and is still the most prevalent approach in the social sciences and the humanities. Yet the concept as used in the discursive and social spheres needs critical examination.

A speech act is not and cannot be synchronic, because its elements do not take place all at once. This can be observed on both the macro and the micro levels. The nature of speech requires that it take place sequentially, piece by piece; otherwise, nothing will be discrete enough to be comprehended. The sounds also have to be sequentially transmitted to listeners in order for them to understand. If speech sounds are transmitted to an audience all at once, the listeners will hear a short noise but not speech.

In discourse, whether written or verbal, letters, words, and sentences are sequentially ordered in time. Speech without such order would be a "word salad." In a conversation, for instance, the speeches of different interlocutors are also sequentially ordered in time. In brief, the elements of speech, as well as the speeches themselves vis-à-vis each other, are temporally positioned and ordered. How is this fundamental feature reflected in our study of speech and narrative? The elements of both speech and conversation are temporally structured on the diachronic axis but not on the synchronic axis. Speakers and interlocutors must abide by the unwritten constitution of this invisible temporal order of speech. Failing this, they risk facing a range of dismissive responses, from shame to exclusion to the accusation of madness.

The temporal structure of speech is more evident in reflexive speech. In this case, the speech a person is reporting must have occurred before he speaks. It is impossible for a person to report something that happens at the same time or later than the time of his speech. The speech that becomes the subject of another speech must precede it. Otherwise, how would it be possible to reflect on it? (Discussion of prophecy constitutes a different realm.)

From this point of view, linguistics is primarily about this temporal order. How are the syllables ordered? How are the words ordered? And how are the sentences ordered? These are the questions linguistics deals with. Finally, on the macro level, how are the elements of a narrative ordered? This is the question narratology deals with. From morphology to syntax and narratology, the underlying preoccupation of these disciplines is to determine the sequential structure of speech on the diachronic axis, on different levels of analysis. For instance, syntax tells us the order of words in time because when we speak their occurrence in time cannot be random or disorderly. Each element of a sentence teaches us syntax and has a fixed place in time that must be respected by the speakers (Hill, Fillmore, Labov).

The observation and questions highlighted above on discursive action apply to a great extent to social actions as well. The temporal structure of social relations poses constraints on social actors. Yet social actors are not for the most part aware of temporal constraints. (This unawareness may be true for scholars who study social behavior as well.) Even if everything else is ripe, if temporal constraints exist, social action is inhibited. For instance, we can do only one thing, or a limited number of compatible things, at a time. Our actions must be put coherently in a sequential order. Also, we have to be careful in our actions about the temporal order required by nature, custom, and morality. Otherwise, our actions are bound to fail. Therefore, social analysis must take into account the temporal constraints that social actors face in their relations.

Sociologists increasingly realize the necessity of coming to terms with temporal constraints, which have been completely ignored by linear causal models. White's work on chains of opportunity (1970) first highlighted temporal constraints, using the vacancy chain model. Abbott (1990, 2001a, 2001b) draws a contrast between causal and narrative approaches in sociology. His efforts have been focused on developing methods that can count for diachronic structures in social process (see also Abbott 1984; Abbott 1988; Abbott and Hrycak 1990; Abbott and Hrycak 1992a; Abbott and Hrycak 1992b; Abbott 1995). Unlike Saussure, who advocated simultaneous usage of diachronic and synchronic methods, Abbott concentrates on a "narrative" approach to social process as an alternative to the prevailing causal approach.

In this connection, one should also consider the case of historical sociology. One might expect that historical sociology would employ diachronic methods. Nevertheless, scholars who specialize in historical sociology do not make use of the distinction between synchronic and diachronic methods. The common practice today in historical sociology is to conflate diachronic process with synchronic laws, on the model of the natural sciences, with the purpose of discovering generally applicable principles. From this perspective, time finds its way into the analyses only as a variable in the causal process.

In sum, we are allowed to undertake synchronic analysis only if we are aware of what we have to sacrifice in the process. Synchronic analysis suppresses time, with the purpose of facilitating certain types of analyses; yet both the researchers and the audience need to be informed about the partial understanding they can gain through such analyses. My emphasis on temporal order should by no means be seen as a reification of time. The best strategy, as I have thus far suggested for the future, is to close the gap between the synchronic and diachronic perspectives on social and discursive structures.

Closing the Loop Back to Synchronic Structures

In the foregoing analysis, I have brought the role of long-ignored diachronic (cross-temporal) networks to the fore along with synchronic (cross-sectional) networks. I have used both concepts simultaneously and have continuously alternated from one to the other according to the analysis.

It is also possible to bring my findings from the analysis of time-stratified organizations to bear on other types of hierarchical social organizations in general. This is because, as I have emphasized many times, social stratification does not derive only from time but also from myriad social and cultural factors. It is quite plausible, then, to understand the concept of the layer, which I have employed in this study, as separating social strata differentiated by virtue of time from strata differentiated by virtue of other factors. Hence, within the context of cross-sectional networks, it became possible to discern "interlayer brokerage" while exploring the vertical ties between layers of superiors and subordinates.

My findings on the macro and micro levels from the analysis of the network of huffaz suggest that social authority comes from extensive external ties. Paradoxically, prominent groups are not so closely connected to each other but are instead densely connected to other groups. Consequently, the power of a group springs from the openness of its network but not from the network's closure. Members of prominent groups are not closely knit among themselves alone; rather, they are extremely open to the outside world. In other words, the social power of individual or corporate social actors comes from outward connections but not from inward connections. Therefore, the extent to which an individual or a group is connected to outside groups determines the level of social prominence that individual or group enjoys. Figure 9.1, which reflects data

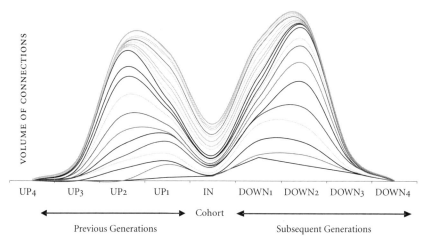

VOLUME OF CONNECTIONS

UP4   UP3   UP2   UP1   IN   DOWN1   DOWN2   DOWN3   DOWN4

◄──────────────────────────────► Cohort ◄──────────────────────────────►

Previous Generations   Subsequent Generations

SPAN OF GENERATIONS

FIG. 9.1. Wave Shape of the Synchronic and Diachronic Structure of Authority Formation. Each line represents a layer. A color version of this figure may be viewed at www.sup.org/senturk.

from 26 layers, clearly summarizes this striking phenomenon; the pattern of the synchronic and diachronic relations reflects the form of a wave.

The opportunities and constraints offered by network closure and openness have been a focus of attention for sociologists. Coleman draws our attention to the opportunities offered by network closure (Coleman 1990; Coleman 1994), whereas Burt stresses openness and claims that "competitive advantage is a matter of access to holes" between networks (Burt 1995). Coleman argues that network closure is a main source of social capital, which he defines as "a resource for action," such as obligations and expectations, information channels, and social norms (Coleman 1994, S95). For him, network closure facilitates two forms of social capital: obligations-expectations and norms. Coleman argues that without network closure the diamond market in New York City could not function so easily, because the trust and norms produced by network closure would be lacking (Coleman 1994; see also Coleman 1990, 318–20).[11]

Unlike Coleman, who focuses on the internal structure of the group in the creation of social capital, Burt focuses on the network environment. For Burt, the internal structure of the network is determined through relations to the network environment in which social actors as well as their network are embedded. He writes:

To explain variation in competitive success, I look beyond the competitors themselves to the circumstances of the relations for which they compete. The terrain on
which competition plays out lies beyond the competitors themselves. It lies in their
efforts to negotiate relations with other players. When those relations are positioned
in the social structure such that there is little room to negotiate, the margin between
success and failure is slim. The social structure of competition is about the negotia-
bility of the relationships on which competitors survive [Burt 1995, 5].

Burt argues that the internal stratification of a group and the results of internal competition are contingent upon relations between networks rather
than on the internal dynamics of the network under investigation. Success
depends on eliminating redundant ties to people with similar resources and
on exploiting holes between networks.[12] In the following excerpt, Burt elucidates the opportunities offered by connections to outside groups to which access is limited:

Network benefits are enhanced in several ways. There is a higher volume of benefits,
because more contacts are included in the network. Beyond volume, diversity en-
hances the quality of benefits. Nonredundant contacts ensure exposure to diverse
sources of information. Each cluster of contacts is an independent source of information. One cluster, no matter how numerous its members, is only one source of information, because people connected to one another tend to know about the same
things at the same time. The information screen provided by multiple clusters of
contacts is broader, providing better assurance that you, the player, will be informed
of opportunities and impending disasters. Further, because nonredundant contacts
are only linked through the central player, you are assured of being the first to see
new opportunities created by needs in one group that could be served by skills in another group. You become the person who first brings people together, which gives
you the opportunity to coordinate their activities. These benefits are compounded by
the fact of having a network contact to other people, thus easing your task of expanding the network to best serve your interests [Burt 1995, 23].

The contrast between the degree of openness and closure of the network can
also shed light on another aspect of an intellectual community. More concretely, it might help us understand the rise of scholasticism and dogmatism.
An intellectual network that is wide open horizontally/synchronically (to other
coexisting networks) and vertically/diachronically (to the networks of previous
and succeeding generations) can hardly fall prey to scholasticism and dogmatism. In contrast, if an intellectual network is closed to horizontal and vertical
relations, it may easily be led into dogmatism.[13]

Furthermore, these groups might be differentiated from each other by virtue of time or other social and cultural reasons. In this study, I have focused on interrelations among groups that are differentiated from each other, and stratified, by virtue of being located in different time periods, which directly bears upon network configuration and patterns of talk within and between them.

I have demonstrated how synchronic network analysis could also be applied to diachronic structures. Here, I will close the loop by tying the argument back in to synchronic network analysis because I believe my findings concerning diachronic networks also bear upon synchronic network structures derived from cross-sectional data. According to my findings, a layer of prominent scholars is thinly connected to itself while thickly connected to past and future layers of prominent scholars. This particular network configuration survives the test of time, since we have observed it in the hadith transmission network among prominent scholars over almost a millennium, ranging from the seventh to the sixteenth centuries and covering a wide terrain, from the steppes of central Asia to the gardens of Spain.

Yet this structure is not one that was envisaged by the scholars who are embedded in it; it is an unintended outcome of an implicit discursive process. Namely, it is metalanguage that inadvertently, and out of sight, shapes the configuration of networks of narrative. The constant effort of social actors to reduce the levels of reported speech, by trying to report speech from the person closest to the original source, is what configured this social network, though this happened without anyone's knowledge or intention. The effect of attention to levels of reported speech is to reduce inward connections and increase outward connections, thereby producing interlayer, or interstratum, brokerage. The former, reducing the levels of reported speech via interlayer brokerage, is applicable to cross-temporal networks; and the latter, reducing the levels of reported speech via interstratum brokerage, is applicable to cross-sectional networks. A circular causality is at work here between literary and social processes that simultaneously and continuously interact with each other.

In a social organization, generally speaking, authority can be perceived as an outcome of vertical ties to social actors above and below in the hierarchy, whether it is a hierarchy created by time or by another factor. Therefore, in overall social and literary processes, in-layer connections play an insignificant role, if they play one at all, by comparison with interlayer connections. In contrast to vertical ties, horizontal connections to peers have either a negative or an insignificant impact on authority formation. On the macro level, aggregate/corporate social actors gain prominence as a cluster not by staying close only to each other but by giving priority to external network connections. Consequently, prominent actors in a social organization will be thinly connected to their own layer but thickly connected to layers above and below.

Is Social Organization Also a Discourse Network?

This book has reconstructed and analyzed a social network through time as a discourse network in which information flowed through speech and reflexive speech, with authorities emerging from the reciprocal interaction of discursive and social relations. The same approach, I believe, is applicable to all social organizations in general, be they historical or contemporary (Kittler 1990). Yet the methods I have used here may need to be modified so as to allow for such replication within the context of particular social organizations under investigation. It will be less challenging to apply this approach to a network that develops around a particular narrative, such as science, with its numerous branches, or religion, or a communication network. However, application of this approach to other social organizations, such as markets, states, families, gangs, sports teams, and the like, may be more challenging. The difficulty comes from the fact that the impact of discourse is equally sweeping and elusive.

Certain features of the data used here favor the reconstruction of a social network as a discourse network, and these features may not exist in other cases. In the preceding discussions, I have analyzed the structure of a discourse network in which the currency was the pieces of narrative transmitted from one generation to another. The rather formalized protocols of narration, and the particular emphasis on recording the network connections of teachers and students in the culture of hadith scholars, made it feasible for me to reconstruct and analyze this monumental social network as a discourse network. Replication of this analysis in other contexts will also require collecting data on both social and discursive relations.

As a further step, there needs to be an organic connection between data collected on the social relations and data connected on the discursive relations in a social organization. I have used metalanguage as a bridge between discourse and social network. Metalinguistic patterns, as demonstrated above, provide helpful tools for showing the connection between network and discourse. If researchers concentrate only on the use of object language, which is what social actors say about the things around themselves, it will be difficult to reveal social connections. However, if researchers concentrate on metalanguage, the way social actors talk about other talk, especially talk by others, it will be easier to capture and analyze the intertwining patterns in discursive and social relations.

Discourse networks are where the discursive action is. Is it possible to imagine a social organization without speech? If not, then we need to revise the Crusoe- or Adam-like image of the "speechless" social actor that we received from classical social theory (see chapter 3). For this purpose, the gap between social and literary structuralism needs to be bridged, and long-uncoupled social and discursive patterns need to be recoupled. Neither social scientists nor scholars in the humanities can deny any longer the synergy between the discursive and social patterns that jointly constitute social structure.

I have thus far unearthed the latent social and discursive mechanisms that produce and reproduce social inequality in a discourse community. A diminutive segment of the social group, because of its position in the social network, controls the movement of narrative. Yet, paradoxically, those who constitute this minute group avoid each other. This is not only because they are competitors but also, and more important, because they are engaged in a constant attempt to reduce the levels of reported speech and eliminate discourse mediators. Regardless of the accuracy of the citation, peers try to take a narrative from the same source their competitors take it from rather than taking it from their friends, thereby remaining independent of their competitors and reducing the levels of reported speech. Eliminating discourse mediators empowers narrators and reduces the levels of reported speech. Therefore, the narrator with the fewest levels of reported speech stands out among his competitors in the narrative social structure. He gains social status and centrality in the network and becomes the most sought-after person in the discourse network. The same is true for his students, or for the ones who take narrative from him, because one's patron determines one's clients. If one obtains a socially authoritative narrative—which is determined for the most part by closeness to the original teller(s)—one will be the most sought-after narrator in the group.

In conclusion, bringing the argument home, we can say that all of us are narrators. Given the reflexivity of our language, we cannot know how aware we are of the consequences that different narratives may have for our social status. Yet we all try to reduce the levels of reported speech. All the while, however, our social network takes shape without our perceiving it. On the one hand, our position in the social structure configures the way we talk, and, on the other hand, the way we talk reconfigures our social position in the structure, and these two factors foster each other.

The ceaseless synergy between action and signification is what makes our day-to-day social life possible. White (1995a, 1995b), who calls action "network" and signification "domain," argues that the structuralist approach is better equipped to investigate their interrelations without reducing one to the other. I have substantiated this claim empirically through an analysis of the interaction, on the macro and micro levels, between discursive action and social action as they related to authority formation in the hadith transmission network of the Prophet Muhammad.

Notes

Chapter 1

1. James Robson, "Hadith," in *The Encyclopedia of Islam*. See also Leonard Librande, *The Encyclopedia of Religion*, vol. 6, 143–51; Sahair El Calamawy, "Narrative Elements in *Hadith* Literature." For the most important classical source, see Ibn Salah, *al-Muqaddimah*. See also Robson's works with Arabic text and English translations (see Bibliography for a list of Robson's works on hadith and its transmission network from a historical perspective). For a bibliographical work on hadith studies in European languages, see Anees and Athar, *Guide to Sira and Hadith Literature in Western Languages*.

2. "The Arabic word *hadith* has the primary connotation of 'new,' being used as an antonym to *qadim,* 'old.' From this derived the use of the word for an item of news, a tale, a story or a report—be it historical or legendary, true or false, moral or scandalous, relating to the present or to the past. The word was employed in this sense by the pre-Islamic poets, and by the Qur'an and the Prophet. Storytellers, also, were called *huddath:* the purveyors of hadith. . . . Since the lifetime of the Prophet himself the Muslims called reports which spoke of his actions and sayings 'the best *hadith*' and, in due course, the word became increasingly confined to such reports" (Muhammad Zubayr Siddiqi, *Hadith Literature,* 1).

3. I use the term *disjointed* to indicate that ahadith are not necessarily organized in any temporal sequence. For the disjointed narrative and its implications, see Umberto Eco, *Six Walks in the Fictional Woods,* 127–28. I explore this issue further in chap. 2.

4. *Muhaddith* (pl. *muhaddithun*) is a generic name for the scholars of hadith. A *hafiz* (pl. *huffaz*), by contrast, is a highly prominent muhaddith whose authority is acknowledged by the overwhelming majority of his colleagues and by the Muslim public in general (see Subhi es-Salih, *Hadis Ilimleri ve Istilahlari,* 58–63). Since no one in Islamic scholarship was seen as immune to criticism, these titles have been contested (see, for

example, the biographical record of al-Tabarani, chap. 4 of this volume). For the concept of the hafiz, loosely translated here as "prominent narrator," see Abu Abdullah Shamsuddin Muhammad al-Dhahabi, *al-Muqizah fi 'Ilm Mustalah al-Hadith* [The Warner on the Science of Hadith](1991a, 67–68).

5. Because this work is primarily intended for nonspecialists in Arabic who are unfamiliar, for the most part, with the Arabic phonetic and transliteration system, I decided against using diacritical marks in the English spellings of Arabic words unless confusion would be likely to arise from the absence of such marks. I have also chosen not to italicize, after first use, a number of Arabic words (including *hafiz* and *huffaz*) because they occur so frequently in the text.

6. Hijrah dates are usually denoted by BH and AH, an era that begins with the flight of the Prophet from Mecca to Medina in 622 CE. Unless otherwise indicated, dates reported in this study are given according to the CE system.

7. For a review of studies on the *ulama,* see R. Stephen Humphreys, *Islamic History: A Framework for Inquiry,* 187–208.

8. For a list of scholars known to be hafiz after Suyuti, the last such figure in this study, see Abdulhay ibn Abdilkabir al-Kattânî, *Fahras al-Fahâris wa Mu'jam al-Ma'âjim wa al-Mashyahâh wa al-Muselselât,* 78–79. I thank my colleague Stephan Reichmuth, Ruhr University, Germany, for drawing my attention to this source.

9. Bulliet, *Islam: The View from the Edge,* 20: "But rare hadith and high isnads gradually became less important as, over a three-hundred-year period, the canonical collections of sound hadith became increasingly authoritative, and hadith classes came to be devoted primarily to teaching them and a few other written texts. Orality in hadith teaching persisted, but by the sixteenth century, the best isnads were considered those that stretched back to the author of a book or to a particularly famous teacher, rather than to an individual reciter of unanthologized hadith. . . . Most hadith deemed by the muhaddithun to be weak died away, and with them dwindled the prominence as teachers of individual reciters with personal isnads going back to the Prophet. After all, if the only worthwhile hadith were those in the books, even including those hadith collections that continued to be consulted occasionally in addition to the six canonical works, what place remained for the scholar who had collected hadith a few at a time on his own?"

10. The following is a striking example: "When the Baal Shem had a difficult task before him, he would go to a certain place in the woods, light a fire and meditate in prayer—and what he had set out to perform was done. When a generation later the 'Maggid' of Meseritz was faced with the same task he would go to the same place in the woods and say: We can no longer light the fire, but we can still speak the prayers—and what he wanted done became reality. Again a generation later Rabbi Moshe Leib of Sassov had to perform this task. And he too went into the woods and said: We can no longer light a fire, nor do we know the secret meditations belonging to the prayer, but we

do know the place in the woods to which it all belongs—and that must be sufficient; and sufficient it was. But when another generation had passed and Rabbi Israel of Rishin was called upon to perform the task, he sat down on his golden chair in his castle and said: We cannot light the fire, we cannot speak the prayers, we do not know the place, but we can tell the story of how it was done. And the story which he told had the same effect as the actions of the other three" (Agnon and Scholem, *Major Trends in Jewish Mysticism*, 349–50).

Chapter 2

1. Commenting on the state of the Science of Hadith in his time, Ibn Khaldun writes: "At this time, traditions are no longer published, nor are the (publications of) traditions by former scholars corrected. Common (experience) attests to the fact that these numerous religious leaders, close to each other in time, were too capable and too firmly possessed of independent judgment to have neglected or omitted any tradition, so that it is impossible that some later scholar might discover one. (Therefore), at this time, one is concerned with correcting the principal written works, with fixing the accuracy of their transmission, and with establishing continuous chains of transmitters leading back to the authors, chains that are sound throughout. With very few exceptions, no attention has been paid to more than five works" (Ibn Khaldun 1967, 2:456).

2. The present approach is particularly interested in the constructive role of reported speech, the most important subsection of reflexive speech, which is defined as language use that re-presents its own structure and use, including everyday metalinguistic activities of reporting, characterizing, and commenting on speech (Lucy 1993, 1–2). Conversely, object language refers to objects, but not to speech. Daily language incorporates both forms, which serve different (meta)semantic and (meta)pragmatic purposes (Lucy 1993; Silverstein 1993; Morson and Emerson 1989, 123–71; Bakhtin 1981, 261–63; White 1995a).

3. See n. 6 to chap. 1 for an explanation of how dates are reported in this study.

4. This hadith was narrated through several chains, slightly differing in the phraseology of the text, with an increasing spread in "depth" and "breadth" (Ayni 1972, 16–35). It reflects the "disjointed" form of hadith genre, which gives the impression that a speech event is separated from its larger context. This complete text is intentionally broken, leaving unaddressed the question of what happened before and after. If we want to reconstruct the sequential order of the events in the story as a whole, we will need to piece together these fragments. These features will be further elaborated later in the discussion.

5. For instance, the term *mu'an'an,* used in connection with ahadith, denotes that in the *isnad* narrators reported a hadith from each other, using the preposition *'an,* which literally means "from." An example would be "From X that he said . . . ." Here, the way

the speech was heard is not specified. This ambiguity may cause ambivalence in the listener toward the hadith reported. Another type is *mu'en'en,* in which case the hadith is reported as "haddethana fulan enne fulan qal" ("such person told me that verily such person said"). The word *enne* (verily) indicates that the connection is stronger.

6.   Here are three examples of ahadith with a large network spread, and more than ten narrators in each generation. The prime example used by hadith scholars is "Whoever lies about me should get ready for his seat in Hellfire." Another is "Water is from water." The last is "The Muslim is the one from whose hand and tongue others are safe." According to the transmission chain, the phraseology may change, and the hadith may be embedded in a brief story contextualizing the text.

7.   Identity came from style. Although the identity "hadith narrator" (*muhaddith*) runs constant, the community of hadith narrators was further differentiated by other identities, depending on narrators' positions in their networks: Companion versus Successor; hafiz versus shaykh; reliable versus unreliable, and so on. Furthermore, multiple identities arising out of membership in more than one network were not unusual: jurist and *muhaddith, muhaddith* and reciter (*qari*), or *muhaddith* and sufi.

8.   "Society is a spectacle he [Barthes] can help explain, by revealing to us some of the mechanisms by which it obscures its artificiality" (Sturrock 1979, 61).

9.   "We shall therefore star the text, separating, in the manner of a minor earthquake, the blocks of signification of which reading grasps only the smooth surface, imperceptibly soldered by the movement of sentences, the flowing discourse of narration, the 'naturalness' of ordinary language" (Barthes 1974, 13). See also White (1987, 35–36); Sturrock (1979, 52–80).

10.   In fact, even in our secondary oral culture, all daily narrative is broken; we have to break it to be able to carry on our daily activities.

11.   Such an example is provided by Reynolds and Wilson (1968, 190): stemmatics produce transmission networks similar to *isnad,* but with a rather limited spread.

12.   See Hart (1992, 632), who cites Ong and Jameson on the usage and role of narrative prior to the arrival of written culture among the Greeks "as members of an essentially oral culture" who used, in the words of Ong (1982, 140), "stories of human action to store, organize, and communicate much of what they [knew]," with, Hart continues, "a way to understand the past and set moral boundaries for future behavior. Narrative in Greece has long been," she says, citing Jameson (1981), "a socially symbolic act," one that reaches, Hart says, "beyond description and into the realm of signification of experience."

13.   The number of biographies of Companions included in the classical works varies. In their biographical dictionaries exclusively dedicated to the Companions, Qurtubi (463/107 AH) included 3,500; Ibn al-Athir (630 AH/1233 CE), 8,000; and Ibn Hajar (852/1448 AH), 12,279. The total number of Companions is reported by conflicting sources to be between 40,000 and 120,000.

14. Sultan Nuruddin Mahmud (d. 569 AH) opened the first *dar al-hadith* (college of hadith) in Damascus and appointed the celebrated Ibn al-'Asakir as its dean. It was followed by al-Kamiliyya College in Cairo in 622 AH, and by Ashrafiyya College in 626 AH and Urwiyya College in 620 AH, both in Damascus. These early institutions provided models for later hadith colleges, which spread quickly around the Islamic world (Okic 1959, 105–7; Makdisi 1981).

15. The impact of distrust of writing and, around the same time, the gradual transition from oral to written narrative can be observed elsewhere in the world as well. According to Kaufer and Carley (1993, 259–60), "the English courts admitted written documents as admissible evidence only when used to corroborate oral oaths and testimonies. It was only since the 12th century that medieval England gradually—over a 200-year period—began to build the infrastructure required to entrust their societal transactions to written records," they report, citing Clanchy (1978). They continue, "A similar ebb and flow of trust and suspicion is evident in the passing of electronic communications" (Kaufer and Carley 1993, 260). See also Ong (1982).

16. This view is in line with the argument that the contribution of non-Arab scholars to the development of Islamic sciences had been greater than that of Arab scholars (Ibn Khaldun 1967, 3:311–15).

17. This structural coherence is distinct from the semantic and text-bound "sense-based coherence" (Silverstein 1993, 45) that actors who are embedded in social structures need in order to interact meaningfully in the context.

18. Other notable treatises by subsequent generations include *Al-Iqtirah* of Ibn Daqiq al-'Iyd (d. 702); *Tanqih al-Anzar* of Muhammad bin Ibrahim al-Wazir (d. 840), the subject of a commentary by al-Amir al-San'ani (d. 1182); *Nukhbah al-Fikr* of Ibn Hajar al-'Asqalani, again the subject of several commentaries, including one by the author himself, one by his son Muhammad, and those of 'Ali al-Qari (d. 1014), 'Abd al-Ra'uf al-Munawi (d. 1031), and Muhammad bin 'Abd al-Hadi al-Sindi (d. 1138) (among those who rephrased the *Nukhbah* in poetic form are al-Tufi [d. 893] and al-Amir al-San'ani); *Al-fiyyah al-Hadith* of al-Suyuti, the most comprehensive poetic work in the field; *Al-Manzumah* of al-Baiquni, which was expanded upon by, among others, al-Zurqani (d. 1122) and Nawab Siddiq Hasan Khan (d. 1307); *Qawa'id al-Tahdith* of Jamal al-Din al-Qasimi (d. 1332); and *Tawjih al-Nazar* of Tahir al-Jaza'iri (d. 1338), a summary of al-Hakim's *Ma'rifah*.

19. These four schools, which outlived several others, were named after their founders: Abu Hanifa (81–150 AH/700–767 CE, Iraq); Malik (90–179 AH/710–795 CE, Medina); Shafii (150–204 AH/767–820 CE, Egypt); and Ahmad ibn Hanbal (164–241 AH/780–855 CE, Baghdad). For an early statement by Shafii, see *al-Shafii's Risala: Treatise on the Foundations of Islamic Jurisprudence,* trans. Majid Khadduri (Cambridge: Islamic Texts Society, 1996).

20. For this debate on the methodology of law, see Şaban (1990, 76). For further de-

tails on the role of network structure in legal reasoning, see Ünal (1994), Koçkuzu (1988), Polat (1985), and al-'Ala'i (1978).

21.   Berman's work itself is a legal metanarrative: "This book tells the following story: that once there was a civilization called 'Western'; that it developed distinctive 'legal' institutions, values, and concepts; that these Western legal institutions, values, and concepts were *consciously transmitted from generation to generation over centuries, and thus came to constitute a 'tradition'* (Berman 1983, 1; emphasis added).

22.   For a detailed discussion of the meaning of layer (*tabaqa*) and the discipline entirely dedicated to it, see As'ad Salim Taym (1978).

23.   The complete title is as follows: *al-Hidaya wa al-Irshad fi Marifah Ahl al-Thiqah wa al-Sadad alladhina Akhraja lahum al-Bukhari fir Jamiih li al-Imam Abi Nasr Ahmad bin Muhammad b. Al-Husayn al-Bukhari al-Kalabazi (363–98 AH).*

24.   We see that not everyone in the network of Abdurrahman was a hafiz. The way to figure this out is to check for all figures, whether they are coded in biographical dictionaries as hafiz or not. It should also be noted that not all teachers and students are mentioned in the biographical entry. In order to avoid repetition, Dhahabi reports ties either in the entry of teachers or in the entry of students. Thus, without a complete survey of the relevant layers in the book, one can never be sure how many students and teachers a hafiz had. Such a survey shows that Abdurrahman had another hafiz teacher, al-Qasim al-Mukhaymira from layer 4 (no. 107), and a hafiz student from layer 7, Abdullah b. Yusuf (no. 408).

25.   While Abdurrahman belonged to layer 5, all his teachers came from layer 4. Among his students, three came from layer 6, two from layer 7. He avoided having ties to narrators from his own layer—an indication of strategic investment in ties and intergenerational brokerage.

26.   Al-Sakhawi wrote (1986b, 19): "As for the hadith scholar [*al-muhaddith*], he is the one who (1) knows the masters of hadith in his homeland as well as other lands; (2) has a precise knowledge of their dates and places of birth and death, their ranking in the sciences, and the various types of narratives they have in their possession; (3) differentiates those with longer chains of transmission from those with shorter ones; (4) is able to spot the hadith masters [*al-huffâz*] in the layers and the chains; (5) records them in writing; (6) recognizes the handwriting of the masters even if the same person's handwriting varies; (7) examines critically the narratives of the masters and extracts what he considers good from their narratives as well as from his own, keeping aware of such qualities of chains as *badal, muwâfaqât, musâwât,* and the like [types of sound grades]; (8) keeps a record of the names of his auditors even if their number is one thousand; (9) is an expert in the names of narrators, particularly those apt to be confused with one another, and obtains this discernment from the leaders in the discipline; (10) knows with precision the unusual words or names one comes across in the texts of hadith, or at least most

of them, to avoid misspellings; (11) knows enough Arabic grammar to protect himself from language mistakes in most cases; (12) masters the terminology of experts in such a way as is sufficient for teaching and explanation; and (13) keeps the proper terminology with respect to this and other disciplines. . . . The *muhaddith* is the one who knows the chains, their defects, the names of the narrators, the short and long chains, and, in addition, has memorized an abundant number of the hadith texts [as distinct from the chains] and heard [directly from a teacher] the Six Books, the Musnad of Imam Ahmad ibn Hanbal, the Sunan of al-Bayhaqi, the Mu'jam of al-Tabarani, and at least a thousand more monographs on hadith. After he has heard what we have mentioned, and written on all the layers of the narrators, and traveled far and wide to see the masters, and lectured about hadith defects, dates of birth and death, and chains of transmission—at that time he attains to the beginning level of hadith narrators."

27. Al-Sakhawi (1986b, 14–17) defines it as follows: "*Shaykh al-Islam,* as inferred from its use as a term among the authorities, is a title attributed to that follower of the book of Allah Most High and the example of His messenger, who possesses the knowledge of the principles of the science [of religion], has plunged deep into the different views of the scholars, has become able to extract the legal evidences from the texts, and has understood the rational and the transmitted proofs at a satisfactory level." Sakhawi traces the evolution of the concept and lists the very few scholars who have been given this title.

28. For a detailed discussion of the titles of hadith scholars, see Sa'd Fahmi Ahmad Bilal (1996). See also al-Sakhawi (1986b).

29. "Islamic law recognizes the physical person alone as endowed with legal personality" (Makdisi 1981, 224) but does not recognize corporate actors as legal persons. Among the prerequisites for a narrator, Ibn Hajar wrote, was "taking knowledge from the mouths of individuals but not from pages" (quoted in al-Dhahabi 1991a, 68). "When he [the teacher] granted the license to the candidate he did so in his own name, acting as an individual, not as part of a group of master-juristconsults acting as a faculty, for there was no faculty" (Makdisi 1981, 274), even though the scholars might be carrying on their teaching activities in a university or college, known as a *madrasa.*

30. This figure is close to the one that Bulliet computed earlier, on the basis of a smaller sample from Nishapur: "In the 47 ascertainable cases, the average age at death was 84.3 years with a standard deviation of 8.9" (Bulliet 1983, 111).

31. For instance, from layer 4 there are 21 ties to layer 4, 130 ties to layer 3, and 115 ties to layer 2, while from layer 5 there are 59 ties to layer 5, 277 ties to layer 4, and 109 ties to layer 3. These numbers indicate the ties to other prominent narrators alone.

32. Interestingly, though, even when the written mode gained the upper hand, the lexica of narrators remained those of oral culture because dictation or reading was usually involved in the transmission of the manuscript. Although there was a text involved

in the transmission, narrators still said, when they reported the transmission, "I was told by 'A,'" which led Sezgin (1956), a philologist of Arabic, to assume, quite naturally, that the transmission had always been oral, until he discovered that the protocol of oral hadith transmission and reporting speech had maintained its sway even in the transmission of manuscripts.

33. Al-Dhahabi (1991a, 53–55) provides an extended list of these utterances (*alfaz al-ada'*) corresponding to the various modes of transmission between layers who came after the generation of the Companions, apparently without noticing the striking distinction between utterances used by eyewitness narrators and those used by later generations.

Chapter 3

1. Schotter's work does not clearly reflect his stand. On the one hand, he argues for "discursive constructionism," but on the other hand he conflates this perspective with conventional social constructionism. These two stands, however, are founded on different perspectives on language. The "discursive constructionism" of Schotter is, of course, social, yet it is more precise in its focus on the mutual relationship between language and social organization because of its stress on the particular ways the two mutually shape each other.

2. William Hanks's work *Referential Practice* clearly reflects the referential approach to language.

3. "A method for obtaining this description is discussed in the following paragraphs. Starting from Barthes's assumption that all fabulas are based upon one model, we can begin to search for a model that is so abstract that it may be considered universal—until, that is, the model in question is either rejected or improved. This model is then 'laid upon' the text that is being investigated; in other words, we examine the way in which the concrete events can be placed in the basis model. The purpose of this method is not to force the text into a general model and then conclude that the text is indeed narrative. Such a procedure could at best be useful for testing doubtful cases when trying to specify the corpus. Rather, a confrontation between a concrete fabula and a general model allows the description of the structure of the fabula of the text in question to be stated more precisely *with regard to* the basis model by which the specific structure is placed in relief and made visible. A 'perfect fit' as well as any deviations from the basis model can influence the meaning of the text" (Bal 1985, 18–19).

4. "In the sprit of a more authentic dialectical tradition, Marxism is here conceived as that 'untranscendable horizon' that subsumes such apparently antagonistic or incommensurable critical operations, assigning them an undoubted sectoral validity within itself, and thus at once canceling and preserving them" (Jameson 1981, 10). Applying this perspective to structuralism, Jameson suggests that there are three, rather than two,

terms to structural analysis. The "absent variable," as he calls it, is history (145–48).

5. "But what is language [*langue*]? It is not to be confused with human speech [*langage*], of which it is only a definite part, though certainly an essential one. It is both a social product of the faculty of speech and a collection of necessary conventions that have been adopted by a social body to permit individuals to exercise that faculty. Taken as a whole, speech is many-sided and heterogeneous; straddling several areas simultaneously—physical, physiological, and psychological—it belongs to the individual and to society; we cannot put it into any category of human fact, for we cannot discover its unity" (Saussure 1994, 9).

6. For Barthes, what is commonly called "society" is an artificial spectacle. However, its artificiality is obscured by some mechanisms that make it look natural. The duty of the literary critic is to unveil at least some of these mechanisms to help us explain this artificial spectacle, which we may tend to see as a natural phenomenon or take for granted (Sturrock 1979, 61).

7. See how Barthes tries to challenge the naturalness of ordinary language (Barthes 1974, 13).

8. The term *semiology* (or *semiotics*) was originally suggested by the Swiss linguist Ferdinand de Saussure. The latter term, deriving from the American philosopher Charles Sanders Peirce, is now more generally accepted than *semiology*.

9. The embedding social organization, for White, must be perceived in its spatial (social and physical) and temporal (synchronic and diachronic) context. In the hadith transmission network, ages later, narrators—whose identities are formed and embedded in the context of the larger structure—are called to take sides as friends and foes to criticize and defend the identities of their predecessors. The ceaseless contention over identities gave rise to the flux of identities for narrators through time, even after their demise. In a clientelist structure, such as the *isnad* system, if the identity of one's patron is in jeopardy, so is one's own. By defending the identity of one's patrons, and their patrons ad infinitum, one defends one's own identity, which derives directly or indirectly from theirs.

Chapter 4

1. An increasing number of sociologists derive data from historical textual sources, with the purpose of reconstructing historical social networks, or networks through time (Burt 1975, 1983; Padgett and Ansell 1993; Bearman 1993; Tilly 1995; Abbott 1992a; White 1970; Zuckerman 1996). These efforts are crucial for the identification and analysis of cross-temporal social structures as well as for extending social network analysis to historical sociology, which offers an alternative perspective to the currently used paradigms (Skocpol). In addition to historical sociology per se, co-citation analysis and diffusion studies are also inherently historical.

2. For instance, Kettani (1994, 280–89, 298–312), in the Turkish edition updated by the translator, provides names and locations for 277 *mashyakhah*s and 72 *mu'jam*s in addition to 13 *mashyakhah*s and 28 *mu'jam*s listed in the earlier editions.

3. Edited and published by Abd al-Majid and al-Zayni (1986).

4. Suyuti writes in *Tabaqat al-Huffaz*: "I have a general diploma [*ijazah 'ammah*] from him. It is possible that I might even have a special diploma [*ijazah khassah*] because my father used to visit him very frequently, and took his place in his absence in the legal consultation [*hukm*]. Even if I could not get the opportunity to attend his lectures, to listen to his talks, and to take hadith verbally and directly [*akhz*] from him, I benefited greatly from his writings in the discipline and profited a lot from them. With his death, the door is closed and this endeavor has come to an end" (Suyuti 1984, 553). Ibn Hajar's goal in life was to achieve the level of authority Dhahabi achieved three generations earlier. Suyuti reports that Ibn Hajar drank water from the sacred Zamzam well in Mecca with the wish in his heart, believed to have been realized with the help of God, to reach the level of Dhahabi. Suyuti (1984, 552) reports this as follows: "The story has it that Ibn Hajar drank from the holy well of Zamzam in Mecca with the wish in his heart to reach the level of Dhahabi in the memorization of hadith. He reached that point and even superseded it." Suyuti, in turn, wished to reach the level of Ibn Hajar and drank the holy water of Zamzam with this wish. In his autobiography he wrote: "When I made my pilgrimage, I drank the water of Zamzam for several wishes. Among them were reaching the level of the master Siraj al-Din al-Bulqini in jurisprudence, and reaching the level of hafiz Ibn Hajar in hadith. I started issuing legal verdicts at the outset of the year seventy one [871 AH], and conducting hadith dictation at the beginning of the year seventy two [872 AH]" (Suyuti 1984, 8).

5. The data were originally collected and organized by Bulliet, who deserves my gratitude for letting me use them (Bulliet 1972, 1979, 1983).

6. One of the two books of Suyuti on the *mutawatir* hadith is published (N=112), the other is still in manuscript form in the Suleymaniye library in Istanbul. The work of the polyhistor Zabidi (1145–1205 AH/1832–1790 CE), famous linguist and lexicographer, is published (N=71).

7. The HADITHNET is designed to construct a multirelational database with its three interrelated components: the record of the narrator, the teacher-student connections, and the record of the narrative. The program aims to store not only the social connections between social actors but also the narratives from which the information about a particular connection is derived and the narrative that was transmitted through this connection.

8. The complete name is rarely used in regular writing and discourse. Instead, various shorter forms of the name are used. For instance, references to al-Tabarani in *Tadhkira* had the following forms: (1) Abu al-Qasim al-Tabarani (in records 648, 683,

684, 685, 688, 709, 710, 720, 729, 737, 741, 742, 745, 747, 752, 754, 760, 799, 976, 994); (2) al-Tabarani (in records 637, 650, 652, 674, 681, 690, 691, 693, 705, 712, 740, 773, 777, 787, 788, 789, 801, 819, 821, 943); (3) Sulayman al-Tabarani (in record 761); (4) Sulayman ibn Ahmad al-Tabarani (in record 682, 696).

9. The following sources have been consulted to complement the data from *Tadhkirah al-Huffaz*. (1) al-Dhahabi, *Siyar 'Alam al-Nubala*; (2) al-Dhahabi, *Tarikh al-Islam*; (3) al-Mizzi, *Tahzib al-Kamal fi Asma al-Rijal*; (4) al-Zirikli, *al-A'lam*; (5) al-Safadi, *al-Wafi bi al-Wafayat*; (6) Ibn al-Khallikan, *Wafayat al-A'yan wa Anba'i Ahl al-Zaman*; (7) Kahhalah, *Mu'jam al-Muallifin*; (8) al-Sam'ani, *al-Ansab*; (9) Ibn Hajar, *Lisan al-Mizan*; (10) Ibn Hajar, *Taqrib al-Tahzib*; (11) Ibn abi Hatim al-Razi, *Kitab al-Jarh wa al-Ta'dil*; (12) al-Bakri, *Mu'jam Musta'jam min Asma al-Bilad wa al-Mawadi'*; (13) Ibn Sa'd, *al-Tabaqat al-Kubra*; (14) Ibn Manzur, *Mukhtasar Tarikh Dimashq*; (15) al-Kattani, *al-Risalah al-Mustatrafah li Bayan Mashur Kutub al-Sunnah al-Musharrafah*; (16) Ibn al-Faradi, *Tarikh Ulama' al-Andalus*; (17) al-Humaydi, *Jayzat al-Muqtabis*; (18) al-Dabbi, *Bughyat al-Multamis*; (19) Ibn Bashkuwal, *al-Silah*; and (20) Ibn Hibban, *Kitab al-Thiqat*. This is far from a comprehensive list; there are many other sources that have been occasionally consulted during the study.

Chapter 5

1. This can be alternatively expressed as follows: $mr_n = L_n + (L_n + 4) + (L_n - 4)$

2. The sociomatrix needs to be broken down to 26 network zones with overlapping membership, each to be analyzed separately. The majority of current social network analysis software is not designed for such a task.

3. In the hadith transmission network, only the Prophet exhausted all the network possibilities because he was, by definition, connected to everyone in his reach. He had personal connections to all of layer 1, his Companions, who in turn were not as densely connected to each other.

4. This can be modeled as follows:

$$LP = \frac{t}{T}$$

where *LP* stands for local prominence, *t* stands for the actual ties of a social actor, and *T* stands for the maximum possible ties of a social actor or the number of connections for the most prominent scholar.

5. The following model reflects this approach:

$$LP_s = \frac{t_t}{T_t}$$

where LP_s stands for local prominence of a student, t_t stands for the total number of actual teacher ties, and T_t stands for the total number of possible teacher ties which is equal to the number of teacher ties for the most prominent student in the layer.

$$LP_t = \frac{t_s}{T_s}$$

where LP_t is local prominence of a teacher, t_s is the total number of actual student ties, and T_s is the total number of possible student ties or the number of student ties for the most prominent teacher.

6. This number is not representative of the portion of in-layer ties within the entire network. In the entire network, there are only 440 in-layer teacher or student connections out of 6,856 ties. The total number of in-layer connections in the entire network is 880 out of 13,712 ties.

7. This reminds us of the famous social network analysis regarding "six degrees of separation" or the phenomenon of a "small world."

8. Since it is a relative measure, the GTP (geodesic distance between teacher and the center/Prophet) value ranges between 0 and 1.

$$GTP = \left(1 + \frac{1}{GD}\right) * \underbrace{\left(1 + \frac{nl}{Nl}\right)}_{0 \leq layervalue \leq 1}$$

where GTP stands for value for geodesic distance between teacher and the Prophet, GD for the geodesic distance or the number of nodes in the shortest chain of a scholar to the Prophet, nl stands for the layer number of the scholar, and Nl stands for the total number of layers.

9. The following model is intended to reflect the role of the network gap bridged by a tie (GTP) on social prominence by taking into account the geodesic values of each tie in the network of scholars:

$$ALP_d = \frac{t}{T} * GTP$$

where ALP_p stands for adjusted local prominence from proximity, t stands for total number of actual ties, T stands for total number of possible ties, and GTP stands for the geodesic value of the distance between teacher and the Prophet.

10. The following model reflects this approach:

$$ALP_d = \frac{t}{T} * gv$$

where ALP_d stands for the adjusted local prominence from distance, t for the number of ties between ego (scholar under consideration) and alter (teacher or student), T for the number of total possible connections that ego can make to scholars of that layer (as teacher and student), and gv for the generation distance value of alter (teacher or student). The variable gv is obtained by taking into account the gap that a teacher tie helps to bridge.

$$ALP_d = \frac{\sum t *g\,v}{\sum T *g\,v}$$

where ALP_d stands for the adjusted local prominence from distance, t for the number of ties between ego (scholar under consideration) and alter (teacher or student), T for the number of total possible connections that ego can make to scholars of that layer (as teacher and student).

Chapter 6

1. For an earlier application of time series analysis in social networks research, see Burt (1975).

2. Al-Dulabi (d. 310) narrated it in *al-Kuna wa al-asma'*. Al-Haythami in Majma' al-zawa'id said: "Al-Tabarani in *al-Kabir* and Ahmad narrate it, but its chain contains Habib ibn 'Amr who, al-Daraqutni said, is unknown." However, Ibn Hibban declared him trustworthy and Ibn 'Adiy said: "There is no harm in him" ("la ba'sa bihi").

3. Because a point cannot be connected to itself, it must be subtracted from the total number of points.

4. Or, in a more detailed way, $D_{in} = c/n(n-1)$; $D_{up1} = c/n(n_{up1})$; $D_{up2} = c/n(n_{up2})$; $D_{up3} = c/n(n_{up3})$; $D_{down1} = c/n(n_{down1})$; $D_{down2} = c/n(n_{down2})$; $D_{down3} = c/n(n_{down3})$; $D_{down4} = c/n(n_{down4})$.

5. It may also be expressed as follows: $Scope_{in} = In$; $Scope_1 = Up_1 + Down_1$; $Scope_2 = Up_1 + Down_1$; $Scope_3 = Up_3 + Down_3$; $Scope_4 = Up_4 + Down_4$.

6. To clarify the reading of the variables, in addition to the definitions provided in the table, I will also provide a key for the way the labels of the series are made up. In the series labels, "t" stands for teacher connections; "s" stands for student connections; "in" stands for in-layer connections; "a" stands for average; "per" stands for percentage; "u" stands for "up," and the number that follows denotes the range of upward connections to the previous generations; and "d" stands for "down," and the number that follows denotes the range of downward connections to the subsequent generations.

7. The null hypothesis is as follows: $H_0: = 0$. Plainly put, in-layer connections have no effect on the number or distribution of student and teacher connections of a layer of prominent scholars. The alternative hypothesis is as follows: $H_1: 0$. In other words, in-layer connections play a significant role in the number or distribution of teacher and student connections of a layer of prominent scholars.

8. Throughout this study, the test results are based on a significance level of 0.05 unless otherwise indicated.

9. Although the total number of layers constituting the network I analyzed is 26, in the regression I used only 24 observations from the 2d to the 24th layer. The first and the

last two layers are not included in the analysis because of the missing data points as a result of the tapering network.

Chapter 7

1. The concept of intellectual used here derives from Max Weber (1978) and Collins (1998).

2. I am grateful to Prof. Collins for the discussions we had during the Networks, Languages and Identities workshop at the Center for the Social Sciences, Columbia University, 1996.

3. This continued until the arrival of Western ideas in the modern period, which instigated another period of dynamism in hadith studies, beyond the concern of this study. The scholars of hadith once again felt the call to defend hadith against denigration by the advocates of secular ideologies.

4. See Ibn Khaldun (1967, 2: 422–23) for a discussion of the knowledge of prophets. In the Qur'an, God orders the Prophet Muhammad to introduce himself as follows: "I am merely a human being like you, to whom it has been revealed that your God is one God; be straightforward with Him and ask Him for forgiveness" (Qur'an 41:5).

5. Abu al-Hasan al-'Amiri (1967). I was led to this quotation by Rosenthal (1975, 63).

6. As commonly known, the hadith transmission network first emerged around the Prophet Muhammad. Owing to his place in the network structure, I consider him the first person in the network and the sole member of the first layer in the HADITHNET dataset, even though he is not a hafiz but the one whose example inspired the huffaz.

7. The following hadith is used to support the method of consensus among scholars in the production of laws: "My community will never unanimously agree on an error."

8. There is a manifold literature about the network of jurists in Islamic history. As in the hadith transmission network, they are also organized in layers, with the Prophet and his Companions standing at the top of the hierarchy. Some of these works are general in their focus, while some others are more specialized; there are biographical dictionaries about jurists from a particular school, or from a particular city. See, as an example, the work of al-Shirazi (393–486 AH), *Tabaqat al-Fuqaha* (Layers of Jurists), and the work of al-Musannif (d. 1014 AH), *Tabaqat al-Shafi'iyya* (Layers of Shafi'is). (Both works are prepared for publication by Khalil al-Miys. Beirut: Dar al-Qalam.)

9. Collins's account of Muslim philosophers is far from conclusive because his data come from recent surveys (mostly textbooks) of Islamic philosophy in English. These modern works derive from classical works by such scholars as Ibn al-Nadim (ca. 990), al-Baqillani (d. 1000), 'Abdulqadir al-Baghdadi (d. 1030), al-Ghazzali (d. 1090), al-Shahrastani (d. 1130), and Ibn Khaldun (d. 1380). The ranking is based on how much space each philosopher occupies in these works. The method can be more useful in mea-

suring the prominence of philosophers in modern English-speaking academia. It is less reliable in measuring their prominence in their own time, or in today's Muslim world. Collins skillfully puts these data to use to demonstrate the "law of small numbers," and the intergenerational character of the network of philosophers. The network patterns demonstrated by the network of Muslim philosophers that Collins analyzes is strikingly similar to the network patterns that the present study has identified and analyzed in the network of huffaz.

10. The first date is for AH, after hijrah, the second for CE, common era.

11. He himself led a very humble life before and after he became a prophet. Although he was the leader of the first Islamic state, he did not have a palace or a comfortable home; instead, he and his family lived in small rooms next to the first mosque in Medina, where people prayed on sand because the floor was not carpeted. He said: "Poverty is my pride." He and his family accepted only the gifts given to them by the Companions, but not a regular salary or compensation from the treasury of the state. He also said: "I am sent only with the purpose of completing good manners." Yet, at the same time, he forbade asceticism and celibacy for his followers.

12. "This science belongs to the sciences of religious law that originated in Islam. Sufism is based on [the assumption] that the method of those people [who later on came to be called sufis] had always been considered by the important early Muslims, the men around Muhammad and the men of the second generation, as well as those who came after them, as the path of truth and right guidance" (Ibn Khaldun 1967, 3:76). Ibn Khaldun himself practiced *tasawwuf* and authored a book on it.

13. These figures may not reflect exactly the actual map of interdisciplinary connections, because they are derived from sources that were composed for other purposes. Neither Dhahabi nor Suyuti and Collins intended to record interdisciplinary network connections, yet their work contains information on the multiple involvement of scholars.

14. Bulliet suggests an alternative to the current perspectives on the history of Islam that cannot account for this diversity. He writes (1994, 8), "For its first five centuries, despite the nominal inclusion of all Muslims in a single conceptual community called umma, Islam was divided into many communities, some doctrinal, some ritual, some geographic. The view from the center, in seeking to explain the apparent homogeneity of Islamic society in later centuries, itself something of an illusion, projects back into the days of the caliphate a false aura of uniformity, leaving untold the complex and strife-ridden tale of how Islamic society actually developed."

Chapter 8

1. Max Weber proposed an inclusive concept of the intellectual, which I also adopt here. He argued that the concept "intellectual" indicates a social type who exists in all

civilizations of the world, across history. He also recognized the hierarchical structure of the intellectual community. See Sadri (1992) on Weber's concept of the intellectual.

2. For a detailed discussion of this aphorism, see Merton (1993).

3. It is reported that Isaac Newton (1642–1727), the British astronomer, mathematician, and physicist, said in a letter, "If I have seen further it is by standing on the shoulders of Giants" (Sills and Merton 1992, 172). Newton's reiteration of the aphorism is significant because it demonstrates that relying on previous generations is important not only in philosophy and the humanities but also in the natural sciences. Yet in the humanities, such as hadith, this feature is brought to the fore. From the time of the Romans to the time of Newton up to the present, the structure of the intellectual community has remained the same. Zeaman (1959) attests to this when he writes that "in the natural sciences each succeeding generation stands on the shoulders of those who have gone before" and that "in the social sciences each generation steps on the faces of its predecessors." A comparison such as the one Zeaman makes, between the natural and the social sciences with respect to differences in relationships to previous generations, would require a monumental research project.

4. A general survey of sacred scriptures would show that most of the prophets and masters of the ancient world who came before the Prophet Muhammad did not claim to have made new discoveries, either. There is thus a striking contrast regarding the concept of originality between ancient and modern intellectual cultures. Traditional cultures gave primacy to authenticity, while modernity gives primacy to innovation. Usually it is a combination of both in varying degrees, depending on the specific social and cultural field concerned.

5. For an easy, readable, yet scholarly biographical work on the life of the Prophet Muhammad, see Lings (1983).

6. See al-Sakhawi (1986b vols. 1, 2). The work is an extended and extremely detailed biography of Ibn Hajar by his close student al-Sakhawi. It is also full of colorful stories, the veracity of which we cannot judge. However, they serve an important purpose by shedding light on the culture of hadith scholars, which would otherwise have remained in the darkness of history. For instance, the legendary story, below, about him sacrificing his love for the sake of knowledge, regardless of its historicity, shows the great emphasis in the culture of hadith students on the pursuit of knowledge.

7. For the medieval technology of transportation, see Bulliet (1990).

8. See chap. 3 for a more detailed discussion of various methods of narration and how they are codified.

9. The title *shaykh al-Islam* is used for different purposes in different contexts. For instance, in the Ottoman government, it meant an official position within the government. The above meaning reflects the way hadith scholars used the term, which may not be identical with its usage in other contexts.

Chapter 9

1. Fig. 3.1 in Mullins's book focuses on the linkages among some persons important to the development of standard American sociology from 1900 to 1950. Applying the perspective I suggest here, it is possible to reconstruct the data as a time-stratified network and analyze the connections between seven layers of sociologists. From this perspective, I reconstructed the Mullins data and looked at the interlayer connections. (1) layer 1: Simmel, Durkheim, Pareto, and Weber; (2) layer 2: Mead, Park, Small, Giddings, and Salin; (3) layer 3: Burges, Ogburn, L. J. Henderson, and Sorokin; (4) layer 4: Blumer, P. Hauser, Staufer, Homans, and Parsons; (5) layer 5: Hawley, Duncan, Merton, and Davis; (6) layer 6: Schnore, Scott, Van der Berghe, Blau, and Ryder.

The most striking pattern in this network, as displayed by fig. 3.1 in Mullins's book, is the prevalent role of the diachronic or out-layer connections, because none of these figures is the student of another from his own cohort. Ties are dominantly diachronic.

2. Zuckerman's data can also be reconstructed and analyzed as a time-stratified network. She mapped the network of masters and apprentices in layers. She organized her data in eight layers in physics and physical chemistry from 1880 to 1959, and five layers in biological chemistry from 1901 to 1972. All ties are diachronic. No in-layer connection in either network is reported; instead, all connections are among scholars from different layers, providing additional evidence from the modern-day scholarly community of the role of interlayer brokerage in the formation of scholarly authority.

3. Of the three authors mentioned above, Collins did the most comprehensive data collection. His data can also be better organized and formally analyzed through the concept of layers. Collins has already divided his data into different periods, yet without exploring its methodological foundations. Nor did he pay special attention to the striking contrast in the volume of connections between and within these generations. It is made easy to show, by the excellent sociograms Collins prepared for each civilization he analyzed to display mentor-disciple connections over time, that diachronic connections are the most dominant type of social connection among intellectuals of all major civilizations. Furthermore, the volume of in-layer connections among intellectuals is strikingly insignificant in all the cultures Collins analyzed. Collins's findings about the network of philosophers in different societies also show striking parallels with the network of huffaz in Islamic culture.

4. It is now possible to analyze the geographical distribution of social variables in the United States, but similar software and detailed data have yet to be produced for the rest of the world. Collection and analysis of what is called GEODATA has recently become a standard part of social research. Analysis of the hadith transmission network can also benefit in the future from this development.

5. In general, however, I had to set aside space variables in favor of time variables, not because I think they are subordinate, but because of the limitations of the present

work. Consequently, I paid limited attention to the geography of the hadith transmission network (see chap. 1). I showed that the center of the social networks continuously moves, over time, between centers of learning, without stability, depicting a polycentric network with moving centers rather than a network with a single and stable center. Yet this analysis of the geographical aspect of the phenomenon is far from exhaustive.

6. I should also note that the list of huffaz in Dhahabi's work is far from complete and precise. Ma'ruf (1976) authored a monograph on Dhahabi and wrote: "Al-Dhahabi did not mean to cover all the huffaz in this book. He apologized for this in several places of his book. At the end of the second layer, he wrote: 'I restricted myself to the presentation of these seventy and some leading scholars [*imam*] with the purpose of making it easy for readers' [1: 244]. He also said at the end of the seventh layer: 'They are many in number, but I selected only the most prominent [*al-A'laam*] [1: 329; see also 2: 529–30; 6:1500].' He referred his readers who desired more detailed information to his grand historical work, *History of Islam* (see, for instance, 2:627; 4:1466) and his autobiographical dictionary (see, for instance, 4:1500). He also mentioned that he presented only limited information about them in this book [1:160]."

7. Kalabazi lists 1,225 names as Bukhari's transmitters, yet three names are missing from the list.

8. Saussure writes, "One [synchronic fact] is a relationship between simultaneous elements, and the other [diachronic fact] a substitution of one element for another in time, that is to say an event" (Saussure 1994, 90).

9. This is a clear example of succession in time conflated with succession in space.

10. Succession in time must be treated differently from succession in space, although there may be commonalities between them (Hill 1977; Fillmore 1975).

11. Coleman's argument is illustrated in the following excerpt: "Inspection shows certain attributes of the social structure. A given merchant community is ordinarily very close, both in frequency of interaction and in ethnic and family ties. The wholesale diamond market in New York City, for example, is Jewish, with a high degree of intermarriage, living in the same community in Brooklyn, and going to the same synagogues. It is essentially a closed community. Observation of the wholesale diamond market indicates that these close ties, through family, community, and religious affiliation, provide the insurance that is necessary to facilitate transactions in the market. If any member of this community defected through substituting other stones or through stealing stones in his temporary possession, he would lose family, religious, and community ties" (Coleman 1994, S99).

12. "I use the term structural hole for the separation between nonredundant contacts. Nonredundant contacts are connected by a structural hole. A structural hole is a relationship of nonredundancy between two contacts. The hole is a buffer, like an insu-

lator in an electric circuit. As a result of the hole between them, the two contacts provide network benefits that are in some degree additive rather than overlapping" (Burt 1995, 18).

13.   Ibn Khaldun explains how "a scholar's education is greatly improved by traveling in quest of knowledge and meeting the authoritative teachers" of his time. The following excerpt shows a high degree of awareness about keeping intellectual networks open by meeting an extended number of teachers, even if it requires traveling abroad. Yet we do not know to what extent this awareness was preserved by subsequent generations of Muslim intellectuals. Ibn Khaldun writes: "The reason for this is that human beings obtain their knowledge and character qualities and all their opinions and virtues either through study, instruction, and lectures, or through imitation of a teacher and personal contact with him. The only difference here is that habits acquired through personal contact with a teacher are more strongly and firmly rooted. Thus, the greater the number of authoritative teachers [*shaykh*s], the more deeply rooted is the habit one acquires. . . . Furthermore, the technical terminologies used in scientific instruction are confusing to the student. Many students even suppose them to be part of a given science. The only way to deliver them from that [wrong notion] is by personal contact with teachers, for different teachers employ different terminologies. Thus, meeting scholars and having many authoritative teachers . . . enable the student to notice the difference in the terminologies used by different teachers and to distinguish among them. He will thus be able to recognize the science itself behind the [technical terminology it uses]. He will realize that [terminologies] are [merely] means and methods for imparting [knowledge]. His powers will work toward acquiring strongly and firmly rooted habits. He will improve the knowledge he has and be able to distinguish it from other [knowledge]. In addition, his habits will be strengthened through his intensive personal contact with teachers when they are many and of various types. This is for those for whom God facilitated the ways of scholarship and right guidance. Thus, traveling in quest of knowledge is absolutely necessary for the acquisition of useful knowledge and perfection through meeting authoritative teachers . . . and having contact with [scholarly] personalities" (Ibn Khaldun 1967, 307–8).

Bibliography

Abbott, Andrew. 1984. "Event Sequence and Event Duration: Colligation and Measurement." *Historical Methods* 17(4): 192–204.

———. 1988a. *The System of Professions.* Chicago: University of Chicago Press.

———. 1988b. "Transcending General Linear Reality." *Sociological Theory* 6: 169–86.

———. 1992a. "From Causes to Events: Notes on Narrative Positivism." *Sociological Methods and Research* 20(4): 428–55.

———. 1992b. "What Do Cases Do? Some Notes on Activity in Sociological Analysis." In Charles Ragin and Howard Becker, eds., *What Is a Case?: Exploring the Foundations of Social Inquiry.* New York: Cambridge University Press.

———. 1995. "Sequence Analysis: New Methods for Old Ideas." *Annual Review of Sociology* 21: 93–113.

———. 2001a. *Chaos of Disciplines.* Chicago: University of Chicago Press.

———. 2001b. *Time Matters: On Theory and Method.* Chicago: University of Chicago Press.

———, and Alexandra Hrycak. 1990a. "Conceptions of Time and Events in Social Science Methods: Causal and Narrative Approaches." *Historical Methods* 23(4): 141–50.

———. 1990b. "Measuring Resemblance in Sequence Data: An Optimal Matching Analysis of Musicians' Careers." *American Journal of Sociology* 96(1): 144–85.

Abbott, Nabia. 1946. "An Arabic Papyrus in the Oriental Institute: Stories of the Prophets." *Journal of Near Eastern Studies* 4(3): 169–80.

———. 1957–1972. *Studies in Arabic Literary Papyri.* 3 vols. Chicago: University of Chicago Press.

———. 1983. "*Hadith* Literature II: Collection and Transmission of *Hadith*." In A. F. L. Beeston, T. M. Johnstone, R. B. Sergeant, and G. R. Smith, eds., *The Cambridge History of Arabic Literature.* Cambridge: Cambridge University Press.

Abdul Rauf, Muhammad. 1983. "*Hadith* Literature I: The Development of the Science of *Hadith*." In A. F. L. Beeston, T. M. Johnstone, R. B. Sergeant, and G. R. Smith, eds., *The Cambridge History of Arabic Literature*. Cambridge: Cambridge University Press.

Abrahamson, Eric, and Charles J. Fombrun. 1994. "Macrocultures: Determinants and Consequences." *Academy of Management Review* 19(4): 728–55.

Abu al-Husayn, 'Abd al-Ghafir bin Ismail al-Farisi. 1982. *al-Halqa al-Ula min Tarikh al-Niysabur* [History of Nishapur]. Ed. Muhammad Kazim al-Mahmudi. Qum, Iran: Ja-ma'ah al-Mudarrisin.

Abu-Lughod, Janet. 1989. *Before European Hegemony: The World System* A.D. *1250–1350*. New York: Oxford University Press.

Agnon, S. J., and G. Scholem. 1961. *Major Trends in Jewish Mysticism*. New York: Schocken Books.

al-'Ala'i, Salahaddin Abi Sa'id Khalil bin Kaykaldi. 1978. *Jami' al-Tahsil fi Ahkam al-Marasil* [On the Hadith with Broken Chain]. Baghdad: Wazarah al-Awqaf.

al-'Amiri, Abu al-Hasan. 1988. *Al-'Ilam bi Manaqib al-Islam*. Ed. A. 'A. Ghurab. Riyadh: Dar al-Isala.

Anderson, Danny J. 1989. "Deconstruction: Critical Strategy/Strategic Criticism." In Douglas G. Atkins and Laura Morrow, eds., *Contemporary Literary Theory*. Amherst: University of Massachusetts Press.

Anees, Muhammad Ahmad, and Alia N. Athar. 1993. *Guide to Sira and Hadith Literature in Western Languages*. New York: Mansell.

Archer, Margaret S. 1989. *Culture and Agency: The Place of Culture in Social Theory*. New York: Cambridge University Press.

Asad, Muhammad. 1981. *Sahih al-Bukhari: Early Years of Islam*. Gibraltar: Dar al-Andalus.

Atkins, Douglas G., and Laura Morrow, eds. 1989. *Contemporary Literary Theory*. Amherst: University of Massachusetts Press.

Austin, J. L. 1962. *How to Do Things with Words*. Cambridge, MA: Harvard University Press.

Ayni, Badr al-Din Abi Muhammad. 1972. *Umdah al-Qari Sharh Sahih al-Bukhari* [Reliance of the Reader: Commentary on the Reliable Compilation of Bukhari]. 25 vols. Cairo: Maktabah al-Halabi.

al-Azami, Muhammad. M. 1977. *Studies in Hadith Methodology and Literature*. Indianapolis: American Trust Publications.

———. 1985. *On Schacht's Origins of Muhammadan Jurisprudence*. New York: Wiley.

Baker, Keith Michael. 1990. *Inventing the French Revolution: Essays on French Political Culture in the Eighteenth Century*. Cambridge: Cambridge University Press.

Bakhtin, M. M. 1981. *The Dialogic Imagination*. Ed. Michael Holquist. Trans. Caryl Emerson and Michael Holquist. Austin: University of Texas Press.

Bal, Mieke. 1985. *Narratology*. Trans. Christine van Boheemen. Toronto: University of Toronto Press.

Barthes, Roland. 1974. *S/Z*. Trans. Richard Miller. New York: Hill and Wang.

———. 1977. *Image, Music, Text*. Trans. Stephan Heath. New York: Hill and Wang.

———. 1988. *The Semiotic Challenge*. Trans. Richard Howard. New York: Hill and Wang.

Bearman, Peter S. 1993. *Relations into Rhetorics: Local Elite Social Structure in Norfolk, England, 1540–1640*. New Brunswick, NJ: Rutgers University Press.

Becker, Henk A. 1992. *Dynamics of Cohort and Generation Research*. Amsterdam: Thesis Publishers.

Beeston, A. F. L., T. M. Johnstone, R. B. Sergeant, and G. R. Smith, eds. 1983. *The Cambridge History of Arabic Literature*. Cambridge: Cambridge University Press.

Berkey, Jonathan. 1992. *The Transmission of Knowledge in Medieval Cairo: A Social History of Islamic Education*. Princeton, NJ: Princeton University Press.

———. 1995. "Tradition, Innovation, and the Social Construction of Knowledge in the Medieval Islamic Near East." *Past and Present* 146: 38–65.

Berman, Harold J. 1983. *Law and Revolution*. Cambridge, MA: Harvard University Press.

Bilal, Sa'd Fahmi Ahmad. 1996 (1417 ᴀʜ). *Al-Siraj al-Munir fir Alqab al-Muhaddithin* [The Illuminating Candle on the Titles of Hadith Scholars]. Riyad: Dar Ibn Hazm.

Bohas, G., J. P. Guillaume, and D. E. Kouloghli. 1990. *The Arabic Linguistic Tradition*. New York: Routledge.

Bonacich, P. 1987. "Power and Centrality: A Family of Measures." *American Journal of Sociology* 92: 1170–82.

Borgman, Christine, ed. 1990. *Scholarly Communication and Bibliometrics*. London: Sage.

Bruner, Jerome. 1986. *Actual Minds, Possible Worlds*. Cambridge, MA: Harvard University Press.

———. 1990. *Acts of Meaning*. Cambridge, MA: Harvard University Press.

———. 1996. *The Culture of Education*. Cambridge, MA: Harvard University Press.

Bukhari, Muhammad bin Ismail. 1995. *Sahih al-Bukhari*. 4 vols. Ed. al-Shaykh Muhammad 'Ali al-Qutb and al-Shaykh Hisham al-Bukhari. Beirut: al-Maktabah al-'Asriyya.

Bulliet, Richard. 1972. *The Patricians of Nishapur*. Cambridge, MA: Harvard University Press.

———. 1979. *Conversion to Islam in the Medieval Period*. Cambridge MA: Harvard University Press.

———. 1983. "The Age Structure of Medieval Islamic Education." *Studia Islamica* 57: 105–17.

———. 1990. *The Camel and the Wheel*. New York: Columbia University Press.

———. 1994. *Islam: The View from the Edge*. New York: Columbia University Press.

Burke, Kenneth. 1966. *Language as a Symbolic Action*. Berkeley: University of California Press.

Burns, Tom. 1977. *The BBC: Public Institution and Private World*. London: Macmillan.

Burt, Ronald. 1975. "Corporate Society: A Time Series Analysis of Network Structure." *Social Science Research* 4: 271–328.

———. 1983. "Stratification and Prestige among Elite Experts in Methodological and Mathematical Sociology circa 1975." *Social Networks* 1: 105–58.

———. 1995. *Structural Holes: The Social Structure of Competition*. Cambridge, MA: Harvard University Press.

Çakan, İsmail Lütfi. 1989. *Hadis Edebiyatı Çeşitleri, Özellikleri, Faydalanma Usulleri*. İstanbul: Marmara Üniversitesi İlahiyat Fakültesi.

———. 1991. *Hadis Usulü* [Methodology of Hadith]. İstanbul: Marmara Üniversitesi İlahiyat Fakültesi.

Chatman, Seymour. 1978. *Story and Discourse: Narrative Structure in Fiction and Film*. Ithaca, NY: Cornell University Press.

Clanchy, M. T. 1978. *From Memory to Written Record in England, 1066–1307*. Cambridge, MA: Harvard University Press.

Cole, Juan R., ed. 1992. *Comparing Muslim Societies: Knowledge and the State in World Civilization*. Ann Arbor: University of Michigan Press.

Coleman, James S. 1988. "Social Capital in the Creation of Human Capital." *American Journal of Sociology* 94, suppl. S95–S120.

———. 1990. *Foundations of Social Theory*. Cambridge, MA: Belknap Press of Harvard University Press.

———. 1994. "A Rational Choice Perspective on Economic Sociology." Pp. 166–82 in *The Handbook of Economic Sociology*, edited by N. J. Smelser and R. Swedberg. York: Russel Sage Foundation.

Collins, Randall. 1998. *The Sociology of Philosophies: A Global Theory of Intellectual Change*. Cambridge, MA: Harvard University Press.

Coulson, N. J. 1964. *A History of Islamic Law*. Edinburgh: Edinburgh University Press.

———. 1983 "European Criticism of *Hadith* Literature." In A. F. L. Beeston, T. M. Johnstone, R. B. Sergeant, and G. R. Smith, eds., *The Cambridge History of Arabic Literature*. Cambridge: Cambridge University Press.

Coward, Harold. 1988. *Sacred Word and Sacred Text: Scripture in World Religions*. New York: Orbis.

Cragg, Kenneth. 1973. *The Mind of the Qur'an: Chapters in Reflection*. London: Allen & Unwin.

Culler, Jonathan. 1975. *Structural Poetics*. Ithaca, NY: Cornell University Press.

———. 1988. *Framing the Sign: Criticism and Its Institutions*. Norman: University of Oklahoma Press, 1988.

Dabashi, Hamid. 1989. *Authority in Islam: From the Rise of Muhammad to the Establishment of the Umayyads*. New Brunswick, NJ: Transaction Publications.

Danto, Arthur C. 1985. *Narration and Knowledge*. New York: Columbia University Press.

Darimi, Abu Muhammad Abdullah. 1987. *Sunan al-Darimi,* Beirut: Dar al-Kitab al-Arabi.

Desan, Philippe, Priscilla Parkhurst Ferguson, and Wendy Griswold, eds. 1988. *Literature and Social Practice*. Chicago: University of Chicago Press.

al-Dhahabi, Abu Abdullah Shamsuddin Muhammad. 1968. *Kitab Tadhkirah al-Huffaz* [Lexicon of Prominent Hadith Narrators]. India: Osmania Oriental Publications Bureau.

———. 1991a. *Al-Muqizah fi 'Ilm Mustalah al-Hadith* [The Warner on the Science of Hadith]. Halab: Maktabah al-Matbu'at al-Islamiyya.

———. 1991b (1416). *Diwan al-Du'afa wa al-Matrukin* [Register of the Weak and the Abandoned]. Beirut: Dar al-Qalam.

Dibbell, Julian. 1993. "How an Evil Clown, a Haitian Trickster Spirit, Two Wizards, and a Cast of Dozens Turned a Database into a Society." *Village Voice* 23 Dec.: 36–42.

Dickey, D. A. and W. A. Fuller. 1979. "Distribution of the Estimator for Autoregressive Time Series with a Unit Root," *Journal of the American Statistical Association* 74: 427–31.

Duri, A. A. 1983. *The Rise of Historical Writing among Arabs*. Ed. and trans. Lawrence I. Conrad. Princeton, NJ: Princeton University Press.

Eco, Umberto. 1994. *Six Walks in the Fictional Woods*. Cambridge, MA: Harvard University Press.

Eickelman, Dale F. 1992. "The Art of Memory: Islamic Education and its Social Reproduction." In Juan R. Cole, ed., *Comparing Muslim Societies: Knowledge and the State in World Civilization*. Ann Arbor: University of Michigan Press.

———, and James Piscatori, eds. 1990. *Muslim Travelers: Pilgrimage, Migration, and the Religious Imagination*. Berkeley: University of California Press.

Eisenstadt, S. N., and R. Lamarchard, eds. 1981. *Political Clientelism, Patronage, and Development*. Beverly Hills, CA: Sage.

El Calamawy, Sahair. 1983. "Narrative Elements in *Hadith* Literature." In A. F. L. Beeston, T. M. Johnstone, R. B. Sergeant, and G. R. Smith, eds., *The Cambridge History of Arabic Literature*. Cambridge: Cambridge University Press.

Ellingson, Stephen J. 1995. "Understanding the Dialectic of Discourse and Collective Action: Public Debate and Rioting in Antebellum Cincinnati." *American Journal of Sociology* 101: 100–144.

Ellis, John M. 1989. *Against Deconstruction*. Princeton, NJ: Princeton University Press.

El-Moudden, Abdurrahmane. 1990. "The Ambivalence of *Rihla*: Community Integration and Self-Definition in Moroccan Travel Accounts, 1300–1800." In Dale F. Eickelman and James Piscatori, eds., *Muslim Travelers: Pilgrimage, Migration, and the Religious Imagination.* Berkeley: University of California Press.

Emirbayer, Mustafa, and Jeff Goodwin. 1994. "Network Analysis, Culture, and the Problem of Agency." *American Journal of Sociology* 99: 1411–54.

Enders, Walter. 1995. *Applied Econometric Time Series.* New York: Wiley.

Es-Salih, Subhi. 1988. *Hadis İtlimleri ve Istılahları.* Trans. Yaşar Kandemir. Ankara: Diyanet İşleri Başkanlığı Yayınları.

Fadel, Muhammad. 1995. "Ibn Hajar's *Hady al-Sari:* A Medieval Interpretation of the Structure of al-Bukhari's *al-Jami' al-Sahih:* Introduction and Translation." *Journal of Near Eastern Studies* 54(3): 161–97.

Feynman, Richard P. 1998. *The Meaning of It All: The Thoughts of a Citizen-Scientist.* Reading, MA: Addison-Wesley.

Fillmore, Charles. 1975. *Santa Cruz Lectures on Deixis.* Bloomington: Indiana University Linguistic Club.

Frye, Richard N., ed. 1965. *The Histories of Nishapur.* London: Mouton.

Geertz, Clifford. 1983. *Local Knowledge: Further Essays in Interpretive Anthropology.* New York: Basic Books.

Gellens, Sam I. 1990. "The Search for Knowledge in Medieval Muslim Societies: A Comparative Approach." In Dale F. Eickelman and James Piscatori, eds., *Muslim Travelers: Pilgrimage, Migration, and the Religious Imagination.* Berkeley: University of California Press.

Gellner, Ernest. 1973. *Cause and Meaning in the Social Sciences.* London: Routledge and Kegan Paul.

Giddens, Anthony. 1987. "Structuralism, Poststructuralism, and the Production of Culture." In Anthony Giddens and Jonathan Turner, eds., *Social Theory Today.* Stanford, CA: Stanford University Press.

Göçgün, Önder. 2001. *Ziya Paşanın Hayatı, Eserleri, Edebi Kişiliği, Bütün Şiirleri ve Eserlerinden Açıklamalalı Seçmeler.* Ankara: TC Kültür Bakanlığı Yay.

Goffman, Erving. 1963. *Behavior in Public Places.* New York: Free Press.

———. 1981. *Forms of Talk.* Philadelphia: University of Pennsylvania Press.

———. 1986. *Frame Analysis: An Essay on the Organization of Experience.* Boston: Northeastern University Press.

Goldziher, Ignaz. 1981. *Introduction to Islamic Theology and Law.* Princeton, NJ: Princeton University Press.

Gombert, Jean Emile. 1992. *Metalinguistic Development.* Chicago: University of Chicago Press.

Graham, William. 1977. *Divine Word and Prophetic Word in Early Islam: A Reconsideration of the Sources, with Special Reference to the Divine Sayings or Hadith Qudsi.* The Hague: Mouton.

———. 1987. *Beyond the Written Word*. Cambridge: Cambridge University Press.

———. 1993. "Traditionalism in Islam: An Essay in Interpretation." *Journal of Interdisciplinary History* 23(3): 495–522.

Granevetter, M. 1973. "The Strength of Weak Ties." *American Journal of Sociology* 81: 1287–1303.

Gujarati, D. N. 1995. *Basic Econometrics*. New York: McGraw-Hill.

Habermas, Jurgen. 1984–87. *The Theory of Communicative Action*. 2 vols. Trans. Thomas McCarthy. Boston: Beacon Press.

Hamidullah, Muhammad. 1974. *Muhammad Rasullullah: A Concise Survey of the Life and Work of the Founder of Islam*. Paris: Centre Culturel Islamique.

———. 1995. *The Emergence of Islam*. Trans. Afzal Iqbal. New Delhi, India: Adam Publishers and Distributors.

Hardy, Barbara. 1975. *Tellers and Listeners: The Narrative Imagination*. London: Athlone Press.

Hart, Janet. 1992. "Cracking the Code: Narrative and Political Mobilization in the Greek Resistance." *Social Science History* 16(4): 631–68.

Hickman, Maya. 1993. "The Boundaries of Reported Speech in Narrative Discourse: Some Developmental Aspects," in Lucy ed. 1993, pp. 63–90.

Hill, Clifford. 1977. *Linguistic Research on Spatial Orientation: African and African-American Continuities*. LC report 91-1. New York: Teachers College, Columbia University.

Hockett, Charles. 1963. "The Problem of Universals in Language." In J. Greenberg, ed., *Universals of Language*, pp. 1–29. Cambridge, MA: MIT Press.

Hodgson, Marshall. 1977. *The Venture of Islam: Conscience and History in World Civilization*. Chicago: University of Chicago Press.

Humphreys, R. Stephen. 1991. *Islamic History: A Framework for Inquiry*. Princeton, NJ: Princeton University Press.

Huntington, Samuel P. 1996. *The Clash of Civilizations and the Remaking of World Order*. New York: Simon and Schuster.

Ibn Hibban, Muhammad. 1987. *Mashahir Ulama' al-Amsar wa A'lam Fuqaha al-Aqtar* [Renowned Scholars of Cities and Outstanding Regional Jurists]. Beirut: Muassah al-Kitab al-Thaqafiyyah.

Ibn Khaldun. 1967. *The Muqaddimah: An Introduction to History*, 2d ed. 3 vols. Trans. Franz Rosenthal. Princeton, NJ: Princeton University Press.

Ibn Salah. 1976. *Muqaddimah Ibn Salah wa Mahasin al-Istilah* [Introduction of Ibn Salah and the Beauties of Terminology]. Ed. Aisha Abd al-Rahman. Cairo: al-Hay'ah al-Misriyyah al-'Ammah li al-Kutub.

Jameson, Fredric. 1981. *The Political Unconscious: Narrative as a Socially Symbolic Act*. Ithaca, NY: Cornell University Press.

al-Jarrahi, Ismail bin Muhammad bin al-'Ajluni. 1932. *Kashf al-Khafa wa Muzil al-Ilbas 'amma Ishtahara min al-Ahadith 'ala Elsinet al-Nas* [Clearing the Mystery and Eliminating Confusion about Ahadith That Are Commonly Known among People]. Beirut: Dar Ihya' al-Turath al-'Arabi.

Jomier, Jacques. 1983 "Aspects of the Qur'an Today." In A. F. L. Beeston, T. M. Johnstone, R. B. Sergeant, and G. R. Smith, eds., *The Cambridge History of Arabic Literature*. Cambridge: Cambridge University Press.

Jones, A. 1983. "The Qur'an II." In A. F. L. Beeston, T. M. Johnstone, R. B. Sergeant, and G. R. Smith, eds., *The Cambridge History of Arabic Literature*. Cambridge: Cambridge University Press.

Jones, J. M. B. 1983. "Maghazi Literature." In A. F. L. Beeston, T. M. Johnstone, R. B. Sergeant, and G. R. Smith, eds., *The Cambridge History of Arabic Literature*. Cambridge: Cambridge University Press.

Junyboll, G. H. A. 1969. *The Authenticity of Tradition Literature: Discussions in Modern Egypt*. Leiden: E. J. Brill.

———. 1982. *Muslim Tradition: Studies in Chronology, Provenance, and Authorship of Early Hadith*. Cambridge: Cambridge University Press.

Kamali, Muhammad Hashim. 1991. *Principles of Islamic Jurisprudence*. Cambridge: Islamic Texts Society.

Kamuf, Peggy, ed. 1991. *A Derrida Reader: Between the Blinds*. New York: Columbia University Press.

al-Kattani, Abdulhay bin Abdilkabir. 1982. *Fahras al-Fahâris wa Mu'jam al-Ma'âjim wa al-Mashyahâh wa al-Museltelât*, vols. 1–3. Beirut: Dar al-Gharb al-Islâmî.

Kaufer, David S., and Kathleen M. Carley. 1993. *Communication at a Distance: Exploring the Effect of Print on Sociocultural Organization and Change*. Mahwah, NJ: Lawrence Erlbaum Associates.

Kettani, al-Sayyid al-Sharif Muhammad bin Jafar. 1994. *Hadis Literatürü* [*al-Risalah al-Mustatrafah li Bayan Mashur Kutub al-Sunnah al-Musharrafah*] [Hadith Literature]. Trans. Yusuf Özbek. İstanbul: İz Yayıncılık.

Khadduri, Majid. 1987. *Al-Shafii's Risala: Treatise on the Foundations of Islamic Jurisprudence*. Cambridge: Islamic Texts Society.

Khalidi, Tarif. *Arabic Historical Thought in the Classical Period*. Cambridge: Cambridge University Press.

al-Khatib al-Baghdadi. 1990. *Sharaf Ashab al-Hadith* [Honor of the People of Hadith]. Ed. Mehmet Said Hatiboğlu. Ankara: Diyanet İşleri Başkanlığı.

Kister, M. J. 1983. "The *Sirah* Literature." In A. F. L. Beeston, T. M. Johnstone, R. B. Sergeant, and G. R. Smith, eds., *The Cambridge History of Arabic Literature*. Cambridge: Cambridge University Press.

Kittler, Friedrich A. 1990. *Discourse Networks 1800/1900*. Trans. Michael Metteer and Chris Cullens. Stanford, CA: Stanford University Press.

Koçkuzu, Ali Osman. 1988. *Rivayet İlimlerinde Haber-i Vahitlerin İtikat ve Tşri Yönlerinden Değeri* [The Value of Single-Chain Hadith in Islamic Law and Theology]. Ankara: Diyanet İşleri Başkanlığı.

Koçyiğit, Talat. 1975. *Hadis Usulü.* Ankara: Ankara Üniversitesi İlahiyat Fakültesi Yayınları.

Kohlberg, E. 1983. "Shii *Hadith.*" In A. F. L. Beeston, T. M. Johnstone, R. B. Sergeant, and G. R. Smith, eds., *The Cambridge History of Arabic Literature.* Cambridge: Cambridge University Press.

Labov, William. 1972. *Language in the Inner City: Studies in the Black English Vernacular.* Philadelphia: University of Pennsylvania Press.

Lanser, Susan Sniader. 1981. *The Narrative Act: Point of View in Prose Fiction.* Princeton, NJ: Princeton University Press.

Lapidus, Ira M. 1988. *History of Islamic Societies.* New York: Cambridge University Press.

Lefkovitz, Lori Hope. 1989. "Creating the World: Structuralism and Semiotics." In Douglas G. Atkins and Laura Morrow, eds., *Contemporary Literary Theory.* Amherst: University of Massachusetts Press.

Levine, Donald N. 1995. *Visions of the Sociological Tradition.* Chicago: University of Chicago Press.

Librande, Leonard, 1987. "Hadith." In Mircea Eliade, ed., *The Encyclopedia of Religion,* vol. 6, 143–51. New York: Macmillan.

Lings, Martin. 1983. *Muhammad: His Life, Based on the Earliest Sources.* London/Cambridge: Allen & Unwin/Islamic Texts Society.

Lucy, John A., ed. 1993. *Reflexive Language: Reported Speech and Metapragmatics.* Cambridge: Cambridge University Press.

Lyons, John. 1992. *Semantics.* Cambridge: Cambridge University Press.

Makdisi, George. 1981. *The Rise of Colleges: Institutions of Learning in Islam and the West.* Edinburgh: Edinburgh University Press.

———. 1991. *Religion, Law, and Learning in Classical Islam.* Hampshire: Variorum.

Margoliouth, D. S. 1929. *Lectures on Arabic Historians.* New York: Burt Franklin.

Martin, Wallace. 1994. *Recent Theories of Narrative.* 3d ed. Ithaca, NY: Cornell University Press.

Ma'ruf, Bashshar 'Awwad. 1976. *Al-Dhahabi wa Manhajuhu fi Kitabihi Tarikh al-Islam.* Cairo: Matba'at 'Isa al-Babi al-Halabi wa Shurakauh.

Marx, Karl, and Fredrick Engels. 1972. *The German Ideology.* Trans. C. J. Arthur. New York: International Publishers.

Merton, Robert. 1965. *Social Theory and Social Structure.* New York: Free Press.

———. 1973. *The Sociology of Science: Theoretical and Empirical Investigations.* Chicago: University of Chicago Press.

———. 1993. *On the Shoulders of Giants: A Shandean Postscript.* Chicago: University of Chicago Press.

———. 1996. *On Social Structure and Science.* Chicago: University of Chicago Press.

Miller, D. A. 1981. *Narrative and Its Discontents: Problems of Closure in the Traditional Novel.* Princeton, NJ: Princeton University Press.

Mitchell, W. J. T., ed. 1981. *On Narrative.* Chicago: University of Chicago Press.

Monroe, James T. 1983. "The Poetry of *Sirah* Literature." In A. F. L. Beeston, T. M. Johnstone, R. B. Sergeant, and G. R. Smith, eds., *The Cambridge History of Arabic Literature.* Cambridge: Cambridge University Press.

Moriarty, M. 1991. *Roland Barthes: Structuralism and After.* London: MacMillan.

Morson, Gary Saul, and Caryl Emerson. 1989. *Rethinking Bakhtin: Extensions and Challenges.* Evanston, IL: Northwestern University Press.

Mullins, Nicholas C. 1973. *Theories and Theory Groups in Contemporary American Sociology.* New York: Harper and Row.

Muslim, Abu al-Husain, al-Qushairi al-Nisaburi al-Hajjaj. 1955–1956. *Sahih-i Muslim.* 5 vols. Cairo: Dar Ihya al-Kutub al-'Arabiyya.

Nash, Cristopher, ed. 1994. *Narrative in Culture: The Uses of Storytelling in the Sciences, Philosophy, and Literature.* New York: Routledge.

Nicholson, R. A. 1993. *Literary History of Arabs.* London: Curzon Press.

Norris, H. T. 1983. "*Qisas* Elements in the Qur'an." In A. F. L. Beeston, T. M. Johnstone, R. B. Sergeant, and G. R. Smith, eds., *The Cambridge History of Arabic Literature.* Cambridge: Cambridge University Press.

Okic, Tayyib. 1959. *Bazı Hadis Meseleleri Üzerine Tetkikler* [Studies on Some Hadith Questions]. Ankara: Ankara İlahiyat Fakültesi.

Ong, Walter J. 1982. *Orality and Literacy: The Technologizing of the Word.* London: Methuen.

Padgett, John F., and C. K. Ansell. 1993. "Robust Action and the Rise of the Medici, 1400–1434." *American Journal of Sociology* 98: 1259–1319.

Paret, R. 1983. "The Qur'an I." In A. F. L. Beeston, T. M. Johnstone, R. B. Sergeant, and G. R. Smith, eds., *The Cambridge History of Arabic Literature.* Cambridge: Cambridge University Press.

Parsons, Talcott. 1964. *The Social System.* New York: Free Press.

———. 1967. *Sociological Theory and Modern Society.* New York: Free Press.

Pedersen, Johannes. 1984. *The Arabic Book.* Trans. Geoffrey French. Princeton, NJ: Princeton University Press.

Poggi, Gianfranco. 1983. "Clientelism." *Political Studies* 31: 662–68.

Polat, Sabahaddin. 1985. *Mürsel Hadisler ve Delil Olma Yönünden Değeri* [Discontinuous Hadith and Its Value in Islamic Law]. Ankara: Diyanet Vakfı Yayınları.

Pratt, Mary Louise. 1977. *Toward a Speech Act Theory of Literary Discourse.* Bloomington: Indiana University Press.

Reinhart, A. Kevin. 1995. *Before Revelation: The Boundaries of Muslim Moral Thought.* Albany: State University of New York Press.

Reynolds, L. D., and N. G. Wilson. 1968. *Scribes and Scholars: A Guide to the Transmission of Greek and Latin Literature.* Oxford: Oxford University Press.

Ricoeur, Paul. 1984–88. *Time and Narrative.* 3 vols. Trans. Kathleen McLaughlin and David Pellauer. Chicago: University of Chicago Press.

Riffaterre, Michael. 1990. *Fictional Truth.* Baltimore: Johns Hopkins University Press.

Robson, James. 1949. "The Transmission of Muslim's Sahih," *JRAS*, pp. 49–60.

———. 1951. "Muslim Tradition: The Question of Authenticity," *Memoires and Proceedings of the Manchester Literary and Philosophical Society* 93 (1951–52): 84–102.

———. 1951. "The Material of Tradition," *Muslim World* 41: 166–80, 257–70.

———. 1951. "Tradition: Investigation and Classification," *Muslim World* 41: 98–112.

———. 1951. "Tradition—The Second Foundation of Islam," *Muslim World* 41: 22–33.

———. 1952. "The Transmission of Abu Dawud's *Sunan*," *BSOAS* 14: 579–88.

Robson, James, trans. 1953. *An Introduction to the Science of Tradition, being Al-Madkhal ila ma'rifat al-Iklil by Al Hakim Abu 'Abdillah Muhammad b. Abdallah al Naisaburi.* London.

———. 1954. "The Transmission of Tirmidhi's *Jami'*," *BSOAS* 16: 258–70.

———. 1955–56. "The Form of Muslim Tradition," *Transactions of the Glasgow University Oriental Society* 16 (1955–56): 38–50.

———. 1956. "Ibn Ishaq's use of *Isnad*," *Bulletin of the John Rylands Library* 38(2) (March 1956): 449–65.

———. 1956. "The Transmission of Nasa'i's 'Sunan,'" *JSS* 1: 38–59.

———. 1958. "The Transmission of Ibn Maga's 'Sunan,'" *JSS* 3: 129–41.

———. 1961. "Varieties of the Hassan Tradition," *Journal of Semitic Studies* 6(1): 47–61.

———. 1964. "Tradition from Individuals," *Journal of Semitic Studies* 9: 327–40.

———. 1965. "The *Isnad* in Muslim Tradition," *Transactions of the Glasgow University Oriental Society* 15: 15–26.

———. 1970. "A Shia Collection of Divine Traditions," *Glasgow University Oriental Society Transactions* 22: 1–13.

———. 1971. "al-Djarh wa'l-Ta'dil." In *The Encyclopedia of Islam*, new ed., vol. 2, p. 462. Leiden: E. J. Brill.

———. 1971. "Hadith," In *The Encyclopedia of Islam*, new ed., vol. 3, pp. 23–29. Leiden: E. J. Brill

———. 1994. *Mishkat al-masabih* (by Khatib al-Tibrizi, Muhammad ibn 'Abd Allah, fl. 1337). English translation with explanatory notes. 2 vols. Reprint. Lahore: M. Ashraf.

Rosenthal, Franz. 1968. *A History of Muslim Historiography.* Leiden: E. J. Brill.

———, ed. 1975. *The Classical Heritage in Islam.* Trans. Emile and Jenny Marmorstein. Berkeley: University of California Press.

Ryder, Norman B. 1965. "The Cohort as a Concept in the Study of Social Change." *American Sociological Review* 30: 843–61.

Şaban, Zekiyyuddin. 1990. *İslam Hukuk İlminin Esasları* [Principles of Islamic Jurisprudence]. Trans. İbrahim Kafi Dönmez. Ankara: Diyanet Vakfı Yayınları.

Sadri, Ahmad. 1992. *Max Weber's Sociology of Intellectuals.* New York: Oxford University Press.

al-Sakhawi, Shams al-Din Muhammad bin Abd al-Rahman. 1986a. *Al-I'lan bi Tawbikh li man Dhamma ahl al-Tarikh* [Publicizing the Critique of the One Who Critiqued the Historians]. Ed. Franz Rosenthal. Beirut: Muassasat al-Risalah.

———. 1986b (1406). *Al-Jawahir wa al-Durar fi Tarjamah Shaykh al-Islam Ibn Hajar (al-'Asqalani)* [Pearls and Diamonds: The Biography of Ibn Hajar of 'Asqalan]. Cairo: Wazarah al-Awqaf.

Sandıkçı, Kemal. 1991. *İlk Üç Asırda İslam Coğrafyasında Hadis* [Hadith in Islamic Geography during the First Three Centuries]. Ankara: Diyanet İşleri Başkanlığı.

Saussure, Ferdinand de. 1966. *Course in General Linguistics.* Trans. Wade Baskin. New York: McGraw-Hill.

———. 1993. *Troisieme Cours de Linguistique General (1910–1911) / Saussure's Third Course of Lectures on General Linguistics (1910–1911).* Ed. and Trans. Eisuke Komatsa and Roy Harris. Oxford: Pergamon Press.

———. 1994. *Course in General Linguistics.* Trans. Roy Harris. La Salle, IL: Open Court Press.

Schacht, Joseph. 1959. *The Origins of Muhammadan Jurisprudence.* Oxford: Oxford University Press.

———. 1964. *An Introduction to Islamic Law.* Oxford: Oxford University Press.

Schank, Roger C. 1990. *Tell Me a Story: Narrative and Intelligence.* Evanston, IL: Northwestern University Press.

Scholes, Robert. 1974. *Structuralism in Literature: An Introduction.* New Haven, CT: Yale University Press.

———, and Robert Kellogg. 1966. *The Nature of Narrative.* New York: Oxford University Press.

Scott, J. 1992. *Social Network Analysis.* Newbury Park, CA: Sage.

Sewell, William Hamilton. 1992. "Introduction: Narratives and Social Identities." *Social Science History* 16: 479–88.

———. 1994. *A Rhetoric of Bourgeois Revolution.* Durham, NC: Duke University Press.

Sezgin, Fuat. 1956. *Buhari'nin Kaynakları Hakkında Araştırmalar* [Studies on the Sources of Bukhari]. Istanbul: Ankara Üniversitesi İlahiyat Fakültesi.

Shakir, Mustafa. 1982. *Aal Qudamah al-Saliha* [Saintly Qudama Family]. Kuwait: Hawliyyat Kulliyah al-Adab.

al-Shirazi, Abu Ishaq. n.d. *Tabaqat al-Fuqaha* [Layers of Jurists]. Ed. Khalil al-Miys. Beirut: Dar al-Qalam.

Shotter, John. 1993. *Conversational Realities: Constructing Life through Language.* London: Sage.

Shotter, John, and Kenneth J. Gergen, eds. 1989. *Texts of Identity.* London: Sage.

Siddiqi, Muhammad Zubayr. 1993. *Hadith Literature: Its Origins, Development, and Specific Features.* Cambridge: Islamic Texts Society.

Sills, David L., and Robert K. Merton. 1992. *The Macmillan Book of Social Science Quotations: Who Said What, When, and Where.* New York: Macmillan.

Silverstein, Michael. 1976. "Hierarchy of Features and Ergativity." In Dixon, *Grammatical Categories in Australian Languages*, 112–71. Canberra: Australian Institute of Aboriginal Studies.

———. 1993. "Metapragmatic Discourse and Metapragmatic Function." In John A. Lucy, ed., *Reflexive Language: Reported Speech and Metapragmatics.* Cambridge: Cambridge University Press.

Simmel, George. 1955. *Conflict and the Web of Group Affiliations.* Trans. Kurt H. Wolf and Reinhard Bendix. New York: Free Press.

Smith, Cantwell Wilfred. 1993. *What Is Scripture? A Comparative Approach.* Minneapolis: Fortress Press.

Somers, Margaret R. 1992. "Narrativity, Narrative Identity, and Social Action: Rethinking English Class Formation." *Social Science History* 16: 591–630.

———. 1995. "What's Political or Cultural about Political Culture and the Public Sphere? Toward an Historical Sociology of Concept Formation." *Social Theory* 13(2): 113–44.

Speight, Robert Marston. 1970. "The Musnad of al-Tayalisi: A Study of Islamic *Hadith* as Oral Literature." Ph.D. diss., Hartford Seminary Foundation.

Stanton, Charles Michael. 1990. *Higher Learning in Islam: The Classical Period, A.D. 700–1300.* Savage, MD: Rowman and Littlefield.

Steinmetz, George. 1992. "Reflections on the Role of Social Narratives in Working-Class Formation." *Social Science History* 16: 489–516.

Sturrock, John. 1979. *Structuralism and Science.* Oxford: Oxford University Press.

———. 1986. *Structuralism.* London: Paladin.

al-Subki, Taj al-Din Abd al-Wahhab bin Ali. 1984 (1404). *Qa'idah fi al-Jarh wa al-Ta'dil wa Qa'idah al-Muarrikhin* [Principle in Wounding and Honoring of Hadith Transmitters and the Principle of the Historians]. Ed. Abd al-Fattah Abu al-Ghuddah. Halab: Maktab al-Matbu'at al-Islamiyya.

Suyuti, Jalal al-Din. n.d. *Al-Azhar al-Mutanathirah fi al-Akhbar al-Mutawatirah* Ed. Ahmad Hasan Jabir Rajab. Cairo: al-Azhar.

———. 1972. *Tahdhir al-Khawass min Akadhib al-Qussas* [A Warning to the Selected Concerning the Lies of the Storytellers]. Ed. Muhammad al-Sabbagh. Beirut: al-Maktaba al-Islamiyya.

———. 1984. *Tabaqat al-Huffaz* [Layers of Prominent Hadith Narrators]. Beirut: Dar al-Kutub al-Ilmiyya.

Taym, As'ad Salim. 1994 (1415). *'Ilm Tabaqat al-Muhadditin: Ahammiyatuh wa Fawaiduh* [Science of the Layers of Hadith Scholars: Its Importance and Uses]. Riyad: Maktaba al-Rushd.

Tilly, Charles. 1995. *Popular Contention in Great Britain, 1758–1834.* Cambridge, MA: Harvard University Press.

Tilly, Charles, Jeff Goodwin, and Mustafa Emirbayer. 1995. *The Relational Turn in Macrosociology: A Symposium.* Working paper no. 215. New York: New School for Social Research.

Tucker, Robert C., ed. 1978. *The Marx-Engels Reader.* New York: Norton.

Ünal, İsmail Hakkı. 1994. *İmam Ebu Hanife'nin Hadis Anlayışı ve Hanefi Mezhebinin Hadis Metodu* [Abu Hanifa's Concept of Hadith and the Hadith Methodology of Hanefi School]. Ankara: Diyanet İşleri Başkanlığı.

Ünal, Yavuz. 1993. "Cumhuriyet Türkiyesi Hadis Çalışmaları Bibliyografyası" [Bibliography of Studies on Hadith in Turkey during the Republican Era]. M.A. thesis, Samsun Üniversitesi.

Volk, Tyler. 1995. *Metapatterns across Space, Time, and Mind.* New York: Columbia University Press.

Wansbrough, John E. 1987. *Res Ipsa Loquitur: History and Mimesis.* Jerusalem: Israel Academy of Sciences and Humanities.

Wasserman, Stanley, and Katherine Faust. 1994. *Social Network Analysis: Methods and Applications.* Cambridge: Cambridge University Press.

Waugh, Patricia. 1984. *Metafiction.* New York: Routledge.

Weber, Max. 1978. *Economy and Society: An Outline of Interpretive Sociology.* Ed. Guenther Roth and Claus Wittich. Trans. Ephraim Fischoff et al. Berkeley: University of California Press.

White, Harrison. 1963. *Anatomy of Kinship.* Englewood Cliffs, N.J.: Prentice-Hall.

———. 1970. *Chains of Opportunity: System Models of Mobility in Organizations.* Cambridge, MA: Harvard University Press.

———. 1992. *Identity and Control.* Princeton, NJ: Princeton University Press.

———. 1993. *Careers and Creativity: Social Forces in the Arts.* Boulder, CO: Westview.

———. 1995a. "Network Switchings and Bayesian Forks: Reconstructing the Social and Behavioral Sciences." *Social Research* 62(4): 1035–1063.

————. 1995b. *Where Do Languages Come From? Switching Talk.* Preprint no. 201. New York: Center for the Social Sciences, Columbia University.

White, Hayde. 1973. *Metahistory: The Historical Imagination in Nineteenth-Century Europe.* Baltimore: Johns Hopkins University Press.

————. 1987. *The Content of the Form.* Baltimore: Johns Hopkins University Press.

Yates, Frances A. 1966. *The Art of Memory.* Chicago: University of Chicago Press.

Zeaman, David. 1959. "Skinner's Theory of Teaching Machines." In Eugene Galenter, ed., *Automatic Teaching: The State of the Art.* New York: Wiley.

Zubaidi, A. M. 1983. "The Impact of the Qur'an and *Hadith* on Medieval Arabic Literature." In A. F. L. Beeston, T. M. Johnstone, R. B. Sergeant, and G. R. Smith, eds., *The Cambridge History of Arabic Literature.* Cambridge: Cambridge University Press.

Zuckerman, Harriet. 1977. *The Scientific Elite: Nobel Laureates in the United States.* New York: Free Press.

Index

In this index an "f" after a number indicates a separate reference on the next page, and an "ff" indicates separate references on the next two pages. A continuous discussion over two or more pages is indicated by a span of page numbers, e.g., "57–59." *Passim* is used for a cluster of references in close but not consecutive sequence.